Specialty Competencies in Counseling Psychology

Series in Specialty Competencies in Professional Psychology

TITLES IN THE SERIES

Specialty Competencies in School Psychology, Rosemary Flanagan and Jeffrey A. Miller

Specialty Competencies in Organizational and Business Consulting Psychology, Jay C. Thomas

Specialty Competencies in Geropsychology, Victor Molinari (Ed.)

Specialty Competencies in Forensic Psychology, Ira K. Packer and Thomas Grisso

Specialty Competencies in Couple and Family Psychology, Mark Stanton and Robert Welsh

Specialty Competencies in Clinical Child and Adolescent Psychology, Alfred J. Finch, Jr., John E. Lochman, W. Michael Nelson III, and Michael C. Roberts

Specialty Competencies in Clinical Neuropsychology, Greg J. Lamberty and Nathaniel W. Nelson

Specialty Competencies in Counseling Psychology, Jairo N. Fuertes, Arnold R. Spokane, and Elizabeth Holloway

JAIRO N. FUERTES
ARNOLD R. SPOKANE
ELIZABETH HOLLOWAY

Specialty Competencies in Counseling Psychology

Oxford University Press is a department of the University of Oxford.
It furthers the University's objective of excellence in research, scholarship,
and education by publishing worldwide.

Oxford New York
Auckland Cape Town Dar es Salaam Hong Kong Karachi
Kuala Lumpur Madrid Melbourne Mexico City Nairobi
New Delhi Shanghai Taipei Toronto

With offices in
Argentina Austria Brazil Chile Czech Republic France Greece
Guatemala Hungary Italy Japan Poland Portugal Singapore
South Korea Switzerland Thailand Turkey Ukraine Vietnam

Oxford is a registered trademark of Oxford University Press in
the UK and certain other countries.

Published in the United States of America by
Oxford University Press
198 Madison Avenue, New York, NY 10016

Library of Congress Cataloging-in-Publication Data

Fuertes, Jairo.
Specialty competencies in counseling psychology / Jairo N. Fuertes, Arnold Spokane,
Elizabeth Holloway.
p. cm. — (Specialty competencies in professional psychology)
Includes bibliographical references and index.
ISBN 978-0-19-538644-8
1. Counseling psychology. 2. Core competencies.
I. Spokane, Arnold R. II. Holloway, Elizabeth. III. Title.
BF636.6.F84 2013
158.3—dc23
2012018786

Printed in the United States of America
on acid-free paper

To my wife, Hnin, and to my daughters, Sofia and Isabella.

JNF

SELECTED EVENTS IN THE HISTORY OF COUNSELING PSYCHOLOGY

1909 Frank Parson's *Choosing a Vocation* is published posthumously.

1912 Jessie B. Davis's work leads Grand Rapids, Michigan, to establish a citywide guidance department.

1927 Edward K. Strong Jr. introduces the "Strong Vocational Interest Blank."

1934 The American Council of Guidance and Personnel Association is formed, later to become the American Personnel and Guidance Association (1952), then the American Association for Counseling and Development (1983), and currently the American Counseling Association (1992).

1938 The *Dictionary of Occupational Titles* is published.

1942 Carl Rogers develops nondirective counseling and publishes *Counseling and Psychotherapy: Newer Concepts in Practice.*

1944 The War Department establishes the Army Separation-Classification and Counseling Program to address the emotional and vocational needs of returning soldiers, and the Veterans Administration establishes counseling centers in their hospitals.

1945 In the rapidly expanding divisional structure of the American Psychological Association (APA) immediately following World War II, the Division of Personnel and Guidance Psychologists is formed and in 1946 it is named the Division of Counseling and Guidance; in 1952 it becomes the Division of Counseling Psychology.

1951 The Northwestern Conference, where issues associated with the refinement of the specialty, including statements on identity, specialization, and training criteria (including the scientist-practitioner model of training), are debated and established.

1951 Carl Rogers publishes *Client-Centered Therapy.*

1952 On January 1 the doctoral program in Counseling Psychology at Teachers College, Columbia University is first accredited by the American Psychological Association.

1954 *The Journal of Counseling Psychology* is published.

1955 The Diploma in Counseling Psychology is established by the American Board of Counseling Psychology.

1958 The National Defense Education Act greatly expands counseling and career development services in schools.

1964 The Greyston Conference of 1964 affirmed the identity of counseling psychology, particularly its commitment to examining person-environment cultural interactions.

1969 *The Counseling Psychologist* is first published.

1984 The first comprehensive book of the profession is edited by Steven D. Brown and Robert W. Lent, *Handbook of Counseling Psychology*.

1987 The Georgia Conference yields recommendations in areas of training and accreditation, research, structure, public relations, and professional practice.

2001 The Houston Conference reflected counseling psychology's history as a leader within the American Psychological Association in addressing issues of racism, sexism, and other forms of oppression.

2003 The Division 17, Counseling Psychology is renamed the Society of Counseling Psychology.

2008 The Chicago Conference reflects an emerging global emphasis in the profession in issues such as scientist-practitioner training, prevention, career, and vocational psychology, and strength-based approaches.

CONTENTS

ACKNOWLEDGMENTS

The authors would like to thank the following colleagues: Dr Joseph Talley, Dr. Norma Simon, Dr. Helen Roehlke, Dr. Charles Gelso, Dr. Clara Hill, and Dr. Linda Subich for their expert feedback on earlier drafts of this book and for their wonderful encouragement and support.

ABOUT THE SERIES IN SPECIALTY COMPETENCIES IN PROFESSIONAL PSYCHOLOGY

This series is intended to describe state-of-the-art functional and foundational competencies in professional psychology across extant and emerging specialty areas. Each book in this series provides a guide to best practices across both core and specialty competencies as defined by a given professional psychology specialty.

The impetus for this series was created by various growing movements in professional psychology during the past 15 years. First, as an applied discipline, psychology is increasingly recognizing the unique and distinct nature among a variety of orientations, modalities, and approaches with regard to professional practice. These specialty areas represent distinct ways of practicing one's profession across various domains of activities that are based on distinct bodies of literature and often addressing differing populations or problems. For example, the American Psychological Association (APA) in 1995 established the Commission on the Recognition of Specialties and Proficiencies in Professional Psychology (CRSPPP) in order to define criteria by which a given specialty could be recognized. The Council of Credentialing Organizations in Professional Psychology (CCOPP), an interorganizational entity, was formed in reaction to the need to establish criteria and principles regarding the types of training programs related to the education, training, and professional development of individuals seeking such specialization. In addition, the Council on Specialties in Professional Psychology (COS) was formed in 1997, independent of APA, to foster communication among the established specialties, in order to offer a unified position to the pubic regarding specialty education and training, credentialing, and practice standards across specialty areas.

Simultaneously, efforts to actually define professional competence regarding psychological practice have also been growing significantly. For example, the APA-sponsored Task Force on Assessment of Competence in Professional Psychology put forth a series of guiding principles for the assessment of competence within professional psychology, based, in part, on a review of competency assessment models developed both within (e.g., Assessment of Competence Workgroup from Competencies

Conference—Roberts et al., 2005) and outside (e.g., Accreditation Council for Graduate Medical Education and American Board of Medical Specialties, 2000) the profession of psychology (Kaslow et al., 2007).

Moreover, additional professional organizations in psychology have provided valuable input into this discussion, including various associations primarily interested in the credentialing of professional psychologists, such as the American Board of Professional Psychology (ABPP), the Association of State and Provincial Psychology Boards (ASPBB), and the National Register of Health Service Providers in Psychology. This widespread interest and importance of the issue of competency in professional psychology can be especially appreciated given the attention and collaboration afforded to this effort by international groups, including the Canadian Psychological Association and the International Congress on Licensure, Certification, and Credentialing in Professional Psychology.

Each volume in the series is devoted to a specific specialty and provides a definition, description, and development timeline of that specialty, including its essential and characteristic pattern of activities, as well as its distinctive and unique features. Each set of authors, long-term experts and veterans of a given specialty, were asked to describe that specialty along the lines of both functional and foundational competencies. *Functional competencies* are those common practice activities provided at the specialty level of practice that include, for example, the application of its science base, assessment, intervention, consultation, and where relevant, supervision, management, and teaching. *Foundational competencies* represent core knowledge areas that are integrated and cut across all functional competencies to varying degrees, and dependent upon the specialty, in various ways. These include ethical and legal issues, individual and cultural diversity considerations, interpersonal interactions, and professional identification.

Although we realize that each specialty is likely to undergo changes in the future, we wanted to establish a baseline of basic knowledge and principles that comprise a specialty, highlighting both its commonalities with other areas of professional psychology, as well as its distinctiveness. We look forward to seeing the dynamics of such changes, as well as the emergence of new specialties in the future.

In this volume, Fuertes, Spokane, and Holloway provide a striking balance of the rich history of the counseling specialty and an outstanding compilation of the professional practice domains conducted by the counseling psychology specialist. For example, these coauthors deliver informative examples of each foundational and functional domain of competency as well as a comprehensive discussion of the historic roots that support the specialty's leadership role in the field with regard to the areas of multiculturalism and diversity. In addition to interested individuals who wish to learn about the specialization of counseling psychology, readers from all specialties who are committed to embracing the philosophies of culturally fair practice, objectivity, and a treatment focus on their clients' areas of strength will also be served well by reading the volume. To assist such readers, the coauthors successfully capture how counseling psychology interfaces, overlaps, yet distinguishes itself from the other psychology specialties. The material in this volume of the series makes clear that counseling psychologists have led the field with regard to humanistic and empowering approaches to treatment. Moreover, the specialization may be one of the broadest, most flexible, and important specialties to the field of applied and professional psychology.

Arthur M. Nezu
Christine Maguth Nezu

ONE

Introduction to Counseling Psychology and to the Current Volume

To borrow and adapt a famous phrase from the early psychologist Hermann Ebbinghaus (1911), the practice of *counseling psychology* has a short history and a distant past. Counseling psychology has been recognized as a profession since after the end of World War II, though its early roots as a profession can be traced back to the vocational work of Frank Parson, a Boston social reformer, in 1909. However, it has only been since the end of World War II, like the other health service professions in psychology (e.g., *clinical psychology*), that counseling psychology has evolved and matured as a broad specialty. In particular, large-scale efforts during and after World War II to assign military personnel—and later to counsel veterans returning to civilian life, enroll in higher education, and find work—stimulated growth in the specialty. Counseling psychology has developed an identity that can be described, at least in part, in terms of five unifying themes to be presented more fully later in this chapter: (a) focus on intact personalities, (b) attention to assets and strengths, (c) emphasis on brief interventions, (d) attention to person–environment interaction, and (e) incorporation of career and educational development (Gelso & Fretz, 2001). Research in counseling psychology and in the related areas to the specialty has provided scientific support for the practice of the profession, and counseling psychologists have developed and refined new treatments and assessment methods for use with an increasingly diverse clientele. The distant past of what we currently do, as per Ebbinghaus, refers to the process that people have engaged in for centuries, in helping others adjust, live, work, and maintain their safety and well-being (Tyler, 1953). It is important to recognize that much of what we do in counseling psychology is deeply rooted in the human experience, and that our profession is ultimately responding to an ancient call deep within our humanity to help one another.

So what is counseling psychology? We offer the long answer in the form of this book. The specialty has matured over some 65 years to the point where a book on the professional practice of counseling psychology is needed to describe, among other things, the foundational and functional competencies associated with professional psychology and our specialty. We present models of professional competence that have been devised for professional psychology and discuss these models in relation to counseling psychology. The reader will learn about the code of ethical conduct that applies to counseling psychology, and about the various areas in which we work, including assessment, intervention, supervision, consultation, and training. Thus, this book is intended for students in psychology who seek further knowledge about the specialty, for graduate students in counseling psychology who may be interested in a book that provides an overview of professional practice, for current practitioners who may be interested in board certification in counseling psychology, and for potential clients and the public as a reference. The volume may also be helpful to health care service professionals outside of counseling psychology who may work in the various settings in which counseling psychologists are found (e.g., college counseling centers, clinics, and hospitals). The book may also add to further refinements in practice and stimulate research in the specialty, and it may inform current and ongoing efforts by programs in counseling psychology to align their training goals with specific competencies.

We begin with a formal definition of counseling psychology, citing various though similar definitions that are found on the Web sites of professional organizations, including the *Society of Counseling Psychology* (Division 17 of the American Psychological Association) and the *American Board of Counseling Psychology* (the certifying board for counseling psychologists in the United States and Canada).

Definitions of Counseling Psychology

The following description is provided by the Society of Counseling Psychology (Division 17 of American Psychological Association) Web site:

> Division 17—Counseling Psychology was founded in 1946 to promote personal, educational, vocational, and group adjustment in

> a variety of settings. Presently, Division 17 brings together psychologists, students, and international and professional affiliates who are dedicated to promoting education and training, scientific investigation, practice, and diversity and public interest in professional psychology. Division 17 advocates for Counseling Psychology within the field of psychology and in the public sector. Division 17 also supports, encourages, and promotes its members and celebrates their diversity. (http://www.div17.org/about.html)

The American Board of Counseling Psychology describes a counseling psychologist as one who

> ... facilitates personal and interpersonal functioning across the life span with a focus on individual, group, and community interventions for emotional, behavioral, vocational, and mental health problems using preventative, developmental, and remedial approaches, and in the assessment, diagnosis, and treatment of psychopathology. Counseling Psychologists participate in a range of activities including counseling, psychotherapy, assessment, teaching, research, supervision, career development, and consultation. They employ a variety of methods closely tied to theory and research to help individuals, groups and organizations to function optimally as well as to remediate dysfunction. A Counseling Psychologist is mindful of diversity and multiculturalism and recognizes the contribution of such broad factors as race, ethnicity, language, sexual orientation, gender, age, disability, class, education, religion/spiritual orientation, and other cultural dimensions to the formulation of the personality and social and mental health problems. A Counseling Psychologist is also aware of issues resulting from physical and mental health concerns. (http://www.abpp.org/files/page-specific/3364%20Counseling/01_Brochure.pdf)

Although other definitions of the specialty have been offered through the years from Super (1957) to Whitely (1984) to Gelso and Fretz (2001) to the Council of Counseling Psychology Training Programs (CCPTP) and the Society of Counseling Psychology SCP (2005) to Packard (2009), they all have consistent and common elements that are described as essential to the profession, such as a particular interest and competence in vocational psychology, a history of work with college students in university counseling centers, and a focus on harnessing the strengths and capacities of the individual even in the face of physical and mental illness.

Counseling psychology has also emphasized brief interventions and developmental programs, as well as an awareness and sensitivity to environmental factors that are deemed necessary to understand and explain individual behavior. We will expand on these themes in this chapter and present an organizational structure to this book that is consistent both with counseling psychology's historical roots and with the contemporary zeitgeist emphasizing competence-based training and practice.

FIVE DEFINING ELEMENTS OF COUNSELING PSYCHOLOGY

Gelso and Fretz (2001) cite five unifying themes whose interplay and complementary nature distinguish counseling psychology from other psychological specialties. These five themes summarize the fundamental underpinnings of counseling psychology (see Table 1.1).

A Focus on Intact Personalities

From its inception as a profession, counseling psychologists have worked with clients in need of vocational guidance, clients in need of psychological help in adjusting to crises and to normal developmental challenges, and with clients who experience normal problems in living or who are seeking personal growth and fulfillment in life. These clients have traditionally been school and college students, people in search of vocational development, and veterans in need of rehabilitation and vocational help as they adjust to life after military service. These clients often have a considerable degree of independence and psychological functioning.

Attention to Assets and Strengths

Our work has been and continues to be guided by the goal of harnessing talents and abilities in the individual to promote psychological growth,

TABLE 1.1 **Five Defining Elements of Counseling Psychology**

1. A focus on intact personalities
2. Attention to assets and strengths
3. An emphasis on brief interventions
4. Attention to person–environment interactions
5. Attention to the educational and vocational development of the person

Source: From Gelso and Fretz (2001).

development, and fulfillment. In part due to the client population with whom we have worked, and in part due to our traditional philosophical focus, counseling psychologists have de-emphasized the centrality of diagnosis and psychopathology in guiding assessment and intervention. However, with certain patient populations, the assessment and diagnosis of psychopathology is done while assessing and accounting for clients' strengths and talents. Despite the influence of modern-day health care models and insurance protocols to diagnose pathology and to tailor treatments to target specific symptoms in virtually all patients, counseling psychologists are trained to guide their work in the direction of promoting the development of psychological strengths and growth of the person.

An Emphasis on Brief Interventions

These interventions tend to be *psychoeducational*, *humanistic*, and *solution oriented*. While counseling psychology is informed by principles of psychology and by empirical scientific evidence, counseling psychology programs are well represented in departments of education and have been informed by principles of education, such as the ideal of lifelong learning and development, and the role of education in personal happiness, psychological hygiene, and adjustment. The early influence of Carl Rogers's humanism and his empathic, *client-centered approach* to treatment on counseling psychology cannot be overemphasized.

Attention to Person–Environment Interactions

This theme has at its root an emphasis on helping clients identify and develop their interests and abilities and the importance of environmental characteristics. In understanding the individual, training in counseling psychology emphasizes an assessment of ecological factors, including the role of family, community, culture, race, and gender; in understanding the development and functioning of the person, factors such as poverty, racism, and sexism are taken into account.

Attention to the Educational and Vocational Development of the Person

Counseling psychology emphasizes the centrality of education and work in people's lives, including their happiness and well-being. Educational concerns and vocational development are usually at the top of the agenda for school and college students, veterans, and clients in private practice. In a country and economy that emphasizes education, competition, and success, the work of counseling psychologists is always in demand whether economic times are good or bad. Even in clinical cases where the client evidences or has experienced significant or prolonged psychopathology, a major component in helping the person recover from dysfunction often involves education, training, and finding productive and manageable work.

Ivey (1979) described counseling psychology as the broadest specialty in applied psychology and the most flexible specialty with respect to focus, application, and the treatment issues and populations with which it deals. We agree with Ivey in his observation because of the breadth of issues that counseling psychology covers. Despite the specialty's traditional focus on personal growth and career development, counseling psychologists also work in hospitals and clinics providing services that cover the entire spectrum of psychological practice, including inpatient, neuropsychological, health, assessment and diagnosis, and psychotherapy services. These services also include manualized, evidence-based, and empirically supported treatments. However, as Gelso and Fretz (2001) point out, even when treating severely disturbed persons, counseling psychologists will assess and account for assets and strengths, and promote positive coping, adjustment, psychological growth, and meaningful work. Gelso and Fretz contrast this approach with the traditional assessment done in clinical psychology, where even a normal person is found to have some level of dysfunction, diagnosis, or pathology that is labeled and targeted in treatment. The specialty of counseling psychology also treats a diversity of clients/patients, including clients who represent the entire life span of human development, from early childhood to very old age, and who represent the broader spectrum of human diversity and social conditions, including the poor, women, racial and ethnic minorities, immigrants, physically disabled persons, and lesbian/gay/bisexual persons.

The Uniqueness of Counseling Psychology

A common effort in defining and describing counseling psychology involves the somewhat challenging exercise of establishing differences between it and clinical psychology. The most frequent distinctions made have to do with the *settings* and types of *populations* with which each specialty has *traditionally* worked. Clinical psychologists tend to be found in hospitals and clinics; they typically work with populations who are more severely affected by mental and physical illness and who require interdisciplinary interventions and coordinated treatment from psychiatry, social work, medicine, and nursing. Counseling psychologists have traditionally worked in educational and university settings, promoting student development, assisting students with normal developmental changes and needs, and helping them adjust emotionally and psychologically during the college years. It is safe to say that these distinctions are now less clear and do not capture the depth and breadth of both professions. Both professions have worked with similar populations in private practice settings for years, and for decades there has been a gradual convergence in terms of the types of places where both clinical and counseling psychologists work, with more counseling psychologists working in hospitals and clinics and clinical psychologists working in increasing numbers in college counseling centers.

In terms of academic training, all states recognize the curricula of both programs as leading to the title of "psychologist" without specification of clinical or counseling. Furthermore, the core training and practicum training requirements for both professions are highly similar, and the level of competence and respectability from other professions and legal organizations is the same for both specialties. The *Association of State and Provincial Psychology Boards (ASPPB)* established the *Examination for Professional Practice in Psychology (EPPP)*, which is the examination taken by both clinical and counseling psychology graduates and which they must pass to obtain licensure as psychologists. Also, the American Board of Professional Psychology has boards certifying psychologists in both areas, which are highly similar in expectations and requirements. The National Register of Health Service Providers in Psychology recognizes both clinical and counseling psychologists without making distinctions between the two specialties. As Leong and Leach (2008) noted in discussing the convergence of the two fields, the clinical psychologist Martin Seligman's call for an emphasis on *positive psychology* (i.e., a psychology focused on human strengths and abilities) has seemingly brought clinical psychology closer to the historical tradition on which counseling psychology is based.

Another example of the convergence between counseling psychologists and other professional psychologists is evident in Division 29, Psychotherapy, of the American Psychological Association (APA). It is now well represented by high numbers of both counseling and clinical psychologists, and its journal, *Psychotherapy*, has been edited by and has published the work of professionals from counseling and clinical psychology for years. Counseling psychologists have also been active members and leaders, alongside clinical psychologists, in Division 42 (Psychologists in Independent Practice) of the American Psychological Association.

Where differences seem apparent are both in the philosophy, the research, and the advocacy that is being promoted by each area. Counseling psychology still professes a focus on strengths and talents, and on optimal human functioning. Furthermore, the research that is being conducted in counseling psychology, in comparison to clinical psychology, is less focused on *The Diagnostic and Statistical Manual of Mental Disorders* and how it terms psychopathology and more concerned with person–environment interactions, student/personal development, vocational psychology, psychotherapy supervision, basic counseling and psychotherapy skill training and development, and group psychotherapy.

COMPARISON OF DOCTORAL PROGRAMS

Robert Morgan and Lee Cohen (2008) recently conducted a study to see whether differences could be gleaned between counseling psychology and clinical psychology programs based on a review of programs' published materials made available to the public and to prospective applicants. They examined recruitment and application materials from 227 APA-accredited doctoral programs (56 PhD counseling psychology, 137 PhD clinical psychology, and 34 PsyD clinical psychology). They found some appreciable differences between these programs in terms of program or faculty characteristics, admissions, and training requirements. Among the differences found were training in counseling psychology in career/vocational counseling, which was not offered in clinical psychology; clinical faculty were more likely than counseling psychologists to conduct research on mental illness; clinical psychology programs were more likely than counseling psychology programs to offer practicum training in inpatient or hospital settings, and clinical PsyD programs admitted larger number of students into their classes. Interestingly, however, PsyD programs did not differ substantially in the research requirements in comparison to PhD counseling and clinical programs. These authors made two observations: first, their study may have been limited by the fact that they only examined published materials which may have been prepared with a broad description in order to attract and recruit a diverse and wide sample of applicants. Therefore, the descriptions provided in the documents by these programs may have contributed to the limited differences found between them; they cautioned that it is possible that other significant differences might emerge if an examination is conducted to see what students actually do, are taught, and are exposed to in a period of 5–7 years by each specialty. The other observation that Morgan and Cohen offer is that perhaps more substantive differences occur within programs than between them, and this may be a function of the personalities and foci of the faculty of the school, the students who populate these programs, and the broader context and environments in which the programs are housed. In our own review of this article and of the training literature in general, we noted the apparent convergence that seems to be occurring between traditional PsyD and PhD programs; the former programs are now emphasizing training in research design and statistics and requiring doctoral dissertations of its graduates, and PhD programs have been increasing the number of semesters, years, and range of clinical competencies achieved by trainees, even prior to the full clinical internship.

REFLECTIONS ON THE CONVERGENCE OF COUNSELING AND CLINICAL PSYCHOLOGY

Some in counseling psychology have written with concern about the convergence between counseling and clinical psychology. For example, Sprinthall (1990) wrote about the possible "road to Armageddon" warning that counseling psychology was losing its distinctive identity and uniqueness as a profession practiced in schools, colleges, and career/vocational counseling centers. He warned about counseling psychologists branching out to traditionally clinical psychology settings such as hospitals, clinics, and private practice, worrying that counseling psychology would never be fully accepted by clinical psychology and that counseling psychology stood to possibly lose greatly if it became indistinguishable from clinical psychology. Twenty-one years later, Sprinthall's vision has not quite materialized, though we believe that the specialty has lost some if its distinctiveness from clinical psychology. This has occurred primarily through the convergence in the *populations* and *settings* with which both specialties now work, and because the convergence has been a two-way phenomenon. Counseling psychologists practice more and more like clinical psychologists due to market needs and demands and due to the expectations for training and competence from licensing state boards and credentialing agencies like the APA. At the same time, the broader field of professional psychology (including clinical psychology) has gravitated to practice in a way that is consistent with traditions in counseling psychology, namely the use of relatively brief interventions and the emergence of the positive psychology movement. And yet, despite the aforementioned convergence, the philosophical flavor and practical tenor of training in counseling psychology is still in some ways characteristic of its early history, in terms of its positive view of the individual, an emphasis on assets and strengths, attention to person–environment interactions and to cultural factors, and a focus on the psychology of work and vocational behavior.

A Brief History of Our Specialty

EARLY INFLUENCES

Vocational Guidance Movement

The *vocational guidance movement* is one of three important early influences in the development of the profession (Woody, Hansen, & Rossberg, 1989). This movement had as its beginning the work of the Boston lawyer and social reformer Frank Parsons. Parsons was the first known or recorded person who took an intense interest in helping people find meaningful work suited to their talents and personalities. He sought to help people find suitable positions that would be conducive to their satisfaction and in which they would be productive. Parsons responded to the demands of the workplace for increasingly skilled workers for increasingly complex jobs, all of which required formal training and greater education. Parsons's scientific approach to matching people to professions, by analysis of the individual, study of occupations, and "true reasoning" is to this day fundamental to career counseling. His interest in helping people find work where they would be productive and satisfied was well received by industries that were growing in size and levels of production, and where tasks were becoming increasingly sophisticated, requiring substantial risk and investments in training.

Mental Health Movement

The *mental health movement* is the second early influence in the early development of counseling psychology (Woody et al., 1989). The work of Sigmund Freud and his collaborators gained public attention and influenced the development of centers where mental illness could be treated, and where the emotional and psychological well-being of the person could be promoted through psychological intervention (Woody et al., 1989). The decision by Lightner Witmer to open the first psychological clinic at the University of Pennsylvania to help treat children with emotional difficulties ushered in the era of outpatient mental health treatment.

Psychometric Movement

Finally, the *psychometric movement*, primarily in the forms of assessment of giftedness, intelligence, and ability provided an early influence to the development of counseling psychology practice as a scientific and empirical enterprise (Woody et al., 1989). As will be discussed in Chapter 2, the parent disciplines of educational, industrial, and personality/individual differences psychologies all contributed to the early development of counseling psychology, and the mental health movement from Freud on contributed to the development of psychotherapies that shaped and still characterize assessment and intervention in counseling psychology practice until today.

WORLD WAR I AND WORLD WAR II

The two world wars were crucial to the development of psychology in the varied areas of education, guidance, training and placement, mental health, and psychometrics. Demand for the testing, recruitment, and placement (and later the treatment and rehabilitation) of young people to various tasks and responsibilities associated with the war fueled the expansion of psychology and created the seeds for the growth of counseling psychology after the war. Psychologists and other professionals became interested in identifying, training, and placing personnel for the most appropriate positions in the war effort, and the federal government funded academic programs to train counselors to serve returning veterans. Concomitantly, pressures and social movements emanating from industry, and new legislation mandating the protection of children and greater awareness about their developmental and educational needs, enhanced the emphasis on education, learning, and guidance. These factors stimulated the growth of counseling and guidance programs in schools, in community agencies, and in colleges and universities. After World War II, there was a sharp increase in the need for psychologists who could help returning soldiers adjust to life back at home, and the GI Bill provided funds for many of these returning soldiers, mostly men in their late teens or early twenties, to finish their high school education and enroll in colleges and technical schools. Counseling centers were established and expanded in these educational settings to help veterans adjust and develop the skills necessary for being productive citizens, and counseling psychology came of age, first within the medicine and neurology units of Veterans Administration hospitals, and soon after as part of outpatient services in community centers and in college counseling centers. The reader is referred to Whiteley's (1984) *The History of Counseling Psychology*, Gelso and Fretz's (2001) *Counseling Psychology*, and Blocher's (2000) *The Evolution of Counseling Psychology* for more in-depth reading on the history of counseling psychology.

MAJOR CONFERENCES/EVENTS

The Boulder Conference of 1949 was convened by the American Psychological Association, the Veterans Administration, and the United States Public Health Service (Baker & Subich, 2008). At this conference, a multidisciplinary group of professionals discussed the future of psychology and the proper training involved in preparing psychologists for public service. The result of their deliberations was the adoption of a model that emphasized training in the absorption and generation of knowledge via scientific methods, and the development of technical skills in assessment and intervention that would make practicing psychologists competent and effective. This model was called the *scientist-practitioner model* and remains to this day one of the primary models of training in both counseling and clinical psychology.

A subsequent conference took place at Northwestern University in 1951 and participants were primarily counselors who debated issues associated with the refinement of the specialty, including statements on identity, specialization, and training criteria in counseling psychology (Baker & Subich, 2008). The result of the Northwestern conference was the reaffirmation of the scientist-practitioner model but stronger statements on the uniqueness of the specialty of counseling psychology and about the training guidelines to prepare psychologists to embody the focus of the specialty. It was also at this conference that the division of Counseling and Guidance within the APA became the division of Counseling Psychology. Soon after the Northwestern conference preparations were made for the development of a scientific journal on the broad topic of counseling psychology, and the *Journal of Counseling Psychology* was launched in 1954.

The Greyston Conference in New York City took place in 1964 and affirmed the identity of counseling psychology, particularly its commitment to examining person–environment–cultural interactions. Perhaps reflecting the sociopolitical movements in the United States in the 1960s, conferees affirmed the opportunities available in both science and practice in counseling psychology to meet the needs of persons living in poverty, and to promote human rights and the educational and developmental needs of those otherwise marginalized in society. The third and fourth National Conferences in Counseling Psychology, in Atlanta in 1987 and in Houston in 2001, reasserted the historical focus of counseling psychology as a specialty centered on developing human potential across the life span; in developing, refining, and using assessment procedures and interventions that uncover and build on the talents and strengths of the person; and in promoting in the individual and society an awareness of social justice, opportunity, and tolerance. Finally, the 2008 conference on international counseling psychology was held in Chicago with the theme "creating the future, counseling psychologists in a changing world." The conference reflected an emerging global emphasis in the profession but promoted papers and workshops on traditional themes such as scientist-practitioner training, prevention, career and vocational psychology, and strength-based approaches.

Today, Division 17 has approximately 2,000 members and an organizational structure that reflects the diversity of the issues with which counseling psychology is concerned (Baker & Subich, 2008). As of this writing there are 69 programs in counseling psychology that are approved by the APA. Sixty-four of these are PhD programs and three are PsyD programs. Two of the 67 are in Canada. The majority of these programs (78%) are housed in schools of education. There also 5 additional programs in counseling psychology that are accredited by the APA in "combined professional-scientific psychology" and all are PhD programs in the United States. The APA surveys graduates from different degrees with respect to where they work. The APA research office reports that in terms of full-time work, counseling psychologists surveyed in 2007 worked in university settings (17.6%), medical schools (2.9%), other academic settings (1.5%), schools and other educational settings (4.4%), independent practice (7.4%), hospitals (17.6%), other human services (32.4%), managed care, (8.8)%, and business/government and other (5.9%).

The Culture of Competence in Professional Psychology

There has been a movement to delineate specific knowledge, skills, and attitudes that characterize reasonable professional standards in professional psychology (Bourg, Bent, McHolland, & Stricker, 1989). On the one hand, there has been the effort by the APA to specify how specialties in professional psychology can be recognized and to establish the type of education and training activities that each specialty offers that culminate in achieved specialization. At the same time, the code of ethics of the APA has specified competency guidelines with respect to scope of practice and continuing education, which has stimulated thinking among professionals, training programs, and professional organizations, such as the American Board of Professional Psychology, to delineate competency guidelines for professional counselors.

BRIEF HISTORY OF THE COMPETENCY MOVEMENT

The competency movement can be traced to the early days of the professional psychology and the Boulder Conference (Raimy, 1950), where professionals discussed the optimal model of training in psychology, including the knowledge and skills that graduates would be expected to master prior to graduation. Since then the National Council of Schools and Programs of Professional Psychology has led the field in proposing and revising a core curriculum for professional psychologists. More recently, clinical, counseling, and school psychology organizations have organized their own conferences and work groups to develop and implement models of competency that cover the education, practicum, and internship training of professional psychologists (see Rubin et al., 2007). The Competencies Conference of 2002 was a pivotal event in the competency movement, and the development of the competency cube in 2005 (Rodolfa et al., 2005) was the seminal article in mapping out the scope of competence. The board-certifying body in professional psychology, the American Board of Professional Psychology, has also implemented its own model of competency with which to evaluate professionals. Increasing attention has also been given to the ethical principle of competence in the code of ethics of the APA, which includes competence as both "an aspirational principle and an enforceable standard" (p. 511; Barnett, Doll, Younggren, & Rubin, 2007). Standard 2 of the APA code of ethics guides psychologists to only provide services for which they have received training and are competent to do so based on "their education, training, supervised experience, consultation, study, or professional experience" (p. 1063), and it guides psychologists to continue their training to maintain an adequate level of competence. The current competency assessment movement has been guided by several principles (see Kaslow et al., 2007), including that competencies be developmental, generic, sensitive to individual and cultural diversity, represent fidelity to practice, and evaluated via various perspectives and methods.

MODELS OF COMPETENCE

A major development in the competency movement has been the publication of a model of competence in professional psychology, The Assessment of Competency Benchmarks Work Group Model (hereafter, CB model; Fouad et al., 2009). This model is based on the extensive work of the Assessment of Competency Benchmarks Work Group convened by the APA Board of Educational Affairs in collaboration with the Council of Chairs of Training Councils. Their charge was to delineate specific competencies that cut across specialties in professional psychology. This work group used as a basis a three-dimensional cube model developed by Rodolfa et al. (2005), which has as its primary axes six foundational competency domains (i.e., reflective practice/self-assessment, scientific knowledge and methods, relationships, ethical and legal standards/policy issues, individual and cultural diversity, and interdisciplinary systems), six functional competency domains (i.e., assessment/diagnosis/conceptualization, intervention, consultation, research/evaluation, supervision/teaching, management/administration), and five stages of professional development (i.e., doctoral education, doctoral internship/residency, postdoctoral supervision, residency/fellowship, continuing competency). Rodolfa et al. in turn based their work and model on the models of education that have been developed over the years by the National Council of Schools and Programs of Professional Psychology (NCSPPP; Kenkle & Peterson, 2010; Rubin et al., 2007). The NCSPPP has continued to develop their model of education, and they recently came out with a model comprised of seven competency areas, which are relationship-based, assessment, intervention, research and evaluation, consultation and education, management and supervision, and diversity competencies (Kenkel & Peterson, 2010). The CB model of professional competence is identical to Rodolfa et al.'s model in terms of foundational and functional competencies except that it delineates competencies across three developmental stages: readiness for practicum, readiness for internship, and readiness for entry to practice (see Table 1.2). Within each of the six foundational and six functional competency areas the work group identified subareas of competence (50 subareas total), and within each subarea and stage of professional development the work group summarized the essential component and highly specific "behavioral anchors" that characterize competence (in total there are 469 specific competencies). They also specified assessment methods per subarea.

The competencies identified in the CB model (Fouad et al., 2009) are by design generic in nature and intended to reflect competence across specialties in professional psychology. Our task has been to review and present sample competencies from this and other models, and to discuss how these competencies pertain to the specialty of counseling psychology. We also describe professional practice in counseling psychology and note what we believe to be the standards of competent practice in the specialty. While we agree with Fouad et al. (2009) that general competencies can be distilled for all professional psychologists, nonetheless, each specialty and

TABLE 1.2 **The Competency Benchmarks (CB) Model**

Developmental Stages: Readiness for Practicum, Readiness for Internship, Readiness for Entry to Practice

Foundational Competency Areas

1. Professionalism—Professional values and ethics as evidenced in behavior and comportment that reflect the values and ethics of psychology, integrity, and responsibility.
2. Reflective Practice/Self-Assessment/Self-Care—Practice conducted with personal and professional self-awareness and reflection; with awareness of competencies; with appropriate self-care.
3. Scientific Knowledge and Methods—Understanding of research, research methodology, techniques of data collection and analysis, biological bases of behavior, cognitive-affective bases of behavior, and development across the life span. Respect for scientifically derived knowledge.
4. Relationships—Relate effectively and meaningfully with individuals, groups, and/or communities.
5. Individual and Cultural Diversity—Awareness, sensitivity, and skills in working professionally with diverse individuals, groups, and communities who represent various cultural and personal backgrounds and characteristics defined broadly and consistent with American Psychological Association policy.
6. Ethical Legal Standards and Policy—Application of ethical concepts and awareness of legal issues regarding professional activities with individuals, groups, and organizations.
7. Interdisciplinary Systems—Knowledge of key issues and concepts in related disciplines. Identify and interact with professionals in multiple disciplines.

Functional Competency Areas

1. Assessment—Assessment and diagnosis of problems, capabilities, and issues associated with individuals, groups, and/or organizations.
2. Intervention—Interventions designed to alleviate suffering and to promote health and well-being of individuals, groups, and/or organizations.
3. Consultation—The ability to provide expert guidance or professional assistance in response to a client's needs or goals.
4. Research/Evaluation—Generating research that contributes to the professional knowledge base and/or evaluates the effectiveness of various professional activities.
5. Supervision—Supervision and training in the professional knowledge base and of evaluation of the effectiveness of various professional activities.

6. Teaching—Providing instruction, disseminating knowledge, and evaluating acquisition of knowledge and skill in professional psychology.
7. Management-Administration—Manage the direct delivery of services (DDS) and/or the administration of organizations, programs, or agencies (OPA).
8. Advocacy—Actions targeting the impact of social, political, economic or cultural factors to promote change at the individual (client), institutional, and/or systems level.

Source: From Fouad et al. (2009). Copyright © 2009 by the American Psychological Association. Adapted with permission. The official citation that should be used in referencing this material is Fouad, N. A., Grus, C. L., Hatcher, R. L., Kaslow, N. J., Hutchings, P. S., Madson, M. B., . . . Crossman, R. E. (2009). Competency benchmarks: A model for understanding and measuring competence in professional psychology across training levels. *Training and Education in Professional Psychology*, 3(4, Suppl), S5–S26. doi:10.1037/a0015832. No further reproduction or distribution is permitted without written permission from the American Psychological Association.

each training program has unique traditions, approaches to intervention, and settings and populations with which it concerns itself, and which give each a particular flavor and distinction; this was noted by Rodolfa et al. (2005) in their development of the competency cube model.

There are several questions that emerge with respect to these models. One is their empirical base, which to date has not been presented in the published literature (Schulte & Daly, 2009). The current set of competencies has been derived as consensus statements from task forces or work groups of professional psychologists. The other question refers to the evidence tying these competencies to better practice or enhanced outcomes for clients/patients. While these competencies have been developed after considerable thought and discussion over a period of years, and while they resonate with clinicians and policy makers, the link between them and enhanced outcome and practice has yet to be made (Lichtenberg et al., 2007). Despite these limitations, the competency models that have been published can serve to highlight specific areas for training programs, for evaluating progress in supervision, for evaluating clinical practice, and can and are being used to evaluate candidates for certification. These competency models can also serve to stimulate psychotherapy research in outcome, process, and clinical training. Already a special issue of the journal *Psychotherapy* was devoted to examining how competencies can be integrated within an array of theoretical frameworks, and a toolkit was published that can be used to assess competencies delineated by the CB model. In sum, the models presented in this volume are not the final word on what constitutes competence in professional psychology, but they appear to be a first step in what appears to be an important phase in future clinical practice (Barnett et al., 2007).

The American Board of Counseling Psychology

Counseling psychology was one of the original certification specialties recognized in 1947 when the American Board of Professional Psychology (ABPP) was founded. The Board was originally organized regionally and, during the beginning decades of the ABPP, exams were administered regionally (e.g., Midwest Board, Eastern Board). The American Board of Counseling Psychology (ABCoP) establishes both qualifications for board certification in counseling psychology and procedures for conducting the review of credentials, practice samples, and the oral examinations in counseling psychology. The ABCoP is governed by a board composed of members certified in counseling psychology and representative of the specialty on a national basis. Board certification in counseling psychology assures the public and the profession that the counseling psychologist has successfully completed the education, training, and experience requirements of the specialty, including an examination designed to assess competencies necessary to provide quality services. During the existence of ABCoP, the central agenda items have remained relatively constant (see Table 1.3).

The counseling specialty board places particular value and emphasis on a rigorous examination process for candidates for board certification.

TABLE 1.3 **Central Agenda Items of the American Board of Counseling Psychology**

(1) Continuous refinement of the criteria used to assess applicants, particularly the practice sample and oral examination criteria.

(2) Demystification of board certification through the development of a criterion-based approach and emphasis on *specialty* competence.

(3) Streamlining the application and examination process without compromising the integrity of board certification.

(4) Development of a more effective mentoring process.

(5) Development of flexibility in the application and examination process.

(6) Inclusion of diversity in the examination criteria.

(7) Maintaining the viability of counseling psychology board certification.

Source: From the American Board of Professional Psychology (2007).

This process includes prescreening of applicants' credentials by the central office; a thorough evaluation and preparation of a practice sample representative of the candidates' typical professional work; and a formal, live examination of these materials that includes ethics and alternative approaches to intervention by a panel of board-certified colleagues. The counseling specialty board emphasizes an examination process that is respectful and challenging for the candidate. Examiners are trained to avoid being argumentative, parochial, confrontational, aloof, or insulting and instead seek to promote an interested, involved, and thoughtful consideration of the candidates' work.

In September 2007, a taskforce of ABCoP met to revise and streamline the examination process and manuals. The revised oral examination is conducted over a half day and consists of an evaluation of competence in eight competency domains: (1) science base and application, (2) assessment, (3) intervention, (4) consultation, (5) interpersonal interactions, (6) individual and cultural diversity, (7) ethical and legal foundations, and (8) professional identification. These domains are examined in six professional practice areas: (1) counseling/psychotherapy, (2) career/vocational counseling, (3) consultation, (4) administration/management, (5) training, and (6) supervision. Specific competencies evaluated by the ABCoP are presented in subsequent chapters of this book.

The Current Volume

The current series of books on the professional practice of psychology highlight the 13 specialty boards that comprise the ABPP (see Table 1.4).

Editors Arthur and Christine Nezu have defined *foundational competencies* as knowledge bases essential to competent practice in counseling psychology. *Functional competencies* refer to actual service delivery abilities that are informed by foundational competencies and other relevant functional competencies. Our thinking as professors of counseling psychology, as licensed psychologists, and as board-certified psychologists by the ABCoP has led us to an organization of this volume as follows. In terms of a *foundational* domain, Chapter 2 presents core foundational areas of counseling psychology; Chapter 3 covers knowledge and application of ethics; and Chapter 4 focuses on issues of human diversity, social justice, and multiculturalism. In terms of a *functional* domain, Chapter 5 covers competencies in assessment and case conceptualization; Chapter 6 discusses competence in intervention, including the role of the professional relationship in treatment; Chapter 7 covers the specialty specific

TABLE 1.4 The Thirteen Specialty Boards of the American Board of Professional Psychology

Clinical Child & Adolescent Psychology
Clinical Health Psychology
Clinical Neuropsychology
Clinical Psychology
Cognitive & Behavioral Psychology
Counseling Psychology
Couple & Family Psychology
Forensic Psychology
Group Psychology
Organizational & Business Consulting Psychology
Psychoanalysis in Psychology
Rehabilitation Psychology
School Psychology

area of functional competence-vocational psychology; Chapter 8 discusses supervision; Chapter 9 considers the professional practice of consultation; and Chapter 10 focuses on competence in research.

Beyond the CB model of competence (Fouad et al., 2009), our discussion of professional competence in the subsequent chapters is also guided by the extensive work that has been done in the area of professional training in counseling psychology by different teams of professional psychologists, including counseling psychologists, over extended periods of time. We cite the work of Murdock, Alcorn, Heesacker, and Stoltenberg (1998) and Stoltenberg, Pace, Kashubeck-West, Biever, Patterson, and Welch (2000) in developing the model training program in counseling psychology. In terms of models of competence beyond counseling psychology, as noted earlier, we are guided by and reference the model of competency-based education for professional psychology, which has been developed for over 30 years by the National Council of Schools and Programs of Professional Psychology, and which was recently updated and published by Mary Beth Kenkel and Roger L. Peterson (2010). We will also discuss the core areas that comprise the EPPP, which is the licensing examination used throughout the United States and Canada and developed by the Association of State and Provincial Psychology Boards. We view this examination as perhaps the ultimate test of foundational competence knowledge in professional psychology, and it is *the* test that counseling psychologists have to pass to become licensed as psychologists in every state in the United States. These models of competency will be referenced throughout the book, and we will present the reader with a summary of the structure of the content and main points of each model by the respective areas in each chapter. We provide sample competencies but refer the reader to the original documents for a comprehensive review of each model and all the respective competencies. Wherever we deem appropriate, we add our own statements regarding competence or professional standards of practice in counseling psychology.

Figure 1.1 presents a graphic depiction of the volume, under foundational domain areas and functional domain areas of professional practice. The figure represents our thinking in terms of the relationship between these different domains. Foundational domains precede the functional domain, but these domains are interrelated and inform one another as depicted with the arrows in the figure. In Figure 1.1 we present how the core areas of psychology, as well as ethics and human diversity, inform assessment and intervention and the professional practice areas of vocational psychology, supervision, and consultation. We also show that assessment informs intervention and that intervention informs practice. We also note that research is informed by the preceding functional and foundational areas, but the returning arrow from research shows that research generates results which inform functional and foundational knowledge.

How is the figure specific to counseling psychology, since it seemingly could relate to other service professions in psychology (e.g., clinical psychology)? To answer this difficult question, we draw upon the unifying principles of the profession identified by Gelso and Fretz (2001). Counseling psychologists tend to focus on helping individuals adjust, cope, function, and thrive. The figure presented is thus harnessed in the service of the strengths of the individual, to promote development and functioning in human relationships and in the world of work. Counseling psychologists also pay close attention to person–environment interactions, so that the focus would not be exclusively on the client and his or her maladaptive internal mechanisms. Counseling psychologists tend to focus as much on the environment as they do on the person and have been influenced by Kurt Lewin's dictum that behavior is a function of the person operating in the environment. Our specialty adheres to the belief that it is a major limitation of psychology or professional practice to try to understand the individual and his or her problems without an analysis

Figure 1.1 Organizational framework of this volume (chapter number in parentheses).

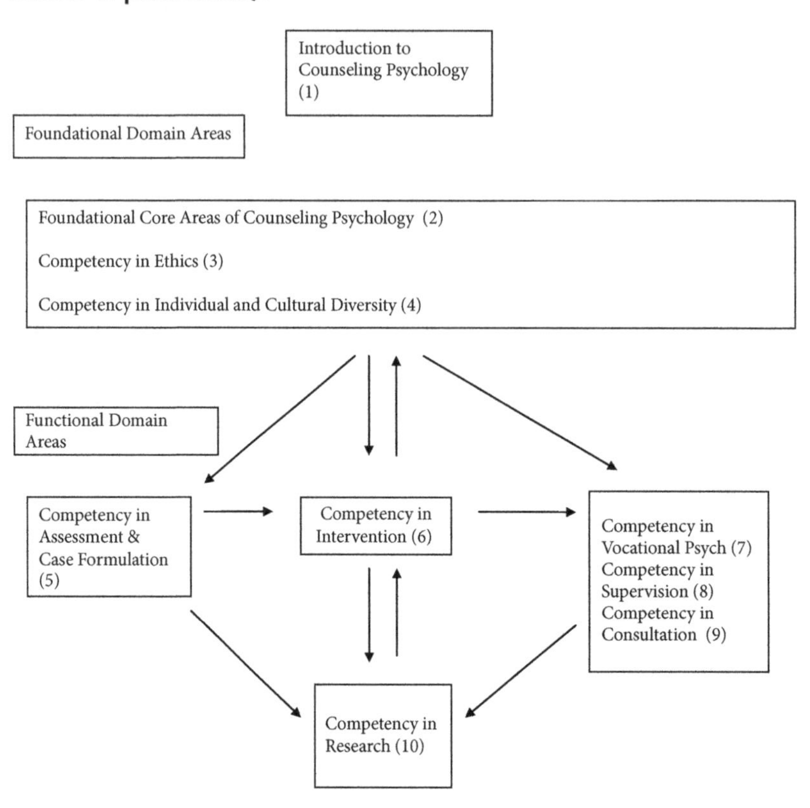

and understanding of his or her environment. This perspective explains the sensitivity of counseling psychology to the context in which the person lives and operates in order to understand behavior. The model presented would also be used by counseling psychologists in programs and interventions that promote life-span development, including the lifelong educational-vocational needs of the individual. As Milton Hahn (1955) observed in the early days of the specialty, "our most nearly unique single function, we are the most skilled professional workers in the assessment and appraisal of human traits for educational-vocational-social living: the casting of a psychological balance sheet to aid our clients to contribute to, and to take from, living in our society" (p. 104). The reader should note what Hahn (1955) makes evident in his quote and which is still true today: that counseling psychologists tend to refer to the people that they serve as "clients" and not as "patients," with the exception being counseling psychologists who work in hospitals. Professional practice in counseling psychology has also been influenced by the human potential and self-actualization paradigms in psychology, as so much of our work in assessment, intervention, supervision, and research is directed at promoting psychological growth and at maintaining and strengthening mental hygiene, or what Super (1957) referred to as "hygeology," the study of human psychological health.

PART I

Foundational Competencies in Counseling Psychology

TWO

Foundational Core Knowledge Areas of Counseling Psychology

This chapter covers fundamental knowledge and foundational competencies in counseling psychology. Consistent with the organizational framework presented in Chapter 1, we include content from the core academic areas in psychology, from the research core foundations, and from the theoretical and empirical bases of psychotherapy. We also cite sample foundational competencies that have been outlined in the literature, including personal and relationship competencies. Two other foundational areas, ethics (Chapter 3) and individual and cultural diversity (Chapter 4), are covered in Part I of this book.

One of the truisms that we have stumbled upon in reading and thinking about this book is the deep connection and interplay between what is foundational and functional in the professional practice of counseling psychology. Making distinctions between foundational competencies and functional competencies in an applied area like ours can seem like the proverbial splitting of hairs. Functional competence is grounded on and intimately tied to foundational knowledge, clinical interventions are based on knowledge and skills honed over several years of incremental study, and the budding professional integrates over time theories and techniques into a personal approach to practice in increasingly complex and demanding clinical training experiences. A review of the current models of competency training and education in professional psychology indicates that foundational and functional competencies are conceived of along a developmental continuum that begins with training at the practicum level and continues through internship and professional practice after graduation. Foundational competence evolves through training, mirroring the complexity that characterizes the evolution of functional competence.

Foundational knowledge has informed professional practice since the beginning days of the profession (American Psychological Association, 1952), and practice has also informed the development of knowledge. Numerous research studies have been conducted based on questions about phenomena observed by clinicians in the field. As an example of this interplay, clinical practice has stimulated research about the role of specific helping skills derived from theory on the process of counseling (e.g., therapist self-disclosure or the use of immediacy), and the results of this research have provided knowledge into how these interventions affect clients, how these skills can be used optimally with certain clients or at varying points in therapy, and how students can be taught to use them as part of training. Of course, many more questions are raised by the results of such research, providing a continuous cycle of research and practice that advances both the knowledge base and clinical effectiveness in the process. Perhaps *because* of the interplay and profound connection between foundational knowledge and competent practice in assessment and intervention, it is useful to delineate the essence of the foundational areas, to delve into their respective qualities, and to examine how the foundational areas have shaped and guided functional competence in counseling psychology. Indeed, it seems valuable to look at the current literature on competence-based practice and examine this literature as it relates to counseling psychology training and practice.

The scientist-practitioner model of training weds knowledge and empirical inquiry with clinical practice, and chief among its aims is the preparation of clinicians who can consume and contribute to the production of knowledge, as well as researchers who can examine questions through science with relevance to clinical practice (Belar, 1992; Belar & Perry, 1992). While it is tempting to call the practice of counseling psychology a craft, or an art form, it is more precise to call it a health care service profession grounded in and guided by psychological theory and rigorous scientific thinking and research. Training in counseling psychology begins with the acquisition of theories about the makeup of the individual—including his or her development, personality, and environment—as well as theories of psychotherapy and the empirical base behind the practice of psychotherapy. Early training also includes teachings on ethics and human diversity, and training in research design, measurement, and statistics. These areas constitute the scientific foundations of the profession and shape the early professional formation of the counseling psychologist. Thus, psychological theory, knowledge, and training in research constitute the foundation on which professional functional competence is built. The *core academic areas* in psychology are developmental psychology, social psychology, cognition psychology, personality/individual differences, and the biological bases of behavior. These knowledge areas have been part of professional training for decades and have been affirmed as central to training in counseling psychology; these areas are part of the *Model Training Program (MTP)* developed by the members of the Council of Counseling Psychology Training Programs (CCPTP) and the leadership of Division 17 of the American Psychological Association (APA), the Society of Counseling Psychology (Murdock et al., 1998). The research core includes training in the scientific method and includes research methods, research design, data analysis techniques, and psychometrics. More recently, programs in counseling psychology have also added qualitative research approaches to the curriculum of training, without supplanting traditional scientific training, and some dissertations and published articles in major journals in the field have now been conducted using qualitative methodologies. Since we note the MTP in counseling psychology (Murdock et al., 1998; Stoltenberg et al., 2000), at this point we will also note that it also includes training in history and systems, and outlines 10 additional professional core areas of training in counseling psychology, including the following: professional issues in the specialty, theories and techniques of intervention, legal and ethical issues, individual and cultural diversity, practicum and internship training, psychological assessment, diagnosis, and appraisal, career development and counseling, consultation, program evaluation, and supervision and training. These core areas, as well as the professional areas outlined in the MTP, are discussed in this chapter and in the other chapters of this volume.

Training in counseling psychology also includes exposure to a variety of theoretical approaches to treatment. While the relevant empirical content in this area is presented and discussed in Chapter 6 of this book, here we will provide a succinct discussion of the rich theoretical bases that guide psychotherapy approaches, and we summarize the extensive research that has been conducted that examines the effectiveness of psychotherapy. We also touch upon the work of counseling psychologists in developing a core knowledge base of helping skills, which are the building blocks of psychotherapy training. These areas, in our view, represent fundamental knowledge domains of early training in our specialty, and they represent foundational competence in counseling psychology.

Much of our work in this chapter—and the entire book for that matter—is informed by the extensive thinking that has been conducted over many years in counseling psychology and by the broader professions of applied psychology. We have searched the literature on training in counseling psychology, and it seems that the preparation of this book is timely and coincides with major developments in the area of competency training in professional psychology. We have reviewed and have been informed by the long-standing and recently revised *model of competency-based education* developed by the National Council of Schools and Programs of Professional Psychology (NCSPPP; Kenkle & Peterson, 2010). We have also tracked the development of highly specific competencies in the competencies benchmarks (CB) model (Fouad et al., 2009), which grew out of the work of a work group convened by the APA Board of Educational Affairs and which was comprised of the Council of Chairs of Training Councils, of which the Council of Counseling Psychology Training Programs is a member. The NCSPP and the CB model work group (Fouad et al., 2009) have made significant strides in identifying and delineating highly specific foundational and functional competencies for professional training in psychology, and they are in essence ushering into the mainstream of professional training what is now called the "culture of competency-based" training in professional psychology (Fouad et al., 2009; Kaslow, 2009). Beyond these two models, we are also guided by the MTP in counseling psychology and by the Examination for Professional Practice in Psychology (EPPP), developed by The Association of State and Provincial Psychology Boards (ASPPB), an association in which counseling psychologists have been active for years. The EPPP is the examination taken for licensure to practice psychology in all 50 states of the United States and in

TABLE 2.1 **Eight General Content Areas Assessed by the Examination for Professional Practice in Psychology (EPPP)**

1. Biological bases of behavior
2. Cognitive-affective bases of behavior
3. Social and multicultural bases of behavior
4. Growth and life-span development
5. Assessment and diagnosis
6. Intervention and prevention
7. Research methods and statistics
8. Ethical, legal, and professional issues

Source: From Association of State and Provincial Psychology Boards (2009).

Canada. We see the EPPP as perhaps the ultimate objective test of foundational knowledge and competence in psychology, including counseling psychology. The eight general content areas assessed by the EPPP via its standardized 225 multiple-choice items are listed in Table 2.1. While we will cite the content areas assessed via the EPPP throughout this volume, for the purposes of this chapter we will review the subareas pertaining to the core areas of knowledge and research.

Theoretical and Empirical Bases

The core academic areas of psychology are supremely important in that they represent the core knowledge of all psychology and in and of themselves represent specialty academic areas with long histories and traditions. As we will show, the core areas of psychology have informed and grounded the practice of counseling psychology, in some instances directly, in others areas indirectly, since the early days of Frank Parsons (1909). Training in the core areas of psychology is required of programs in counseling psychology that are approved by the APA. These areas of psychology represent central aspects of human behavior and are at the core of training in other health service specialties. Doctoral students in counseling psychology will often find themselves with students in other academic (e.g., developmental psychology) and applied psychology areas (e.g., clinical psychology) while taking these courses. These core areas are so fundamental to the early development of a psychologist that they can be considered the sine qua non of professional training, providing students with foundational knowledge with respect to theory and research in psychology.

A brief statement on the content of these core areas is in order. With respect to learning and cognition, counseling psychology students are exposed to theories of learning, theories of intelligence, fundamentals of perception, reasoning, the psychology of language, and the vast research on memory. Didactic instruction in the biological bases of behavior includes lectures on neuron and brain anatomy and functioning and research on brain–behavior relationships; many programs also cover the fundamentals of neuropsychological assessment and the nature of common neuropsychological disorders. Doctoral-level training in human development throughout the life span includes theory and research on emotional development, cognitive and language development, and affective and moral development. Social psychology covers interpersonal relations, social learning, social motivation, communication, attitudes, groups and organizations, behavior, and social/cultural change. A course on personality/individual differences includes readings on theories and research that cover dimensions of personality and the measurement of differences in the psychological makeup of individuals, including personality, intelligence and other talents and abilities, interests, and values. While these core areas represent separate academic areas of psychology and are separate courses in graduate training, they are nonetheless interrelated. For example, theories of learning can be understood in the context of human development, individual differences, affect and motivation, and brain anatomy and neuron functioning. These core areas, therefore, have considerable overlap and, as part of the curriculum in counseling psychology, provide a foundational and rich intellectual basis for early training.

LITERATURE ON THE RELATIONSHIP BETWEEN CORE AREAS OF PSYCHOLOGY

The relationship among the core areas of psychology was discussed in a series of articles published in the *Journal of Counseling Psychology* to commemorate the centennial of the APA in 1992. In the words of the guest editors (Richardson & Patton, 1992), the "centennial of the APA provides a unique opportunity to critically examine the relationship of counseling psychology ... to its parent discipline of psychology" (p. 3). In addition to the guest editors' introduction and summative reflections, three separate seminal papers were published in which the connection between counseling psychology and core areas of psychology was described. For the purposes of the current chapter, we provide a succinct review of the three papers that delved into the connection between counseling psychology and the academic areas of psychology. While these papers were published nearly 20 years ago, a review of them indicates that they remain extremely important in understanding the foundation and development of counseling psychology, and that many of the observations and research ideas presented by the authors still seem relevant and important today. Moreover, we believe that a discussion of these articles may provide further insights into the connection between counseling psychology and its "parent" disciplines and may stimulate further thinking about this legacy.

Individual Differences Tradition in Counseling Psychology

The first paper was entitled "The Individual Differences Tradition in Counseling Psychology" and was authored by Rene V. Dawis. As Dawis (1992) argues, counseling psychology is essentially applied *individual differences psychology*. He traces the history of counseling psychology to educational psychology and industrial psychology. Early in the 20th century, psychologists in these two areas were concerned with assessing abilities and functioning in individuals, and they delved into the development of *trait-factor theories*. With the idea of matching the abilities of the person with the characteristics of the environment, they began the assessment of individuals along psychological and behavioral traits and began to define and measure educational and work environments in terms of factors. These assessments had real-life implications for the selection, training, and placement of these individuals into school/educational settings or professions.

Both educational psychology and industrial psychology were heavily influenced in their beginnings by even earlier advances in psychological measurement and earlier innovations in *psychometrics*. Dawis (1992) notes that the very earliest minds in the field of psychometrics and test construction provided the foundation on which individual differences psychology was built; men such as Francis Galton, Alfred Binet, Edward Lee Thorndike, and Karl Pearson can be claimed as the forefathers of counseling psychology. He also notes that the early advocates for the specialty of counseling psychology, such as Donald Super and Edmund Williamson, C. Gilbert Wrenn, and Leona Tyler, were in fact individual differences psychologists who saw vast opportunities for the application of individual differences psychology to the world of education and work.

A review of Dawis's (1992) paper makes the connections between individual differences psychology and the five unifying themes characteristic of counseling psychology (Gelso & Fretz, 2001) appreciable. The foundations in educational and industrial psychology explain our focus and traditional work in guidance and counseling in schools and colleges, as well as our theoretical and empirical contributions to the literature on vocational behavior. Guidance and counseling in schools and colleges invariably entailed a careful consideration of the environment, leading to the development of trait and factors theories of vocational psychology, and propelling our research into the assessment of human interests, talents, and abilities (as opposed to work on defining, classifying, and assessing dysfunction and pathology). To maximize the fit between the student/worker and his or her environment, counseling psychologists were involved in the education, training, and placement process, thereby placing our work in schools and colleges at the early phase of intervention (i.e., prevention). The early history of our work in clinics and hospitals was in vocational rehabilitation, and while our work in clinics and hospital has broadened to all facets of psychological assessment and care, our work continues to be characterized by the conduct of assessments and interventions that are grounded in the psychology of individual differences.

Social Psychology and Counseling Psychology

The second paper in the series was entitled "Social Psychology and Counseling Psychology: The History, Products, and Promise of an Interface" and was authored by Stanley R. Strong, Josephine A. Welsh, Jean L. Corcoran, and William T. Hoyt (1992). Strong et al. discussed the overlap between social psychology and counseling psychology and pointed out that an interface between these professions occurred early on in the development of the counseling psychology specialty, when researchers examining the process and mechanisms of change realized that therapy was a special form of a social encounter. Strong et al. note that it became possible for counselors to use theories of social psychology because clients in therapy were similar to the subjects in social psychology research (i.e., relatively psychologically normal college students) and because both disciplines were essentially interested in the dynamics of normal encounters. Another significant point of convergence was researchers' realization that therapy was a form of a social influence process, social influence being the foundational hallmark of social psychology research (Ross & Nisbett, 1991). The earliest names associated with the study of psychotherapy using theories of social psychology are Jerome Frank (1961) and Harold Pepinsky (1963; Pepinksy & Karst, 1964); the former wrote extensively about the interpersonal process of persuasion in treatment, and the latter developed a program of research examining convergence in language, attitudes, and views between clients and counselors. Stanley Strong's (1968) paper on therapy as a social influence process stimulated numerous studies on the role of counselor attractiveness, trustworthiness, and credibility in facilitating client perceptions of the counselor as a credible source of help. Indeed, a significant amount of research in psychotherapy conducted by counseling psychologists has examined the role of constructs from social psychology, such as cognitive dissonance, casual attributions, impression management, bias, and strategic self-presentation in the process and outcome of treatment. Strong et al. noted that a considerable amount of research on psychotherapy has been developed along the lines of social psychology constructs, namely an interest in (a) the convergence of attitudes/beliefs, language, and agreement between therapist and client; (b) the role of discrepancy on client change, based on therapist interventions such as questions, interpretations, self-disclosures, and feedback; and (c) client dependence and responsiveness, which has been anchored in research on the motivational role of the relationship in client change and clients' responsiveness to being open to change as a consequence of such a relationship. Many of the studies anchored in social psychology principles were published in the *Journal of Counseling Psychology* and have been designed as analog studies using quasi-experimental methodology, adapted by counseling psychologists from the laboratory studies conducted in social psychology.

The interplay between social psychology and counseling psychology has been evident in contemporary writings and nascent research on the psychology of human diversity and multiculturalism. This latter work deconstructs the role of the environment and societal forces on the development and worldview of the individual, and advances the view that clients and therapists are socialized beings with biases and prejudices that may be unconscious and manifested in the social encounter of the session. The new psychology of human diversity has raised serious questions about the traditional role of the therapist as a legitimate source of social influence, credibility, and trust, particularly when the counseling dyad is diverse or when the content of the sessions has to do with racism, oppression, or bias. The social emphases of research conducted by counseling psychologists in the last 15 years can also be discerned in studies examining the role of the therapy relationship in treatment. One dimension of the relationship that has received considerable attention is the construct of the working alliance, which is theoretically characterized by a convergence of views and agreement between therapists and clients on the goals and tasks of treatment, and the development of trust between them. Strong et al. (1992) noted that due to the persistence of counseling psychologists in studying the therapy relationship, it has become the most studied and understood human relationship in all of psychology.

Personality, Development, and Counseling Psychology

The third paper in the series was entitled "Personality, Development, and Counseling Psychology: Depth, Ambivalence, and Actualization" and was authored by Charles J. Gelso and Ruth E. Fassinger (1992). These authors discussed the influence and interplay between counseling psychology and personality and developmental psychology, and were particularly attentive to discussing how counseling psychology has been *influenced by and influenced* personality and developmental psychology. They chronicled the history of applied psychology to the early days of Freud and psychoanalysis, through Watson's behaviorism, the humanistic theories of Maslow and Rogers, the typological or trait-factor theories of Eysenck and Raymond Cattel, to the more recent developments in cognitive psychology, particularly Kelly's theory of personal constructs. Gelso and Fassinger note that the field of counseling psychology has been most influenced by humanistic, cognitive, and behavioral theories. Humanistic theories present a highly optimistic view of human nature that rhymes with the view of counseling psychologists on the strengths of the individual, and both cognitive and behavioral theories direct therapists to relatively brief interventions. Gelso and Fassinger also note that in the realm of vocational psychology, the early work of Donald Super (1953, 1957) was clearly informed by and modeled after the research of personality and development psychologists. This is evident in Super's theory of the self-concept progressing through several developmental stages of career exploration. The approach and method of the trait-factor theories clearly influenced the work of John Holland (1973, 1985). And other vocational theorists, particularly the psychoanalytic camp of Bordin (1984) and Roe (1984), were directly influenced by the personality and development tenets of Freud's theory of psychoanalysis.

Gelso and Fassinger (1992) proposed that the knowledge bases in personality and developmental psychology have been extended by thinking and research spearheaded by counseling psychologists. They note theoretical and empirical contributions along a construct that they term the "cultural self," specifically the development of theories, measures, and research on gender identity and gender-aware theories of therapy, theories of gay/lesbian identity development, and theories of racial identity. They also note theoretical and empirical work on adult development, including theory and research on positive aging, the postwork transition, and the psychological experiences and needs of a graying America. Gelso and Fassinger also noted that research conducted by counseling psychologists has informed the knowledge bases in understanding personality and lifespan development, for example, via (a) theories, assessment instruments, and research in vocational psychology; (b) by theoretical statements and related research conducted on the development of personal identity; and (c) by research in counseling that has examined the nature of psychological attachment. Gelso and Fassinger ended their paper by noting the potential for a future and deeper convergence between personality, developmental, and counseling psychology around the construct of a healthy or effective self. The potential for personality constructs to inform the characteristics of such a self, and for developmental psychology to outline its growth and maturation, seem ripe for future research. In fact, since 1992, counseling psychology has made significant contributions in research and theory in areas such as the development of optimal human functioning (Walsh, 2003) and the dimensions of human agency/well-being (Lopez & Magyar-Moe, 2006).

Foundational Competencies in the Core Areas of Psychology

The previous section discussed counseling psychology in the context of the history of psychology, particularly the core areas of development, personality, social, and individual differences psychology. At this point, we turn to discussing the foundational competencies in these areas, as per the literature on professional competence. Our review of the model training program in counseling psychology (MTP; http://www.ccptp.org/trainingdirectorpage5.html), the CB model (Fouad et al., 2009), and the National Council of Schools and Programs of Professional Psychology (NCSPPP; Kenkel & Peterson, 2010) model of education indicate that they have not extrapolated specific competencies with respect to these core areas, though the CB model mentions the core academic area under the foundational competencies of "Scientific Knowledge and Methods." However, the EPPP outlines very clearly the knowledge assessed with respect to core psychology; the ASPPB has a public document available on their Web site (http://www.asppb.net) entitled the *ASPPB Information for Candidates*, which includes all the information an applicant would need to prepare and take the exam. Appendix A in this document summarizes the content areas in the exam. As readers will note, 49% of the items in the EPPP assess knowledge in the four core areas of psychology: *Biological Bases of Behavior*, *Cognitive-Affective Bases of Behavior*, *Social and Multicultural Bases of Behavior*, and *Growth and Life-Span Development* (see Table 2.2). These are the content areas that counseling psychologists would have to know at a level considered "passing," usually 70% correct or higher, as determined by the psychology board in the state in which the exam is taken. Appendix A goes on to list 37 specific content domains, complete with detailed examples of content assessed, for each of the four core areas just described.

Foundational Competencies in Research

As has already been discussed, training in counseling psychology is guided by the science-practitioner model, which requires training in research methods, research design, data analysis techniques, and psychometrics. The typical course content in a counseling psychology program includes course work in research design covering the process of identifying and implementing research topics, as well as the classification of research designs such as experimental, quasi-experimental, single-subject designs, and qualitative research approaches (Heppner, Kivlighan, & Wampold, 1999). Students are usually also taught statistical

TABLE 2.2 **Coverage of the Four Core Areas of Psychology in the Examination for Professional Practice in Psychology (EPPP)**

Core Area	Percentage of Items in Exam	Knowledge Assessed
Biological bases of behavior	12%	(a) Biological and neural bases of behavior (b) Psychopharmacology (c) Methodologies supporting this body of knowledge
Cognitive-affective bases of behavior	13%	(a) Cognition and its neural bases (b) Theories and empirical bases of learning, memory, motivation, affect, emotion, and executive function (c) Factors that influence cognitive performance and/or emotional experience and their interaction
Social and multicultural bases of behavior	12%	(a) Intrapersonal, interpersonal, intragroup, and intergroup processes and dynamics (b) Theories of personality (c) Issues in diversity
Growth and life-span development	12%	(a) Age-appropriate development across the life span (b) Atypical patterns of development (c) The protective and risks factors that influence developmental outcome for individuals

Source: Adapted from Appendix A (Association of State and Provincial Psychology Boards, 2009).

concepts and analyses, including variability, standardized distributions, probability, hypothesis testing, statistical inference, analysis of variance, correlation design and analysis, and in more advanced courses multivariate statistical techniques and psychometric theory. While the MTP does not delve into specific areas associated with the research core, foundational competencies have been identified in the EPPP, and the CB and NCSPPP models.

EPPP ASSESSMENT OF RESEARCH CORE

We begin with the EPPP, which in Appendix A of the ASPPB lists an area called *Research Methods and Statistics*, and notes that 8% of the items in the examination assess "knowledge of (a) research design, methodology, and program evaluation, (b) instrument selection and validation, and (c) statistical models, assumptions, and procedures." Specific examples of content assessed within these areas are provided as part of Appendix A; for example, under "statistical and analytic methods" the following is given: "Requires knowledge of ... qualitative, quantitative, descriptive, probability theory, univariate, bivariate, and multivariate methods; meta analysis, parametric and non-parametric statistics, regression analysis; casual modeling; time-series designs) and related issues (e.g., power, effect size, selection of appropriate statistical methodologies, interpretation of findings, casual vs. association, sensitivity and specificity, degree and nature of generalizability, clinical versus statistical significance)."

THE CB MODEL: SCIENCE KNOWLEDGE AND METHODS

The CB model identifies an area called "Science Knowledge and Methods" as representing foundational competence (Fouad et al., 2009). This area is organized along three subcategories called "Scientific Mindedness," ."Scientific Foundation of Psychology," and "Scientific Foundation of Professional Practice." Each subcategory is further divided into three developmental levels: readiness for practicum, readiness for internship, and readiness for entry to practice. Within each subcategory and by developmental level an "essential component" is presented, along with specific behavioral anchors (these are the competencies). For example, under the subcategory "scientific mindedness" the essential components for each of the three developmental levels are as follows: "critical scientific thinking," "values and applies scientific methods to professional practice," and "independently applies scientific methods to practice." Ten behavioral anchors are described across developmental levels. A sample behavioral anchor under "scientific mindedness" at the developmental level "readiness for entry to practice" is the following: "independently accesses and applies scientific knowledge and skills appropriately and habitually to the solution of problems."

THE NCSPPP MODEL: LOCAL CLINICAL SCIENTIST

The NCSPPP model (Kenkel & Peterson, 2010) has a broader aim beyond training in science-practice to include scholar-practitioners and students in PsyD programs throughout the country. There are now 81 professional schools/programs that are part of the NCSPPP, and currently there are three doctoral counseling psychology programs that follow the scholar-practitioner model of training and award the PsyD. The NCSPPP model is directed at training the "local clinical scientist" (Kenkel & Peterson, 2010, p. 125). This model does not distinguish between foundational and functional competencies but makes distinctions between knowledge, skills, and attitudes. The NCSPPP model specifies three developmental levels, called "begin practicum, begin internship, and complete doctoral degree," and for Research and Evaluation Competency area, three domains, "critical evaluation of research," "conducting and using research in applied settings," and "ethics and professional competence" are specified (Trierweiler, Stricker, & Peterson, 2010). In all, 18 knowledge, 29 skills, and 16 attitudes are the competencies specified for the Research and Evaluation Competency area. A sample knowledge competency under the "critical evaluation of research" domain at the level of "begin practicum" level is "familiarity with difference research methodologies (e.g., qualitative, quantitative)."

Counseling and Psychotherapy Theory and Outcome Research

In this section we provide a succinct discussion of the rich theoretical bases that guide psychotherapy approaches and then summarize the research that has been conducted on the outcome of therapy. A significant part of the foundational training in counseling psychology involves exposing students to a variety of theoretical approaches to psychotherapy. These approaches have been described as belonging to one of three camps: *psychoanalysis* and its derivative psychotherapies, *cognitive and behavioral treatments* and *humanistic/existential psychotherapies* (Gelso & Fretz, 2001). While the bulk of the training in counseling psychology is on individual therapies, all programs include courses that cover theory and technique in group and family systems approaches.

THE MTP AND TRAINING IN THE VARIETY OF TRADITIONS

The MTP outlines the importance of training students in the knowledge base within each of these psychotherapy traditions, their respective philosophies, their theoretical approaches to assessment and intervention, and their associated techniques. However, of equal importance is training students to integrate theory and technique into their own approach, one that is personally meaningful and in which the student becomes increasingly proficient, comfortable, and effective. Training at this level also includes exposure to the empirical research base associated with various psychotherapy approaches, including the research that each has stimulated with respect to the efficacy of specific techniques for specific problems and disorders. Students are exposed to research that has been conducted across approaches to uncover common factors in psychotherapies, and the research base with respect to outcome of psychotherapy. There is an emphasis on getting trainees to think critically about theories and techniques of psychotherapy, including limitations or constraints based on their fundamental assumptions, limitations in efficacy in the treatment of specific disorders, and limitations with respect to their use or applicability across populations. The reader interested in learning more about the history, development, and content of the various theories and techniques of psychotherapy is referred to Gelso and Fretz (2001), Corsini and Wedding (2008), and Murdock (2009).

PSYCHOTHERAPY OUTCOME

There is extensive evidence that is based on research examining the effectiveness of therapy, and as Cooper (2008) points out, the "facts are friendly." Lambert and Ogles (2004) reviewed the extensive literature on outcome research in psychotherapy and presented 10 conclusions based on the evidence. Among their conclusions based on an extensive review of hundreds of studies, including numerous meta-analyses of the relevant literature, is that psychotherapy is efficacious, benefiting on average a range of 40% to 70% of clients across client/patient groups and treatment conditions, and that these benefits persist beyond the end of therapy. Therapy speeds up the process of psychological recovery and helps clients stay better longer, when compared to control populations that do not receive psychotherapy care. They also note that anywhere between 21 to 50 hourly sessions of psychotherapy is sufficient to help up to 75% of patients recover from psychological dysfunction. They also note that well-developed and implemented therapies, irrespective of theoretical or philosophical foundation, are equally effective across patient and treatment conditions but do confirm longer standing evidence that cognitive and behavior approaches show some incremental level of effectiveness for certain problems, such as panic and anxiety disorders. They also noted the consistent supporting evidence for the role of the psychotherapy relationship in explaining variance in outcome. A reading of the outcome literature, including several meta-analyses of thousands of studies going back several decades, leads to us to reaffirm the conclusion that psychotherapy is highly effective for most people who seek it, and that the benefits of psychotherapy are efficacious in that they can be obtained in a relatively short period of time with the effects lasting well after treatment is terminated. Perhaps the authoritative text on psychotherapy research, including outcome evidence, is *Bergin and Garfield's Handbook of Psychotherapy and Behavior Change* (5th ed.), edited by Michael J. Lambert. The reader interested in further detailed reading on this topic is referred to this text, as well as Mick Cooper's (2008) *Essential Research Findings in Counselling and Psychotherapy: The Facts Are Friendly.* Both of these texts also include up-to-date summaries on the vast amount of research that has been conducted on the process of psychotherapy, a good amount of which has been conducted by counseling psychologists in the last 30 years.

Relevant Foundational Competencies

The relevant *foundational* competencies in the area of psychotherapy and outcome are as follows.

INTERVENTION

The EPPP devotes 14% of its items to the assessment of knowledge in an area called "Treatment, Intervention, Prevention, and Supervision" (p. 20). As per Appendix A of the *ASPPB Information for Candidates* (ASPPB, 2009), the area is summarized as follows: "knowledge of (a) individual, couple, family, group, organizational, or community interventions for specific problems/disorders in diverse populations, (b) intervention and prevention theories, (c) best practices and practice guidelines, (d) consultation and supervision models, and (e) evidence supporting efficacy and effectiveness of interventions" (p. 20). The ASPPB Appendix delineates 12 specific knowledge domains, each with specific content for this section, including, for example, knowledge of "Treatment decision making based on best available data (e.g., matching treatment to assessment/diagnosis, matching client/patient and therapist characteristics, cost and benefit, readiness to change)" (p. 20).

The CB model (Fouad et al., 2009) lists knowledge of interventions, intervention planning, skills, intervention implementation, and progress evaluation as *functional* competencies of intervention, with a strong emphasis made on evidence-based practice. These will be discussed in Chapter 6 of this book. However, a subarea in the CB model under "Science Knowledge and Methods" is called "Scientific Foundation of Professional Practice" and appears relevant to the current discussion. Under the developmental level of "readiness for entry to practice," the essential component is summarized as "knowledge and understanding of scientific foundations independently applied to practice." A sample behavioral anchor at this same developmental level is the following: "reviews scholarly literature related to clinical work and applies knowledge to case conceptualization" (p. S12).

For its part, the MTP in counseling psychology specifies the following under the area called theories and techniques of counseling psychology: "competencies in this area include skills and knowledge theories of counseling and psychotherapy (individual, group, family, or systems theory) and the integration of theory, research, and practice in the activities of counseling psychologists. Students demonstrate knowledge about the efficacy of counseling psychology interventions and awareness of and appreciation for culturally appropriate evidence-based practice" (Murdock, Alcorn, Heesacker, & Stoltenberg, 1998, p. 666).

The NCSPPP model, in contrast, has several knowledge competencies that seem relevant to this section. Again, the model is organized into knowledge, skills, and attitudes. We focus on the knowledge competencies as they seem foundational to practice. The broad area of Intervention in the NCSPPP model is organized along three developmental levels of "begin practicum, begin internship, complete doctoral degree" and into four domains, "intervention planning, intervention implementation, intervention evaluation, and ethics." A sample knowledge competency from the planning domain at the complete doctoral degree developmental level is: "understanding of the influence of a chosen theory and interventions on the process of therapy" (p. 108). A knowledge competency from the implementation domain at this same level is: "knowledge of the appropriate treatment intervention for particular clients and presenting problems including some knowledge of appropriate psychopharmaco-therapy" (p. 109). Overall, 48 knowledge, 61 attitude, and 70 skill competencies are specified in the area of Intervention in the NCSPPP model, and we will return to cite samples of skills and attitude competencies as we discuss intervention competency in Chapter 6.

HELPING SKILLS

Another area that must be discussed in the context of foundational competence in counseling psychology is the *helping skills* area. Much of the thinking and research in this area has been conducted by counseling psychologists, and it represents the earliest form of training in counseling and psychotherapy. Training in counseling psychology (and the broader field of counseling as well) usually begins with prepracticum courses where students role play the use of basic intervention helping skills; usually they start by using them in writing in response to clinical vignettes, they then start using them in pairs in class, and by the end of training at this early level they are using them in front of their class and receive feedback from their instructor, or audiotape role plays outside of class and turn them in to their professors for feedback. From then on, training moves to practice counseling sessions with client-volunteers, usually for just two to three sessions, and then at the level of practicum training students start seeing actual clients in therapy. The basic helping skills usually include practicing the proper physical sitting posture with clients (e.g., the SOLER posture; Egan, 2010), the use of minimal encouragers, paraphrasing, reflection of feeling, the use of open-ended questions and other types of probes, the use of empathy, immediacy, self-disclosure, and summary (Egan, 2010; Hill, 2004). Competence in these basic skills is essential to the development of competence in counseling and psychotherapy, and usually competence is evaluated via in-class examinations, in-class demonstrations, and assignments such as the taping and transcription of a mock counseling interview where these skills are demonstrated. Besides presenting her model of helping skills (Hill, 2004), Clara E. Hill has also published as a separate book the empirical base behind her model (Hill, 2001); this effort highlights not only the contributions of counseling psychologists to the knowledge base in foundational clinical competence but also exemplifies the interplay between science and practice in our field.

OTHER AREAS OF FOUNDATIONAL COMPETENCIES

The CB model outlines foundational competencies in several other areas, called "professionalism," "reflective practice/self-assessment/self-care," "relationships," "individual-cultural diversity," "ethical-legal standards-policy," and "interdisciplinary systems." We will discuss competence in ethics and diversity in the next two chapters. Professionalism and relationship competencies will be discussed in Chapter 6 as part of our discussion on intervention, and competencies in work with interdisciplinary systems are discussed in Chapter 9. The CB model describes "Reflective Practice/Self-Assessment/Self-Care" as "Practice conducted with personal and professional self-awareness and reflection; with awareness of competencies; with appropriate self-care" (p. S10). Our review of the competency area indicates that it taps personal health, self-care, and self-knowledge/awareness. This area cannot be overemphasized in counseling psychology. Professionals and students alike are taught it is impossible to divorce the person from the professional, that so much of our effectiveness with clients is based on our being "fit" psychologically, and that our own psychological business must be taken care of and attended to in order for us to be effective as psychologists. Every student in counseling psychology has heard at some point in training the old adage, "counselor know thy self." This competency area highlights the importance of awareness, reflection, and care in the practice of professional psychology.

Conclusion

In sum, a great deal of work has been conducted by teams of scholars and clinicians to specify foundational competencies in professional psychology, including counseling psychology. We have discussed the associated models of competence, along with the MTP and the EPPP, to give the reader a flavor for the latest and most specific knowledge bases on this topic. We have also discussed the foundational bases in the context of the development of the profession, and we have presented brief summaries of what we believe are two additional empirical bases for the profession: the evidence from the outcome literature in psychotherapy, and the knowledge base associated with the development of basic helping skills. We now turn to discussing ethics and human diversity as the next chapters in this volume; for us, these constitute foundational training in counseling psychology.

THREE

Competence in Ethical Practice in Counseling Psychology

This chapter discusses the ethical principles and issues involved in the professional practice of counseling psychology. It is important to note that the specialty adheres to the principles and ethical code of conduct of the American Psychological Association (2011), which apply to all aspects of professional practice in professional psychology. Thus, there are no specialty-specific principles or a code of ethical conduct specific to counseling psychology. A discussion or even cursory presentation of every standard in the code of conduct is beyond the scope or space allotted to this chapter, and so the reader is referred to the APA's *The Ethical Principles of Psychologists and Code of Conduct* (hereafter "code of ethics"; American Psychological Association, 2011). Here we limit ourselves to a presentation of what we deem to be the most salient and frequently emerging standards of practice as well as the management of risk in counseling psychology practice. We present sample foundational and functional competencies in the knowledge and application of ethics in psychology and provide some examples of how these principles are used in the profession.

A clear distinction must be made between ethics and law. The ethical code is an agreed-upon imprimatur for behavior, intended to be used as a guide for psychologists, whereas a legal standard is established in court precedent or by legal statute, which may be the basis for a civil suit or criminal prosecution. Although the APA may impose sanctions upon a psychologist who violates the ethical code, legal action is generally taken at the state level, and it may be influenced by case law at the state or federal level. In terms of competence, while it is always an ethical issue, at times it can also be a legal one based on state laws (Barnett, Doll, Younggren, &

Rubin, 2007). We begin by discussing the code of ethics, and then discuss relevant material from legal precedents.

APA Code of Ethics

APA GENERAL ETHICAL PRINCIPLES

The APA code of ethics (American Psychological Association, 2011) stipulates five general principles that guide ethical practice for all psychologists. These five general principles are (a) *beneficence and nonmaleficence*, (b) *fidelity and responsibility*, (c) *integrity*, (d) *justice*, and (e) *respect for the rights and dignity of clients/patients.*

Beneficence and Nonmaleficence

This principle instructs to "do no harm" and to safeguard the rights of others. Psychologists are expected to act on behalf of the best interests of their clients and others who may be affected by the behavior of their clients. We are expected to behave professionally in accordance with the code of conduct and all applicable laws to prevent harm and promote the well-being of our clients. The APA states the following:

> Psychologists strive to benefit those with whom they work and take care to do no harm. In their professional actions, psychologists seek to safeguard the welfare and rights of those with whom they interact professionally and other affected persons, and the welfare of animal subjects of research. When conflicts occur among psychologists' obligations or concerns, they attempt to resolve these conflicts in a responsible fashion that avoids or minimizes harm. Because psychologists' scientific and professional judgments and actions may affect the lives of others, they are alert to and guard against personal, financial, social, organizational, or political factors that might lead to misuse of their influence. Psychologists strive to be aware of the possible effect of their own physical and mental health on their ability to help those with whom they work. (American Psychological Association, 2011, General Principles section, Principle A)

Fidelity and Responsibility

This principle guides psychologists to behave in a professional manner in contact with others, including working on behalf of clients and taking proper responsibility for the welfare of clients. The APA states:

> Psychologists establish relationships of trust with those with whom they work. They are aware of their professional and scientific responsibilities to society and to the specific communities in which they work. Psychologists uphold professional standards of conduct, clarify their professional roles and obligations, accept appropriate responsibility for their behavior, and seek to manage conflicts of interest that could lead to exploitation or harm. Psychologists consult with, refer to, or cooperate with other professionals and institutions to the extent needed to serve the best interests of those with whom they work. They are concerned about the ethical compliance of their colleagues' scientific and professional conduct. Psychologists strive to contribute a portion of their professional time for little or no compensation or personal advantage. (American Psychological Association, 2011, General Principles section, Principle B)

Integrity

This principle means that psychologists act in a truthful manner, honoring commitments and interacting professionally with other professionals. The APA states the following:

> Psychologists seek to promote accuracy, honesty, and truthfulness in the science, teaching, and practice of psychology. In these activities psychologists do not steal, cheat, or engage in fraud, subterfuge, or intentional misrepresentation of fact. Psychologists strive to keep their promises and to avoid unwise or unclear commitments. In situations in which deception may be ethically justifiable to maximize benefits and minimize harm, psychologists have a serious obligation to consider the need for, the possible consequences of, and their responsibility to correct any resulting mistrust or other harmful effects that arise from the use of such techniques. (American Psychological Association, 2011, General Principles section, Principle C)

Justice

This principle ensures that all persons have access to the services of psychologists without bias. The APA states:

> Psychologists recognize that fairness and justice entitle all persons to access to and benefit from the contributions of psychology and to equal quality in the processes, procedures, and services being conducted by

> psychologists. Psychologists exercise reasonable judgment and take precautions to ensure that their potential biases, the boundaries of their competence, and the limitations of their expertise do not lead to or condone unjust practices. (American Psychological Association, 2011, General Principles section, Principle D)

Respect for People's Rights and Dignity

This last principle guides psychologists to respect individual rights and cultural differences. The APA states:

> Psychologists respect the dignity and worth of all people, and the rights of individuals to privacy, confidentiality, and self-determination. Psychologists are aware that special safeguards may be necessary to protect the rights and welfare of persons or communities whose vulnerabilities impair autonomous decision making. Psychologists are aware of and respect cultural, individual, and role differences, including those based on age, gender, gender identity, race, ethnicity, culture, national origin, religion, sexual orientation, disability, language, and socioeconomic status and consider these factors when working with members of such groups. Psychologists try to eliminate the effect on their work of biases based on those factors, and they do not knowingly participate in or condone activities of others based upon such prejudices. (American Psychological Association, 2011, General Principles section, Principle E)

APA STANDARDS OF PROFESSIONAL PRACTICE

The APA Code of Conduct delineates 10 standards of professional practice, and within each, specific codes are presented. The standards are as follows: Resolving Ethical Issues, Competence, Human Relationships, Privacy and Confidentiality, Advertising and Other Public Statements, Record Keeping and Fees, Education and Training, Research and Publication, Assessment, and Therapy. A recent set of amendments to the APA Code (American Psychological Association, 2011) further defines the responsibilities of psychologists in all practice settings. All members of the APA, and in most circumstances, all psychologists, must be aware of these standards. Lack of awareness or the misinterpretation of an ethical obligation does not excuse psychologists from an ethical obligation. Of the 10 standards noted earlier, Competence is of particular relevance to this chapter and book. The APA has identified professional competence as an ethical issue, and as Barnett et al. (2007) note, competence is not a dichotomous concept but one that spans a continuum from a clearly delineated "floor" of basic competence as well as an "aspirational" ceiling of competence to be continually sought, a ceiling that is not static but evolves at a personal level just as the code of ethics has evolved over the years. Barnett et al. describe the floor as the minimally acceptable standards of practice that have also evolved and are outlined in the code of ethics and enforced in state licensure laws.

Although as Gelso and Fretz (2001) observe, ethical standards and codes are continually evolving and may require decisions in which ethical and legal axioms conflict, the various standards specified within the general ethical principles detail what a "reasonable" professional should do when faced with ethical dilemmas. Training in ethics and, therefore, examination of ethical awareness and skills are fundamental to board certification in counseling psychology (Nezu, Finch, & Simon, 2009). Gelso and Fretz (2001) detail 14 potential violations of the APA ethical code in addition to the more flagrant and sensational violations involving sexual misconduct and fraudulent billing (see Table 3.1).

APA ETHICS COMMITTEE

The report of the Ethics Committee (2008) summarizes the activities of the Committee, and, of most interest to practitioners, the number and nature of ethics cases before the Committee in six broad categories. In most instances, cases before the Committee fall in more than one (i.e., multiple) category. In 2008, 16 new cases were opened, a number that has been relatively steady since 2002. Cases in 2008 fell largely in the category of dual relationship ($n = 4$), child custody ($n = 2$), and cases from other jurisdictions that involved loss of licensure ($n = 10$). Over the past decade, although the categories into which the cases fell remained consistent (e.g., child custody, multiple relationships [including sexual misconduct], insurance/fee problems, and testing practices), the number of cases has declined dramatically from a peak of 137 cases in 1995. This decline might be attributable to improved education programs and revisions and enhancements to the ethical code, or, simply to an improvement in the manner and skill in which psychologists resolve disputes with clients. Whatever the case, however, a modest number of ethics cases come before the Ethics Committee.

Critical Areas of Ethics

Kitchener and Anderson (2000) discuss five critical but complex areas of ethics and their implications for therapeutic practice. We summarize these five critical areas next.

TABLE 3.1 **Potential Violations of the American Psychological Association's Ethical Code**

1. Discrimination
2. Lack of knowledge about human differences
3. Multiple relationships
4. Unresolved personal problems and conflicts
5. Inappropriate use of assessment instruments
6. Use of testimonials in advertising
7. Not appropriately structuring the therapy relationship
8. Failing to obtain informed consent to therapy
9. Failing to minimize intrusion into clients' privacy
10. Inappropriate disclosures of clients' information
11. Use of unjustified deception in research
12. Taking on unjustified publication credit
13. A lack of truthfulness and candor in forensic activities
14. Not reporting ethical violations

Source: From Gelso and Fretz (2001).

MULTIPLE-ROLE RELATIONSHIPS AND BOUNDARY ISSUES

Multiple-role relationships are broad terms that encompass instances in which a psychologist acts in more than one capacity with an individual, and, which can be potentially harmful to the client. Consider, for example, the psychologist who works in a university counseling center and teaches as an adjunct professor in that university's graduate training program in counseling psychology. An undergraduate student, who was a client one year before, is now a master's student and appears in the psychologist's class as a student. The psychologist is then in a potential dual-role situation, albeit sequential, with that student and must resolve the multiple-role problem (i.e., evaluative vs. therapeutic roles). The primary obligation of a therapist in multiple-role situations is to the welfare of the client (Kitchener& Anderson, 2000).

Perhaps the most flagrant and troublesome multiple-role violation is one of sexual intimacy with a client. Although 97.8% of psychologists would consider such a relationship to be a violation of ethical boundaries (Pope, Tabachnick, & Keith-Speigel, 1987), sexual intimacy violations unfortunately still top the list of complaints to the Board of Ethics of APA by a factor of 2:1 (Bennett et al., 2006). The ethical code prohibits sexual intimacy with a current client under any circumstance. Posttherapy relationships with clients are discouraged for many reasons (Kitchener & Anderson, 2000) and the APA ethical code places a severe responsibility on the therapist to show that:

> ... there has been no exploitation, in light of all relevant factors, including (1) the amount of time that has passed since therapy terminated; (2) the nature, duration, and intensity of the therapy; (3) the circumstances of termination; (4) the client's/patient's personal history; (5) the client's/patient's current mental status; (6) the likelihood of adverse impact on the client/patient; and (7) any statements or actions made by the therapist during the course of therapy suggesting or inviting the possibility of a posttermination sexual or romantic relationship with the client/patient. (American Psychological Association, 2011, Standard 10.08 Sexual Intimacies with Former Therapy Clients/Patients)

Although the same sexual intimacy prohibition generally applies between the supervisor and supervisee, and faculty member and student, a limited set of extraclassroom dual relationships (e.g., accepting an invitation to a party) is not only common (Kitchener & Anderson, 2000) but may be of benefit to both parties.

INFORMED CONSENT

Informed consent implies that the client (or in research situations, the participant) is fully aware of the nature, potential risks, and benefits of any procedures or interventions to which he or she might be exposed. The process of informed consent is one of communication and clarification (Pope & Vasquez, 1991) and should be incorporated throughout the process of therapy (Bennett et al., 2006). A client must be capable—that is, have the ability to give consent. Although in most cases this consent in given in written form, such forms are increasingly complicated and intimidating for the client, and, in many cases, uncomfortable for the therapist (Pope & Vasquez, 1991). It is incumbent, therefore, upon the psychologist to ensure that the client/participant both understands and agrees to the situation that he or she is about to undertake. Welfel (1998) provides a helpful listing of the specific elements of informed consent for therapy (see Table 3.2).

In addition to the aforementioned information, the material discussed under HIPAA in the next subsection should also be incorporated into the informed consent form. Each of these elements should be detailed in clear nonjargonized language that clients can readily understand. If a counseling psychologist works in an institutional setting, the informed consent in use in the setting can be utilized. If, however, the professional believes that such consent is insufficient to satisfy the requirements of informed consent, the psychologist has an obligation to bring the form in use into compliance. There may be settings, such as postdisaster mental health intervention, in which counseling psychologists may work and make very appropriate use of their skills, but for which comprehensive informed consent is difficult or even at odds with the sponsoring organization under which the psychologist is practicing (e.g., American Red Cross; SAMSHA). This is a difficult problem for which no clear guidelines exist (Spokane et al., 2011).

CONFIDENTIALITY AND PRIVILEGED COMMUNICATIONS

Two terms, often mistakenly used interchangeably, bear on the ethical behavior of psychologists. *Confidentiality* refers to the circumstances under which a communication arises, whereas *privileged communication* is accorded to the client/patient when there is a professional relationship with a psychologist. Privileged communication statutes are interpreted and cover in-court testimony and are, therefore, not absolute (Knapp & VandeCreek, 1987; Knapp, Tepper, & VandeCreek, 1993). Clients or their representatives may waive privilege (preferably in writing) for a specific purpose; this waiver should be differentiated from a "Release of Information" form for other purposes such as insurance claims.

TABLE 3.2 **Specific Elements of Informed Consent for Therapy**

(a) Goal, techniques, procedures, limitations, risks, and benefits
(b) Use of diagnoses tests, and reports
(c) Billing and fees
(d) Confidentiality
(e) Training status of therapist and involvement of supervisors or colleagues
(f) Access to records
(g) Right to choose or refuse treatment and the implications of each
(h) Right to ask questions and receive clarification

Source: From Welfel (1998).

Mandatory reporting laws may differ from state to state, but a psychologist, as a mandated reporter, has an ethical, if not a legal obligation to report child abuse when acting in a professional capacity with children/minors as defined by the state. In Pennsylvania, to illustrate, prior to 1995, a mandated reporter was required to report abuse if there was "*reason to believe*" that abuse was an issue. After 1995, the language in the Pennsylvania law changed to "*reasonable cause to suspect*" child abuse (Knapp & Tepper, 1995). The most recent reporting requirements in Pennsylvania further increase responsibilities for mandated reporters such as psychologists (Gold, 2009). Psychologists must report suspected abuse even when the child does not "come directly before the mandated reporter" and "regardless of the relationship between the alleged abuser and the child" (Gold, 2009). Penalties for failure to report also increased in the most recent Child Protective Services Law. These significant changes in language probably encouraged more reports of suspected abuse, but mandated reporters continue to have immunity in good faith reports of abuse (Knapp & Tepper, 1995). Most states have child protective services hotlines, and reporters can both report suspected instances and request clarification or information.

In child abuse, as in most other legal/ethical dilemmas, psychologists should consult with appropriate colleagues wherever possible and appropriate. It is incumbent upon the psychologist to understand the statutes, precedents, and laws governing professional practice in their setting and state, and to maintain currency on ethical legal issues in counseling psychology practice.

HEALTH INSURANCE PORTABILITY AND ACCOUNTABILITY ACT

Privacy regulations under *Health Insurance Portability and Accountability Act (HIPAA)* are designed to limit access to patient records and information. Beginning in 2003, this sweeping legislation covers virtually all health care records, including the electronic transfer of patient information to insurance companies. Compliance with HIPAA regulations is an obligation for any psychologist who provides services and does not operate on a strictly cash basis. The HIPAA "Privacy Rule" and "Security Rule" outline policies and procedures for physical office considerations, file storage, and so on that protect confidential patient information and records (American Psychological Association, 2002). The privacy rule covers psychotherapy notes, but it excludes information that must be transmitted in a claim—for example, diagnosis, treatment plan, prognosis and progress, and so on (American Psychological Association, 2002). The HIPAA "Transaction Rule" governs any psychologist who submits claims electronically. HIPAA guidelines require that psychologists comply in the following ways: "provide information to patients about their privacy rights and how the information can be used, adopt clear privacy procedures for their practices, train employees so that they understand the privacy procedures, designate an individual to be responsible for seeing that privacy procedures are adopted and followed, and, secure patient records" (American Psychological Association, 2002).

ETHICAL ISSUES IN PSYCHOLOGICAL ASSESSMENT

Psychologists use tests that are valid and reliable for the purpose and the population (e.g., socioeconomic status level, special populations, or subgroups) for which they are used. Furthermore, full informed consent should be obtained prior to testing, and it should include the purpose of the testing, and, if the findings are to be released, a specific consent to do so. If findings are to be conveyed, they should be released in such a way as to minimize any possibility of misinterpretation or misuse of test results. Psychologists ensure that the test taker receives an explanation of the findings unless stipulated to the contrary in advance in the informed consent, for some specific reason. Tests should be current, and scoring and interpretive services should have evidence supporting their validity.

Competence to Practice in Professional Counseling Psychology

The Ethical Principles of Psychologists and Code of Conduct stipulate that psychologists practice only within their boundaries of competence: "Psychologists provide services, teach, and conduct research with populations and in areas only within the boundaries of their competence, based on their education, training, supervised experience, consultation, study, or professional experience" (American Psychological Association, 2011, 2.01 [a]). Competence is a complex concept that includes ethical content as stipulated in the code of ethics, legal connotations, and relevance for training and education. The APA code of ethics stipulates that even when providing services in an emerging area in which strong evidence is not yet available, or in practicing in a crisis or in an area wherein services would not otherwise be available, a psychologist strives to work in an informed manner and to ensure that referral is made when a crisis ends. Furthermore, the APA code states that psychologists seek continuing training and education to maintain competence and do not practice when they are impaired from a mental health or personal perspective in ways that would adversely affect their ability to provide competent professional services.

Although *competence* is a broad term that has both ethical and legal connotations, a growing concern over competence is both more specific and based in scientific evidence. Competency, then, implies the regular level of performance of specific professional responsibilities in scientifically supported ways (Fouad et al., 2009; Rodolfa et al. 2005). Recently, as well, there has been a substantial increase in the literature in professional journals, including a new APA journal entitled *Training and Education in Professional Psychology*. The history of the current competence movement—which began in the mid 1980s and received a significant boost with the 2002 Competencies Conference—is well articulated in Fouad et al. (2009). This conference generated a graphic (i.e., a cube) that has been widely adopted as a basis for stipulating these competencies (see Rodolfa et al., 2005).

Several documents produced by psychology-related organizations stipulate specific professional competencies that all psychologists should possess (ASPPB, 2009; Fouad et al., 2009; Kaslow et al., 2007; Rodolfa et al., 2005). These documents outline core foundational and functional competencies across levels of training and professional development for practicing psychologists that are being progressively adopted in Counseling Psychology Training programs. The CB model (Fouad et al., 2009) identifies a foundational area entitled "Ethical Legal Standards and Policy," which is described as "application of ethical concepts and awareness of legal issues regarding professional activities with individuals, groups, and organizations" (p. S14). This area is subdivided into three domains called:

> a) *knowledge* of ethical, legal, and professional standards and guidelines; b) *awareness* and application of ethical decision making; and c) *ethical conduct*.
>
> Each of these three domains specifies benchmarks (or competencies) at three developmental levels, readiness for practicum, readiness for internship, and readiness for entry to practice. Each domain is also summarized by an "essential component." A sample competence at the level of readiness for entry to practice in the domain "ethical conduct" is the following: "Integrates an understanding

> of ethical-legal standards policy when performing all functional competencies" (p. S15).

Role of Supervision and Consultation in Ethical Training

It is important to note that in counseling psychology, the practical use of ethics is learned through supervision and consultation. This learning usually takes place in the early phase of training via training clinics where students are taught to resolve ethical dilemmas as they arise in clinical situations. Through close supervision, the process of making and resolving a conflict of interest or an ethical dilemma is discussed. Thus, learning goes beyond studying the rules to applying the rules, and the role of consultation is inevitably involved in ethical decision making and in resolving potential ethical dilemmas. Of course, training, supervision, and consultation continue through graduate school and in postgraduation training, and even as licensed psychologists, counseling psychologists continue to use supervision and consultation to examine potential ethical dilemmas and to make sound decisions as informed by the code of ethics. The point to emphasize is that by being exposed to consultation early in training, counseling psychologists develop good practices with respect to knowledge and competence in ethical behavior and ethical decision making.

Testing in Ethics

The Association of State and Provincial Psychology Boards (ASPPB) has detailed five content knowledge areas that are evaluated via the EPPP Examination with respect to ethics. The area is entitled "Ethical/Legal/Professional Issues" and approximately 15% of the items in the exam (i.e., 30 items) assess knowledge of the following: (a) codes of ethics; (b) professional standards for practice; (c) legal mandates and restrictions; (d) guidelines for ethical decision making; and (e) professional training and supervision. For its part, the Model Training Program (MTP) in Counseling Psychology dictates training in legal and ethical issues, stating:

> ... students are presented with current information regarding legal and ethical aspects of the profession. Relevant case studies are used to explore the application of ethical standards and guidelines as they apply to scientific and professional practice. A variety of issues are addressed under this domain, such as research with human subjects, relations with health systems,

> risk management, malpractice, and licensure.(Murdock, Alcorn, Heesacker, & Stoltenberg, 1998, p. 666)

The examination for board certification in counseling psychology assesses competency in ethical and legal foundations. The primary component is described as "knowledge about ethical standards is apparent and there is evidence that these standards guide all of their professional functioning; knowledge about legal standards is apparent and there is evidence that these standards guide all of their professional functioning" (http://www.abpp.org/files/page-specific/3364%20Counseling/02_Candidate_Exam_Manual.pdf, p. 14). The American Board of Counseling Psychology (ABCoP) provides applicants with examples of passing and failing levels in this area. Two examples of passing level of competence are the following: "demonstrates awareness of the ethical implications of various situations and can cite an ethical quandary from own practice and describe appropriate responses" and "demonstrates awareness of statutory reporting and other legal requirements that practitioners must follow in their jurisdiction, can cite example from own practice when these requirements were relevant, and can describe appropriate behaviors in response" (p. 14). Examples of failing levels include "is unaware of important ethical implications or does not comply with ethical guidelines and principles" and "is unaware of relevant legal standards or these standards do not inform their practice behavior" (p. 14).

Assessment and Management of Risk in Counseling Psychology Practice

ASSESSMENT OF DANGEROUSNESS

In 1976 the Supreme Court of California reviewed its earlier decision on a case that would alter the practice of Counseling and Psychology in significant ways. The specifics of the Tarasoff decision (*Tarasoff v. Regents of the University of California*, 1976) are carefully described in detail in Knapp and VandeCreek (1982) and VandeCreek and Knapp (1993), but the essence of the decision and its aftermath was that a psychologist had a *duty to warn* in order to protect an identifiable victim from a dangerous patient/client, and he or she could be liable for "failure to commit." Although in the past physicians had been sued for failure to commit such a patient when the circumstances were foreseeable, the Tarasoff decision upended what for decades had been the assumption of psychologists that the content of psychotherapy sessions was immutably confidential. Prior to Tarasoff few psychologists would have considered breaching the therapeutic relationship to reveal a client's intentions or propensities. Following Tarasoff, psychologists face "a complex task of balancing the need of the patient for the need of society for safety," though VandeCreek and Knapp conclude that the threats to clinical practice are "more apparent than real" (VandeCreek & Knapp, 1993, p. 57). Subsequent to Tarasoff, the *assessment of dangerousness* when treating patients/clients has become increasingly important and is a factor in the some tenfold increase in malpractice insurance rates for psychologists.

TWO PRINCIPAL TYPES OF RISK

Two very different types of risk are relevant in the professional practice of counseling psychology. The first is the risk that a client may pose in injuring self or others (i.e., dangerousness). In this first type of risk, both the ethical codes and accumulated legal precedents (e.g., Tarasoff decision) must be considered in making decisions about client care. Protecting the client and/or others from harm by the client is an evolving matter of concern to all practicing mental health professionals. Predicting dangerous behavior and the potential for violence, however, is a very inexact science (Groth-Marnat, 2009), largely because there are relatively few instances of such behavior from which to generalize. As Groth-Marnat notes, repeated assessment using psychological tests validated for this purpose and aggregate over time ratings are more likely to be considered sufficient by the courts as compared with clinical interview assessments. The second type of risk is that posed in providing services to clients/patients who may take retributive action against a professional psychologist as a result of treatment received or omitted. Both types of risk should be carefully considered by the counseling psychologist.

Bennett et al. (2006) provide a thorough treatment of this second type of risk-practice risk assessment paired with an online education module and outline a risk management formula as an aid to reducing clinical, ethical, and legal risks in psychological practice. The risk management formula, which is used to calculate the likelihood that a mental health intervention may have "bad outcomes" for the practitioner and patient, is depicted below:

$$\text{Clinical Risk} = \frac{(\text{Patient Characteristics} \times \text{context} \times \text{disciplinary consequences})}{\text{Therapist factors}}$$

According to Bennett et al. (2006), high-risk patients include those with serious personality disorders, posttraumatic stress disorder, identity disorders, history of abuse, those posing threat of harm, the wealthy, and patients/clients involved in prior lawsuits. Institutional settings may buffer some risks and increase others, and divorce or custody contexts may pose additional risk. Finally, therapists who work beyond the limits of their expertise, as well as those who fail to consult or keep accurate records, may increase their risk of negative outcomes. One particularly troublesome area of psychological practice that continues to result in ethical complaints involves divorce and child custody (see Report of the Ethics Committee, American Psychological Association, 2008). The APA has published guidelines for forensic child custody evaluations, and issues of support, visitation, and parental rights. These guidelines underscore that legal custody disputes occur in only 10% of cases, but in these cases, psychologists provide the courts with unbiased input in the best interests of the child. The guidelines stipulate that parental issues and personality are secondary to the cultural and social context that may influence the welfare of the child. Psychologists who work in this area are expected to remain impartial, avoid conflict of interest and multiple relationships, and demonstrate competence and expertise both of the psychosocial and legal issues involved. Procedural requirements in custody evaluations include timely reporting with complete evaluation data, accurate records, and appropriate recommendations in the interest of the child. In addition to disciplinary actions by licensing boards and ethics committees, psychologists whose conduct falls below accepted standards face civil actions. Bennett et al. note that 1% of psychologists face some formal action each year with board action four times more likely than a lawsuit. The likelihood of such actions can be minimized by thorough continuing education and study of the ethics code and consultation with an ethics consultant as soon as possible conflict or violation is identified.

Conclusion

In summary, the code of ethics of the APA guides professional practice in counseling psychology. Counseling psychologists are trained very early in their graduate programs, usually the first semester, to develop a comprehensive knowledge of this code, as well as to develop clinical competence in its application and use in practice. Through formal course work and supervision counseling psychologists are trained to practice ethically and to conduct ethical decision making, to maintain professional liability insurance, to know state and federal laws that pertain to psychology practice, and to reach out and consult regularly with trusted colleagues, supervisors, and experts when ethical dilemmas arise.

FOUR

Competence in Individual and Cultural Diversity

The Model Training Program (MTP) in counseling psychology identifies the area of *individual and cultural diversity (ICD)* as a professional core area in training (Murdock, Alcorn, Heesacker, & Stoltenberg, 1998; Stoltenberg et al., 2000). The MTP notes: "counseling psychology's tradition of emphasizing the value of human diversity dictates that significant attention to individual and cultural diversity is evident in course content, practica, and research experiences" (Murdock et al., 1998, p. 666). In fact, counseling psychology has demonstrated sensitivity to ecological factors in the development and well-being of the individual since the beginning of the specialty (American Psychological Association, 1952).

As noted in Chapter 1, one of the unifying themes in counseling psychology is the attention given to person–environment interactions (Gelso & Fretz, 2001), and the importance of understanding the individual within his or her current and developmental context. Counseling psychologists in service areas such as counseling services, education, and vocational psychology have sought to explain how race, culture, and sociopolitical factors influence the development of identity, values, and conceptions of normal and pathological behavior. In this chapter we rely on a recently completed chapter on the topic of *multicultural counseling* by the first author of this book (Fuertes, 2012) and discuss individual and cultural diversity and summarize the research that has accumulated on this topic in about the last 20 years. We also review the competency statements that have been developed in the field with respect to ICD.

It can be argued that of all the professional specialties in psychology, counseling psychology has led the field in terms of thinking, research, and activism for awareness, sensitivity, and inclusion of matters of ICD in professional psychology. However, by no means has counseling psychology been alone in this endeavor. As evident in the recently revised model of competency-based education developed by the National Council of Schools and Programs of Professional Psychology (NCSPPP; Kenkel & Peterson, 2010) and in the competencies developed in the competencies benchmarks (CB) model (Fouad et al., 2009), as well as by the guidelines on multicultural education and practice developed by the American Psychological Association (2003), the concern with matters of individual and cultural diversity goes beyond counseling psychology and has been addressed as essential by all of professional psychology.

Why the Focus on Individual and Cultural Diversity?

Population growth (including the high birth rate among Hispanics) and immigration patterns for the United States in the last few decades (including the daily influx of approximately 3,000 legal immigrants a day [US Department of Homeland Security, 2011]), the growing number of professionals in the field of professional psychology, and the globalization of psychology to international markets have led to increases in the services and research that is conducted with and for racial, ethnic, and other minority groups in the United States (Fuertes, 2012). To meet the psychological needs of an increasingly diverse clientele, the field has seen the development of theories and models proposed on the topic of multicultural counseling (see Fuertes, 2012; Fuertes & Gretchen, 2001; Ponterotto, Fuertes, & Chen, 2000). There has been a steady flow of research on topics such as ethnic and racial identity, multicultural competence, multicultural psychotherapy, and social justice in a variety of specialized and generic journals in professional psychology. New practice models and research venues have also been developed in areas related but outside counseling and psychotherapy, such as consultation, training, and supervision.

RELATED FACTORS TO INDIVIDUAL AND CULTURAL DIVERSITY

Factors surrounding ICD go beyond the study of individual or cultural factors and involve attempts at addressing and solving social problems that are unique and significant for racial, ethnic, and other minority groups, including immigrants in the United States. For example, there is evidence of outcome disparities for racial/ethnic minorities (and immigrants) who receive mental health services in the United States (Fuertes, 2012). There is also disproportionate poverty, unemployment, educational gaps, violence, and other problems that affect these populations, problems that are compounded by lingering racism and discrimination (Department of Health and Human Services, 2001). Racial/other minority groups do not experience psychiatric disorders in greater proportion or intensity than the majority population; however, the lack of quality and availability of services to them, the lack of insurance, and the limited access to care lead many clients/patients to not receive adequate treatment, to experience worsening of symptoms, and to experience worsening of the poverty, unemployment, and marginalization that already surrounds them (Department of Health and Human Services, 2001).

The Surgeon General of the United States released a comprehensive report in 2001 addressing the state of mental health for ethnic and racial minorities within the United States and in which the disparity in the quality of mental health care for underserved minority patients was documented. This report highlighted associations between race, ethnicity, racism, poverty, and mental health treatment. The Surgeon General's report revealed that severe mental illnesses, such as bipolar disorder, depression, and schizophrenia, are found within every group in the United States and in the world, but barriers to mental health services exist in the United States in disproportionate scale for racial and ethnic minority groups (Fuertes, Mislowack, & Mintz, 2005). The high cost of care, limited availability of services, and the social stigma of mental illness are common barriers that all patients face, but these factors are exacerbated for racial and other minority group members (Fuertes, Mislowack, & Mintz, 2005).

In education, the percent of culturally and linguistically diverse children in schools in the United States is now approximately 30, and this percentage is estimated to rise dramatically in the next 50 years (National Center of Educational Statistics [NCES], 2000). NCES reports suggest that almost 5% of school-age children in the United States speak a language other than English at home and these same reports suggest that cultural and linguistic diversity will continue to rise in schools due to demographic changes in the general population (Fuertes, Alfonso, & Schultz, 2005). The increasing cultural and linguistic diversity in the US educational system presents challenges that include significantly lower academic performance of racial/ethnic minority and immigrant students, culminating in insufficient learning and unacceptably high dropout rates (with the exception of some Asian American subgroups), in comparison with White American students (NCES, 2000). Additionally, ethnic minority and immigrant students (particularly low socioeconomic status African Americans and Mexican Americans) experience disproportionably higher rates of psychosocial difficulties (e.g., teen pregnancy, gang membership, drug use) in the United States. Poverty, poor quality of education, unsupportive or uninvolved parents, marginalization, and the inherent difficulties associated with acculturation and second-language acquisition have been discussed as causes for the educational gaps and sociodevelopmental problems that disproportionately affect these populations (Fuertes, Alfonso, & Schultz, 2005, 2007).

FOCUS OF THE CURRENT CHAPTER

In sum, the problems and mental health needs of racial and ethnic minority groups are significant, costly, and of importance for the future of the country. These problems are being addressed at all levels of government and by various professions, including medicine and psychology. Having presented a brief rationale for examining matters of ICD in professional psychology, in the remainder of this chapter we return to the focus of the current chapter, which is to present the competencies that have been identified with respect to ICD and professional practice. We discuss the competencies outlined by the American Psychological Association, the MTP in counseling psychology, and the relevant sections of the competency models that have been cited in the previous two chapters, the NCSPPP model (Kenkel & Peterson, 2010) and the CB model. We also note the relevant knowledge areas of ICD assessed by the Examination for Professional Practice in Psychology (EPPP), which as we noted in Chapter 1, is probably the ultimate measure of foundational competence in professional psychology. We end the chapter by reviewing the available research on two of the major areas in the field of multicultural counseling, that is, *racial/ethnic identity* and *multicultural competence.* In presenting this review, we cite heavily from a chapter just completed for another book by the first author, which at the time of this writing is "in press" (i.e., Fuertes, 2012). The research on racial and ethnic identity accounts for factors associated with identity, development, well-being, and cognitive processes, including assumptions based on socialization, race, and racism. This research is important, because it is considered essential to understanding and promoting psychologists' (and clients') self-awareness about race, ethnicity, racism and oppression, and related factors. The area of multicultural competence includes research on racial/ethnic identity development but, more so, examines the provision of services, the experiences of both psychologists and clients, and attempts to connect factors of ICD to process and outcome in the delivery of services.

It seems extremely important and relevant to highlight the research on identity and multicultural competence in the context of discussing professional psychology competencies, since much of the research has been directed at enhancing exactly that very topic: provider competence. While the "culture" of competence may be the current zeitgeist (Kaslow, 2009), ironically, the topic of multicultural competence has been stressed now for almost three decades (see Sue et al., 1982).

Guidelines of the American Psychological Association

The American Psychological Association (APA) in 2003 published guidelines for psychologists to follow to improve service delivery with respect to individual and cultural diversity. These are the guidelines that counseling psychologists must also adhere to and, in fact, have been active in promoting in psychology for decades (Fuertes, 2012). The APA's *Guidelines on Multicultural Education, Training, Research, Practice, and Organizational Change for Psychologists* are relevant to the current topic in that they were derived to address issues of ICD and standards of care with respect to service delivery in mental health. By using the term "cultural" these guidelines are relevant to more than just racial and ethnic minority groups and include groups such as gay/lesbian/bisexual populations, the physically disabled, and low socioeconomic status groups of any race. The guidelines emphasize the importance of multicultural competence at the individual level, particularly with respect to provider self-awareness, knowledge of specific cultures and needs of clients/patients, and sophisticated use of skills that are tailored to the beliefs, needs, and unique circumstances of clients. The APA guidelines also emphasize education, research, and training activities that may further the establishment of competence across mental health settings and population needs.

FIRST GUIDELINE: ISSUES OF BIAS, RACISM, AND DISCRIMINATION

The first guideline addresses issues of bias, racism, and discrimination, and other cognitive errors that appear to affect access to health care and the quality of care for minority patients. As the report of the Surgeon General (Department of Health and Human Services, 2001) uncovered, racism and bias diminish quality of service. The APA states, "*Psychologists are encouraged to recognize that, as cultural beings, they may hold attitudes and beliefs that can detrimentally influence their perceptions of and interactions with individuals who are ethnically and racially different from themselves*" (p. 382, italics added). The adage "Counselor know thy self" applies here. Psychologists must realize that they are vulnerable to cognitive errors in perception and judgment, that these errors are often fueled by biases, stereotypes, or lack of information about their patients, and that these errors can affect their approach and care of their clients. These errors can affect providers' interpersonal style with their patients, and they may very well affect the questions they ask (or do not ask), the information that they elicit from patients, their interpretation of patients' reports, their decision making with respect to diagnosis or treatment plan, or their ability to "partner" or foster trust with their patients. Beyond good service and professional psychological practice, this guideline may help keep professionals from becoming embroiled in ethical and legal problems due to malpractice.

SECOND GUIDELINE: MULTICULTURAL SENSITIVITY/RESPONSIVENESS

The next APA guideline encourages psychologists "*to recognize the importance of multicultural sensitivity/responsiveness to and knowledge and understanding about ethnically and racially different individuals*" (p. 385, italics added). This guideline emphasizes the central role of culture in clients' experiences, perceptions, and values, particularly in relation to mental health and problems in living. The APA "recognizes the broad scope of dimensions of race, ethnicity, language, sexual orientation, gender, age, disability, class status, education, religious/spiritual orientation, and other cultural dimensions" (p. 385). It appears that it is important for psychologists to not only have a psychological understanding of the clients' problems but also to have empathy for the *person* experiencing those problems. As the Surgeon General concluded in his report (2001), "culture counts" in psychological service delivery, and the client/patient's culture-based beliefs and perspectives have to be at least acknowledged and at times negotiated in order to engage the client in the treatment of the problem. This level of communication seems crucial in helping the client understand how the problem will be treated and to win his or her consent and commitment.

THIRD GUIDELINE: PSYCHOLOGISTS AS EDUCATORS

The third guideline refers to psychologists as educators: "*As educators, psychologists are encouraged to employ the constructs of multiculturalism and diversity in psychological education*" (p. 386, italics added). Multicultural education strategies are anchored in the first two guidelines outlined in the APA report: understanding one's own cultural lenses, biases, as well as being empathic of others' cultural beliefs, backgrounds, biases, and formative influences. Training, according to the APA, is the utilization of psychological education for advancing practical and research expertise. Indeed, this third guideline may also stimulate continuing education practices, in workshops, conferences, or readings in journals and professional magazines that may further educate providers on effective multicultural service delivery. Education becomes important in the long run in diminishing racism and discrimination. Education can also increase the number of psychologists who are members of racial and ethnic minority groups in the United States and who speak languages other than English.

FOURTH GUIDELINE: INVOLVEMENT WITH RESEARCH

To keep practitioners abreast with the latest innovations and culturally sensitive interventions, guideline 4 recommends involvement with research: "*Culturally sensitive psychological researchers are encouraged to recognize the importance of conducting culture-centered and ethical psychological research among persons from ethnic, linguistic, and racial minority backgrounds*" (p. 388, italics added). This guideline addresses the importance of examining needs, barriers, and effective interventions through research. The vast amount of clinical research in applied psychology has historically been conducted with predominantly European American populations, although new initiatives and incentives are in place to encourage research with minority, underserved populations. For example, the National Institute of M ental Health (NIMH) and other National Institutes of Health (NIH) agencies now require gender and minority inclusion estimates on all projects prior to approving or releasing funding. The Surgeon General's report specifically outlined the lack of evidence and knowledge base for established treatments and effective interventions with racial and ethnic minority populations.

FIFTH GUIDELINE: APPLYING CULTURALLY APPROPRIATE SKILLS

Research including minority populations may inform some of the issues raised in the fifth guideline of the APA report: "*Psychologists strive to apply culturally-appropriate skills in clinical and other applied psychological practices*" (p. 390, italics added). These issues include *best practices* and *optimal conditions* for effective mental health treatment to the burgeoning minority and ethnic subgroups/communities in the United States.

SIXTH GUIDELINE: PSYCHOLOGISTS AS ADVOCATES

The sixth and last guideline states: "*Psychologists are encouraged to use organizational change processes to support culturally informed organizational (policy) development and practices*" (p. 392, italics added). This guideline encourages psychologists' role as advocates. For instance, psychologists working in an environment with few cultural indicators are encouraged to advocate for changes that incorporate cultural sensitivity and diversity. According to the National Center for Cultural Competence (NCCC),

TABLE 4.1 **ITEMS ON THE EXAMINATION FOR PROFESSIONAL PRACTICE IN PSYCHOLOGY (EPPP) PERTAINING TO INDIVIDUAL AND CULTURAL DIVERSITY**

(a) Cultural issues (e.g., cross-cultural and social comparisons, universal and culture-specific formulations, political differences, international and global awareness)
(b) Causes, manifestations, effects, and the prevention and reduction of oppression (e.g., racism and antiracism, sexism, homophobia)
(c) Racial and ethnic minority issues (e.g., theories of racial/ethnic identity, effects of culture on school motivation)
(d) Sexual orientation (e.g., sexual identity development, gay/lesbian/bisexual/transgender perspectives)
(e) Psychology of gender (e.g., psychology of women, psychology of men, gender identity development)
(f) Disability and rehabilitation issues (e.g., inclusion, accessibility, psychological impact of disability)

Source: From Appendix A (Association of State and Provincial Psychology Boards, 2009).

cultural competence must be systematically incorporated at every level of a health organization, for example, by having a written strategic plan that outlines goals, policies, and operational plans, by maintaining proper patient health information, and by maintaining participatory and collaborative partnerships with their respective communities. The NCCC recommends that clinicians make sure the organization they are representing has the following: (a) continuing multicultural competency training for all staff members; (b) economical backing to enhance cultural competence in all levels of the organization; (c) an ongoing evaluation process to assess current population needs; (d) means of attaining translation and interpretation assistance; and (e) guidelines that promote community outreach (http://www11.georgetown.edu/research/gucchd/nccc/foundations/frameworks.html).

Competency Models on Individual and Cultural Diversity

THE EPPP: ITEMS ON INDIVIDUAL AND CULTURAL DIVERSITY

Specific knowledge areas pertaining to ICD are included in the EPPP. The ASPPB has a public document available on their Web site (http://www.asppb.net) entitled the *ASPPB Information for Candidates*, which includes all the information an applicant would need to prepare and take the exam. Appendix A in this document summarizes the content areas in the exam.

This appendix shows an area entitled *Social and Multicultural Bases of Behavior*, which constitutes 12% of the items of the exam. The items that pertain to individual and cultural diversity are described in six areas, and we summarize them in Table 4.1.

As we mentioned earlier, since the EPPP is the examination that all psychology graduates in the United States must pass in order to be licensed, we see it as *the* measure of foundational knowledge in professional psychology. The six areas highlighted in the examination are extensive and appear to us to be up to date and consistent with the training in counseling psychology and the expectations from the specialty, and adequately reflect the literature in the broader field of multiculturalism and of ICD.

THE MTP: GOALS FOR THE EXAMINATION FOR PROFESSIONAL PRACTICE IN PSYCHOLOGY

The MTP (Murdock et al., 1998) in counseling psychology outlines one broad objective in training with respect to ICD: "*The Program recognizes the importance of cultural and individual differences and diversity in the training of psychologists*" (p. 669, italics added). Three goals follow this objective. The first goal can be summarized as follows: "students are taught to take a systematic, person-environment approach ... the interaction of factors such as culture, ethnicity, gender, sexual orientation, socio-economic status, physical ability ... are given special attention" (p. 669). The second goal includes the following: "students and faculty demonstrate sensitivity to social, economic, and political factors that diminish, marginalize, or otherwise limit a client's access to full participation in the society. Counseling psychology training programs promote the development of competencies through which counseling psychologists may assist clients in overcoming barriers to education, employment, and health services" (p. 669). The third goal is the following: "program faculty implement a thoughtful and coherent plan for recruiting a diverse faculty and student body. In addition, counseling psychology integrates concepts related to cultural and individual differences in both science and practice" (p. 669). These three goals are important in that each program in counseling psychology must demonstrate achievements reached with respect to student training with respect to each goal, and the achievements noted by the program are used by The Commission on Accreditation of the APA in evaluating the quality of the program, its success in properly training psychologists, and ultimately weighs in on the decision by the committee to reaccredit the program.

THE CB MODEL: FOUNDATIONAL COMPETENCY AREA OF INDIVIDUAL AND CULTURAL DIVERSITY

The CB model (Fouad et al., 2009) identifies ICD as a foundational competency area, described as "Awareness, sensitivity, and skills in working professionally with diverse individuals, groups and communities who represent various cultural and personal backgrounds and characteristics defined broadly and consistent with APA policy" (p. S13). As noted in Chapter 2, the CB model is organized into three developmental levels (i.e., readiness for practicum, readiness for internship, and readiness for entry to practice, and each level delineates an "essential component," and specific behavioral anchors or competencies). There are four general competency areas in the CB model with respect to ICD; the first three can be summarized as "Self, Others, and Interaction of Self and Others as shaped by individual and cultural diversity ... and context" and the fourth is "Applications based on individual and cultural context" (p. S14). Under "Self," the essential component at the developmental level of "readiness for entry to practice" is "independently monitors and applies knowledge of self as a cultural being in assessment, treatment, and consultation" (p. S13). A sample behavioral anchor under this same developmental level is "independently articulates, understands, and monitors own cultural identity in relation to work with others" (p. S13). A prominent theme in this foundational area is clearly psychologist self-awareness and knowledge as a cultural, racial, ethnic, and socialized being, and maintaining an open stance to develop such an awareness and appreciation about others. There is also a theme of sensitivity to socialization and cultural patterns, including oppression and privilege in all interactions, and the use of supervision and consultation about ICD as needed.

THE NCSPP MODEL: DOMAINS RELEVANT TO INDIVIDUAL AND CULTURAL DIVERSITY

The NCSPPP model (Kenkel & Peterson, 2010) does not distinguish between foundational and functional competencies but distinguishes between knowledge, skills, and attitudes, at three developmental levels: practicum, internship, and completion of the doctoral degree. The ICD section of the overall NCSPPP model is entitled "Knowledge, Skills, and Attitudes and Domains for the Diversity Competency" and is divided into five domains: "Multiple Identities; Power, Oppression, and Privilege; ICD-Specific Knowledge; Culturally Competent Service Provision; and Ethics." In total there are 35 knowledge competencies, 28 skill competencies, and 27 attitude competencies outlined throughout the five domains and developmental levels. A sample knowledge competency under "multiple identities" and at the level of "complete doctoral degree" is "recognition that professional and institutional roles interact with personal identities and biases, which impact professional work" (p. 181). A sample skill competency under "power, oppression, and privilege" and at the level of "complete doctoral degree" is "ability to reflect on and responsibly use own experiences of power, oppression, and privilege in professional roles to promote social justice" (p. 182). A sample attitude competency under "culturally competent service provision" at the level of "complete doctoral degree" is "commitment to the critique and modification of traditional models of intervention for use with diverse populations" (p. 185).

SUMMARY OF INDIVIDUAL AND CULTURAL DIVERSITY COMPETENCIES

A review of these models and their competencies indicates that factors associated with ICD are central to professional psychology and essential to competent psychological practice. Since so much of service delivery involves the interpersonal processes of communication, understanding, trust, and encouragement, the ICD competencies reflect the importance for psychologists to be highly self-aware and attuned to the values, beliefs, and experiences of clients/patients. These competencies address the interpersonal process of service provision as well as an important layer in the individuality of the client, whose race, ethnicity, or worldviews must be understood and respected in order for psychological services to make sense to them and to be of help. These competencies also appear to be essential to all psychologists, including minority psychologists who work with either minority or majority populations (e.g., European Americans, women). The competencies also speak about the legitimate role of psychologists as advocates for their clients/patients (given the barriers noted here), the imbalances in privilege and power, and other injustices that many minority, oppressed, and immigrant populations experience in living in the United States.

Review of Multiculturalism Research

Having presented the most direct and relevant literature on the topic of competence in ICD, we now present a review of the research in the field of multiculturalism, much of which has been led by teams of counseling psychologists throughout the United States. We believe this research provides important, though preliminary evidence about the role of ethnic and racial identity as well as counselor/therapist multicultural competence in effective and competent treatment of individuals from various racial and cultural backgrounds. One clarification that we would like to make at this point is that in our view, multicultural competence and attention to issues of diversity supplement do not supplant traditional therapist training and clinical competence. Thus, for a counselor/therapist to be multiculturally competent, he or she must first be a good clinician, who is able to account for and use traditional psychological theory and standard methods of assessment and intervention. With that level of competence as a core, the counselor/therapist can then embellish and refine his or her approach to assessment and intervention, as well as his or her interpersonal style and treatment planning, with theory and techniques that have been proposed by multicultural counseling researchers.

RECENT RESEARCH ON RACIAL AND ETHNIC IDENTITY

As Fuertes (2012) recently pointed out, there has been considerable and substantial theoretical and empirical work done in the areas of ethnic and racial identity. Phinney and Ong (2007) noted overlapping lines of theoretical development in both areas. In both areas the theories attempt to describe and explain how individuals' perceive and value themselves and their group memberships. Theories of racial and ethnic identity also attempt to explain individuals' values and beliefs and how these inform their worldviews. However, the focus of racial identity has been on responses to racism and on the internalization of racism using African American and European American samples. Phinney and Ong (2007) point out that theory and research on ethnic identity has had a broader focus, beyond race and ethnicity to factors such as gender, sexual orientation, and disability. Fuertes (2012) recently noted that a review of the literature shows that studies of ethnic identity tend to include a more diverse set of participants among minority groups in the United States, including subgroups of Hispanics and Asian Americans (e.g., Lee, Noh, Yoo, & Doh, 2007; Umana-Taylor & Shin, 2007). Studies on ethnic identity have implemented elegant models with clearly delineated antecedents and outcomes. Fuertes (2012) pointed out that:

> ... ethnic identity has been examined as a moderating effect of psychological distress (Yip, Gee, & Takeuchi, 2008), well-being (Yoo & Lee,

> 2005), self-esteem (Lopez, 2008), race-related stress and quality of life (Utsey, Chae, Brown, & Kelly, 2002), situational well being (Yoo & Lee, 2008), alcohol and marijuana use (Pugh & Bry, 2007) and depression and suicidal ideation (Walker, Wingate, Obasi, & Joiner, 2008). Ethnic identity has also been examined as a mediator with respect to delinquency and violence (Le & Stockdale, 2008), and academic grades, pro-social behaviors, and externalizing symptoms (Schwartz, Zamboanga, & Jarvis, 2007). The results of this literature generally point to a significant effect for ethnic identity, in some instances as a buffer from psychological illness and in other instances in theoretically predicted ways as a contributor to distress. (Fuertes, 2012, p. 578)

Fuertes (2012) also found that studies of racial identity have focused on African Americans, European Americans, and people with multiple racial identities (Miville, Constantine, Baysden, & So-Lloyd, 2005), Asian American racial identity (Chen, LePhuoc, Guzman, Rudem, & Dodd, 2006; Liu, 2002), and American Indian racial identity (Bryant & LaFromboise, 2005). In studies of White racial identity the focus has been on examining multicultural competence demographic correlates of professionals or trainees in counseling (Constantine et al., 2005; Middleton et al. 2005; Neville, Spanierman, & Doan, 2006). The results from these studies are clear: More sophisticated statuses of racial identity are correlated with higher therapy and supervision multicultural competence (Fuertes, 2012). Carter, Helms, and Juby (2004) developed White racial identity profiles and examined racial identity profiles with respect to racist attitudes for 217 White college students. Students with flat profiles were the most frequently observed where no racial identity status dominates, and along with a profile called Autonomy, correlated with the high scores on the New Racism Scale (Jacobsen, 1985). Silvestri and Richardson (2001) reported inverse associations between Reintegration and Agreeableness, and positive associations between Reintegration and Neuroticism and Openness while examining racial identity in relation to personality. Gushue and Constantine (2007) reported that attitudes which downplay the experience of racism were associated with less developed forms of racial identity (Fuertes, 2012).

Fuertes (2012) noted that research on Black racial identity has examined primarily the negative effects of racism on African Americans. Mahalik, Pierre, and Wan (2006) found that among men higher levels of racial identity were associated with higher self-esteem and that higher levels of racial identity were inversely associated with psychological distress

(Fuertes, 2012). Sellers and Shelton (2003) found that racial identity moderated the relationship between discrimination and distress. Fuertes (2012) also cites a study by Johnson and Arbona (2006) who found that racial identity, but not ethnic identity, was correlated with race-related stress (Fuertes, 2012). Also, Anglin and Wade (2007) found that among African American college students an internalized-multicultural identity was related to adjustment to college, where as an Afrocentric racial identity was inversely correlated with adjustment (Fuertes, 2012).

RESEARCH ON MULTICULTURAL COMPETENCE

Fuertes (2012) noted that a considerable amount of theoretical and empirical work has been directed at studying multicultural competence. Since the publication of the Division of Counseling Psychology (17) Education and Training Committee report (Sue et al., 1982), steady progress has been made to identify and define counselor multicultural competencies as part of a multicultural competency model (see Sue et al., 1998 for a complete list of the competencies). The work of Derald Wing Sue and his collaborators for 20 years has led to the identification of 34 competencies that specify counselor beliefs and attitudes, knowledge, and skills in three broad areas (see Sue et al., 1982, 1992, 1998). The first area includes counselors' racial and cultural self-awareness, which includes counselor understanding of racially or culturally based beliefs and attitudes about themselves and others. The second area is centered on counselor understanding of clients' worldviews, beliefs, cultural values, and sociopolitical experiences and influences, and how these inform case conceptualization and treatment planning. The third area focuses on counselors' ability to use intervention strategies that are sensitive to the cultural and contextual factors of the client, such as clients' spiritual beliefs and cultural traditions.

Quite a few studies have examined multicultural competence in counseling, and most of these are summarized here, following on the observations of Fuertes (2012) in his recent review. Constantine, Fuertes, Roysircar, and Kindaichi (2008) found that multicultural training and education lead to increased levels of multicultural competency. New and even experienced psychotherapists who receive multicultural training exhibit higher levels of multicultural competence (Arthur, 2000; Constantine, Ladany, Inman, & Ponterotto, 1996; Pope-Davis, Reynolds, Dings, & Ottavi, 1994; Sodowsky, Kuo-Jackson, Richardson, & Corey, 1998; Spanierman, Poteat, Wang, & Oh, 2008; Vereen, Hill, & McNeal, 2008). Fuertes and Ponterotto

(2003) surveyed the literature and found that multicultural training works for a diverse group of counseling professionals. Even one course alone in multicultural counseling leads to counselors demonstrating higher levels of multicultural competence (Fuertes, 2012). It has also been found that multicultural competence, racial identity development, and confidence levels in working with racially and culturally diverse clientele are related (Constantine, Juby, & Liang, 2001; Cumming-McCann & Accordino, 2005; Neville, Spanierman, & Doan, 2006; Ottavi, Pope-Davis, & Dings, 1994). It has also been found that minority group members who are psychotherapists, in comparison to European American psychotherapists, express more interest and skill in the area of multicultural competence (see Bernal et al., 1999; King & Howard-Hamilton, 2003; Sodowsky et al., 1998).

Constantine et al. (2008) examined the role of counselor multicultural competence in therapy and found a correlation between minority clients' ratings of counselors' multicultural competence and their general competence, and between multicultural competence and their satisfaction with treatment. Fuertes and Brobst (2002) further uncovered that multicultural competency explained a large and significant amount of variance for ethnic minority clients only, above and beyond counselor general competence and empathy. Fuertes et al. (2006) examined the relationship between therapist multicultural competence and ratings of working alliance, therapist empathy, social influence, and satisfaction. Among their findings they found that clients' ratings of counselor multicultural competence were related to satisfaction and therapist empathy and social influence. This research suggests that there is a level of overlap between therapist competence, broadly defined, and multicultural competence. Fuertes, Bartolomeo, and Nichols (2001) discussed this association and suggested that the reason multicultural competence and general competence are associated is because multicultural competence can only be developed and use in therapy after a solid foundation in general competence skills has been established. As Fuertes et al.(2001) note, the basic and advanced skills used by multicultural counselors are the same (e.g., empathy or probing) as in any other form of counseling, but the topics addressed and the dynamics of the interactions in multicultural counseling are more of a race-based or group membership–based nature. In research outside of psychotherapy but involving similar constructs and processes, the only predictor of adherence to medical treatment of racial or ethnic minority medical patients was their perceptions of their doctors' multicultural competence. In explaining this result, Fuertes et al. suggested that physicians' multicultural competence communicated respect to the patients, and thus enhanced the perceptions of the doctors as competent and trustworthy, leading to higher respect and so the patients complied with the treatment.

TENTATIVE FORMULATIONS

The research on racial and ethnic identity development and on multicultural competence is not yet well developed and it is too early to derive competency statements based on single studies, many of which have been based on small samples and to date have not been replicated by independent researchers. However, Fuertes (2012) presented two tentative formulations about the role of ethnic/racial identity on psychological functioning and psychologist/counselor clinical competence. The first is that *there is a significant effect for ethnic and racial identity; in instances where ethnic and/or racial identity is well developed it can serve as a buffer against psychological illness, and in instances where ethnic and/or racial identity is not well developed it can be a contributor to distress.* Another formulation is that *more sophisticated statuses of racial identity are positively correlated with psychologist/counselor therapy competence as well as competence in clinical multicultural supervision.* Based on our review of the literature on multicultural competence and building on the observations made by Fuertes and Ponterotto (2003) and Fuertes (2012), we offer the following tentative formulations: Competence in ICD entails counseling psychologists being *proficient in a theoretical and technical stance with respect to assessment and intervention, knowing how to integrate and supplement their theoretical stance with knowledge and findings gleaned from the multicultural counseling literature, and being able to establish core conditions in service delivery regardless of theory or approach to intervention.* In our view, competence in ICD also entails counseling psychologists being able to *establish and sustain rapport and working alliances with a diverse set of clients, being open to criticism from or to being tested by the client, and being able to communicate openness to and able to discuss issues associated with gender, race, ethnicity, culture, socioeconomic background, sexual orientation, and other human diversity factors with their clients.* Competence in ICD also entails counseling psychologists being able to *sensitively, respectfully process differences in race, culture, worldviews, or beliefs when such a discussion is clinically indicated for the client, and they are able to name or identify for their clients experiences that may be of a racist or oppressive nature.* We offer these tentative formulations based on our review of the research, in the hope of stimulating psychologists' reflection and analysis of their stance with respect to ICD and in the hope of directing research in this fast-growing area.

A Meta-Analysis on Culturally Adapted Approaches

Griner and Smith (2006) published a meta-analysis of studies that examined culturally adapted approaches to counseling. Their database included 76 studies and 25,225 participants. These researchers included studies that compared a culturally adapted treatment with a treatment that was not culturally adapted. They classified culturally adapted treatments as those that "involved explicitly including cultural values/concepts into the intervention" (p. 535), as well as matching by group and language used or which included family consultation. The findings of their meta-analysis indicated an effect size of .43 for culturally adapted treatments, which indicates a substantial positive effect. As part of their meta-analysis, Griner and Smith also examined the role of potential moderators between the treatments and outcome. They found that for Hispanic clients who were not highly acculturated and for whom services were offered in Spanish, culturally adapted services were particularly important. This study is extremely important in that it catalogues in a scientific and elegant manner a precise effect and benefit of adapting treatments to meet the needs of racial and ethnic minority clients and patients. Limitations noted by Griner and Smith (2006) included that researchers did not specify how treatments were in fact modified, and so this needed to be inferred by the researchers, and that potential confounds of researcher bias and other related effects were not accounted for in their analyses.

Conclusion

We close this chapter by reminding the reader of the changes taking place in the population of the United States, where current racial and ethnic minorities are expected to outnumber European Americans by 2050, and it is by about this date that the United States will become the largest Spanish-speaking country in the world. Issues of ICD in health care and specifically in mental health treatment will increase in magnitude in the next few decades, making competence in diversity and multiculturalism, and the need for far more research in the realm of ICD, an even higher priority for all professional psychologists.

PART II

Functional Competencies in Counseling Psychology

FIVE

Competence in Assessment and Case Conceptualization

Competency in assessment and case formulation are fundamental components of board certification for every psychological specialty. As the following excerpt from the American Board of Counseling Psychology (ABCoP) Examination Manual reflects, "assessment" is a broad term that cross-cuts virtually every aspect of practice as a counseling psychologist:

> Successful candidates conduct assessments that can range from the administration and interpretation of standardized tests to behavioral observations and counseling interviews. Assessment cases may come from any developmental level or domain across the lifespan. In some forms of professional practice, assessment and intervention are integral parts of the same process. Examiners explore candidates' level of competence in discussing choice of assessment methods or approaches to address diagnostic issues and/or case formulation consistent with whatever theoretical foundation and evidence base guides assessment work. Interpersonal interactions, individual and cultural diversity, ethics and legal foundations, and professional identification are examined as they relate to assessment. (American Board of Professional Psychology, 2011, p. 8)

Assessment, Testing, and Case Conceptualization

Assessment describes the overall process of psychological appraisal using multiple samples and sources of input, including, potentially, clinical judgments, across domains of human behavior. Assessment methods are driven in large part by the purpose of the assessment and the audience or the party to which the assessments will be reported (e.g., the client, a court, an employer, etc.). Assessment is typically conducted for a designated purpose or directed to a specific audience. *Testing*, in contrast, refers to the use of psychological instruments structured around one or more psychological constructs, and having a demonstrated set of psychometric qualities documented in technical and professional manuals. Finally, *case conceptualization* refers to the process of aggregating information from assessment and testing to formulate a clinical picture of the client. Case conceptualizations are useful in establishing diagnoses, predicting behavior in novel settings, synthesizing treatment plans, organizing information about the client for consultation or communication with the client or with outside sources, and for training and supervision purposes. All three of these activities—assessment, psychological testing, and case conceptualization—are fundamental aspects of the professional practice of counseling psychology and complement treatment and intervention. Competency in each of these areas is judged in the examination for board certification in counseling psychology. In each case, culturally concordant and ethically appropriate practice is expected.

A Brief History of Assessment and Cultural Context in Psychology

Considerable growth in testing occurred during and following World War I and World War II with the necessity for placing and counseling returning war veterans. Criticism of assessment became more common during the 1960s with the advent of the civil rights movement and a series of court precedents limiting the use of tests in selection and placement (Thorndike, 2005). There is little argument, however, that culture fair assessment (including gender fair) is the most critical and problematic issue in psychological assessment in the present day. Therefore, we devote attention in this text to how test and assessments can be used in culturally concordant ways.

Culturally Appropriate Psychological Assessment

Many definitions of mental health are possible. As Sue and Sue (2007) have argued, however, the choice of such a definition can place minority groups in a disadvantaged position simply on the basis of the definition chosen. If, for example, a Western definition of psychological health dominates practice, then independence, autonomy, and self-reliance will be prized, and individuals not exhibiting such qualities may be pathologized. Thus, an individual acculturated in a collectivistic as opposed to an individualistic culture and who values remaining a part of a group may be seen as less than healthy. When psychological tests or assessment procedures are utilized that are based in Western or individualistic cultures and are neither culture free nor unbiased, then the findings from such assessments invariably lead to outcomes that disadvantage individuals from diverse cultures (Sue & Sue, 2007). This problem is particularly acute the more probabilistic any diagnostic decisions or implications from testing are (Melton, Petrila, Poythress, & Slobogin, 2007), or the more likely any findings will be used to make diagnostic formulations, and in particular to the differential diagnosis of psychopathology and mental illness (Sue & Sue, 2007). Standardized tests, therefore, may contribute to the "perpetuation of social, economic, and political barriers" facing minority subgroups, especially when used for screening or selection purposes in "high stakes" testing (Padilla & Medina, 1996). Padilla and Medina (1996) warn, further, that mental health professionals may be entirely unaware of their biases and how they affect the interpretations they derive from instruments normed on dominant culture individuals, and how those inferences may then influence the client's outcomes. Nonetheless, psychological interventions and assessments can be adapted for use in culturally appropriate ways. In a recent meta-analysis, for example, Benish, Quintana, and Wampold (2011) found that psychotherapy was a third of a standard deviation more effective for minority clients when adapted interventions did not make inferences about specific symptoms, assumptions about the etiology of an illness, or estimations of illness course, consequences, or treatment expectations.

CONSIDERATIONS FOR TEST USAGE

Geisinger (1998) cautioned that mental health professionals should carefully review test manuals prior to the usage or adaptation of a test for diverse populations. Geisinger posed four concise questions to be answered before using a test with a given population:

1. What is the composition of the test-taking population?
2. To what extent can the assessment instrument be administered without encumbrance to all members of the population?

3. Has the test publisher or a subsequent test user or researcher used the instrument in a translated version, adapted version, or accommodated version, or are there any recommended alternative testing procedures?
4. Has the planned accommodation been assessed in terms of the meaningfulness of the score it yields? (Geisinger, 1998, pp. 20–22)

DIAGNOSTIC CLASSIFICATION VERSUS ASSESSMENT OF ASSETS AND STRENGTHS

Conclusions about the disadvantage of culturally biased testing have led to court precedents that prohibit certain psychological tests under some circumstances or when they lead to biased outcomes (Sireci & Geisinger, 1998). Additionally, concerns about the link between tests and assessment to treatment planning and intervention appear to be leading to less categorical assessment and more assessment of continuous symptoms and behaviors across time. Although there are several systems of diagnostic classification, most are based in the assessment of problems, mental health concerns, or negative attributes (Berg, 2009). Thus, we address both diagnostic classifications as well as the assessment of assets and strengths—a foundational concept in counseling psychology and one that engenders fewer potentially detrimental consequences for minority populations (Benish et al., 2011). A counseling psychologist can be expected to be competent both in diagnostic classification and in the assessment of assets and strengths (Gelso & Fretz, 2001).

EXAMPLE OF THE NEED FOR CULTURALLY APPROPRIATE PSYCHOLOGICAL ASSESSMENT

A particularly powerful and timely example of the need to view psychological health and assessment from a cultural perspective can be seen in Stephens, Hamedani, Markus, Bergsieker, and Eloul (2009). Stephens et al. (2009) interviewed survivors who evacuated from the Gulf Coast area following Hurricane Katrina and those who stayed through the storm. Using grounded theory, common themes were extracted for "leavers" and "stayers." Among leavers themes included "choice," "assessing risk," "future focus," and "fear of loss of independence." Stayers, in contrast, emphasized "strength," "caring for others," "maintaining faith," "connection to others," and "underestimating the hurricane." Thus, although outside observers derogated the choices of "stayers," compelling social and cultural rationales for stayers and leavers can be seen as equally agentic. The analysis of Stephens et al. (2009) is important because it highlights the importance of cultural ways of coping that are relevant to psychological and mental health.

Clinical Versus Actuarial Assessment of Human Behavior

In addition to an understanding of the cultural issues in psychological assessment, a competent counseling psychologist must understand the interface between assessment data garnered from clinical or interview sources of data and data drawn from structured psychological tests and inventories (Antony & Barlow, 2002). The utility of these two kinds of data (clinical vs. actuarial) and their integrated use in psychological assessment is a fundamental aspect of competence and, thus, is discussed in some detail.

More than 60 years ago, Meehl catalyzed a debate over the accuracy and utility of inferential versus probabilistic models for assessing and predicting behavior (Grove & Lloyd, 2006). The question Meehl posed—is clinical judgment equal to or superior to judgments based upon test scores—has been addressed repeatedly and clarifies the twin processes by which assessment information is synthesized. *Clinical judgment* involves inference or the generation of hypotheses about the client from behavior and information observed during interviews. *Actuarial* or "statistical" methods, in contrast, involve data-based estimates of the probability of the occurrence of a behavior or outcome. An example of the actuarial method might be estimating the likelihood of entry into a particular occupation based upon a pattern of scores from an interest inventory or the probability of a suicide attempt based upon scores on a scale measuring depression. Research comparing clinical and actuarial methods to the prediction of behavior in novel situations consistently shows the actuarial method to be superior (Dawis, Faust, & Meehl (1989), even though inferential clinical judgment is far more commonly utilized (Meehl, 1996). Furthermore, there is evidence that although human inferential judgments are flawed, some clinicians are much more accurate than others (Groth-Marnat, 2009). A reasonable conclusion from this voluminous literature is that in situations where a specific behavioral outcome can be identified for which a base of empirical evidence is available (e.g., managerial performance), actuarial methods based upon specific psychological tests should form the basis for diagnostic judgments and predictions even when multiple sources of input are available. As actuarial formulas are not widely available for most purposes, and case conceptualizations are rarely specific to a narrow range of behavioral predictions, clinical appraisal is appropriate and can improve with experience and feedback (Skovholt & Jennings, 2004). In actuarial or clinical prediction, it is essential to establish validity and utility across cultures and subgroups. Neither actuarial nor clinical judgment should be considered viable unless evidence confirming cultural utility supports the use of either model for the population being examined. Despite the long history of debate, and the reasonableness of the idea, compelling evidence supporting a combination of statistical and inferential models is not yet available. To minimize errors in clinical judgment, Groth-Marnat (2009) compiled eight recommendations for conducting psychological assessments (see Table 5.1).

BIAS AND FAIRNESS IN INFERENTIAL (CLINICAL) AND PROBABILISTIC (ACTUARIAL) ASSESSMENT

Clearly, however, each assessment method has idiosyncratic sources of bias and validity. While some psychologists eschew the use of formal actuarial tests, especially when they have not been validated for the subgroup under consideration, there is obvious bias inherent when an assessor from one culture or gender makes inference on the basis of self-report data from assessment interviews. Thus, neither clinical nor actuarial methods are free of bias, nor is one more fair than the other. For example, while a score on an interest inventory (e.g., accountant) may have considerable predictive validity for a college-educated male in Columbus, Ohio, that same score may have little utility for a high school–educated woman raised in a rural area of the Appalachians. Similarly, an item endorsement indicating

TABLE 5.1 **Recommendations for Conducting Psychological Assessments**

(a) Use structured approaches to interviews
(b) Consider disconfirming evidence
(c) Base inferences on evidence
(d) Avoid memory in formulating inferences
(e) Attend to base rates of disorders
(f) Solicit feedback on judgments made
(g) Familiarize oneself with the population of subgroup from which the client comes
(h) Stay current on relevant literature

Source: From Groth-Marnat (2009).

that the respondent "hears voices" may be a valid marker of psychosis for a group of dominant culture individuals from Minnesota, whereas that same score may mean that an individual from the Caribbean was raised in a culture where meta-communication with one's ancestors was considered normal. Evidence may accumulate in the future to address this question of which source of assessment data is more fair (i.e., clinical vs. actuarial), but for the present, a reasonable professional should be aware of the contributions and limitations of each method and consider any possible effects on the client or examinee when incorporating either method.

TESTING AS AN ASPECT OF PSYCHOLOGICAL ASSESSMENT

A *psychological test* is a highly structured sampling of behavior under controlled conditions that should be distinguished from the more generic term "psychological assessment," which may include testing. The term test, here, is used to denote a fully manualized and reliably implemented measure that meets standards for a psychological test. Any test employed in professional practice can be expected to demonstrate acceptable psychometric qualities, including *standardization* and *norming, validity, reliability,* and *utility* for the examinee being tested.

Standardization and Norming

When tests are developed for general use, a standardization sample is collected that represents the population to which the test should generalize. In most cases this standardization involves administering the test to a representative sample (usually in proportion to census data when done in the United States), and then constructing population norms using standard scores. The composition of the norming sample and the score distributions are published in the test manual. Psychologists should be particularly cautious in utilizing any test with a client who is not adequately represented in the norming sample.

Reliability

Reliability refers to the degree to which a particular test will consistently tap the concept in question. Simply stated, reliability detects the level of error contained in a measure (Groth-Marnat, 2009). There are several types of reliability, including *test-retest reliability* or the stability of the scores of a test when taken over discrete time periods (typically 2–4 weeks apart); *internal consistency* (measured by Cronbach alpha or split-half reliability), which refers to the degree to which items in a test measure a concept in similar ways (i.e., items cohere); and *parallel or equivalent test forms*, which contain different items but measure a concept reliably.

Validity

Validity connotes the degree to which the measure actually taps the construct it purports to tap. Here again there are several types of validity, including face validity, content validity, construct validity, and criterion validity (concurrent and predictive). *Face validity* is the degree to which items on a test are recognized as reflecting the construct being assessed. For example, an item on a depression scale may tap degree of low mood. *Content validity* is the degree to which test items fully represent the content of the construct being assessed—that is, all aspects of a construct. *Criterion validity* measures the degree to which a scale or test is associated with a specific measure, behavior, or outcome—either presently (concurrent) or in the future (predictive)—for example, to what extent does the "accountant" scale on an interest inventory predict who is or who will become an "accountant." *Construct validity*, often deemed the "acid test" of a psychological scale or inventory, is the degree to which the construct purported to be measured can be demonstrated to be measuring that construct. Construct validity can be demonstrated in a variety of ways (Groth-Marnat, 2009).

Typically, mental health professionals who are concerned with construct validity will examine the *nomological net* in which the construct is embedded. Thus, correlations with other variables that can reasonably be expected to relate to the construct in question should be evident in the nomological net. For example, a measure purporting to tap self-esteem could be expected to relate positively (e.g., overlap) with a measure of ego strength and negatively with a measure of poor self-image. New methods of establishing validity probabilistically at the item level such as Rasch Modeling (Bond & Fox, 2001) open additional ways to demonstrate validity. Additionally, construct validity can be demonstrated through data reduction techniques such as factor analysis, which captures the structure underlying a subset or group of items across individuals. Groth-Marnat (2009) adds *incremental validity*, or the degree to which a test explains additional variation beyond either clinical judgment and inference or probabilistic determinations from other tests or assessment procedures.

Utility

Utility is a relatively recent form of validity. Two types of utility (*clinical utility* and *cultural utility*) are increasingly important in psychological assessments. Although dated, but still relevant, Tinsley and Heesacker (1984) reviewed studies of the effects of test interpretation on the client which they found to be unusually sparse considering the importance of the topic. The effects of a psychological test, either on the client or upon the counseling process, constitute clinical utility. A test may meet all of the traditional psychometric standards of validity and reliability but still not have evidence of clinical utility. To illustrate this problem, consider the extreme example of the Weschler Adult Intelligence Scale instruments, which have acceptable indices in most areas, but because they are rarely interpreted to the examinee in research studies, have little evidence that supports any positive (or negative) effect upon the client. At the other extreme are self-directing inventories such as the Holland Self-Directed Search (SDS), one of the few inventories cited by Tinsley and Heesacker (1984) as presenting substantial clinical utility.

GUIDELINES FOR SELECTING TESTS AND ASSESSMENTS

If a test is selected, that test should demonstrate some advantage over the use of a clinical assessment for the purpose of the assessment (i.e., incremental validity; Groth-Marnat, 2009). Furthermore, tests used for specific purposes must be valid for both the purpose and the population being tested. Messick (1980) asserted that the adequacy of a test as a measure of a specific construct can be determined empirically and is reflected in construct validity. Appropriateness of a test for some specific purpose, in contrast, is an ethically laden issue that should be based upon the consequences of the assessment for the individual or population group being tested, or the consequential validity of the assessment (Messick, 1980). Validity of a test is a general feature based upon "the overall degree of justification for test interpretation and use" (Messick, 1980). We want to underscore the conclusion that equity in testing and assessment, a broader and more generic term for psychological appraisal, is an increasingly complex undertaking as the diversity among client populations increases (Sandoval et al. 1998). Counseling psychologists, therefore, are careful to consider the consequences of any assessment procedure or psychological test for the client, the purpose, and the context in question.

The actual and potential array of psychological tests and assessments is vast, and the technology, scaling, and analytic methods employed in these assessments are quite remarkable. In virtually every domain of human functioning, some manner of assessment can be conducted. Indeed, psychological measurement is generally regarded as the most important contribution of psychology to everyday life. The broad domains of psychological tests and assessments commonly utilized by counseling psychologists include personality and interpersonal functioning; career and vocational behavior; cognitive and intellectual functioning; adjustment and psychopathology; personal assets and effectiveness in educational, work, and family contexts; forensics; health, stress, and coping; and therapeutic process and outcome. Groth-Marnat (2009) has compiled a list of the 10 most frequently utilized psychological tests (see Table 5.2) and the pattern of usage appears to be stable. Thus, the assessment of personality, psychopathology, and cognitive functioning are most often conducted with psychological tests. The usage of psychological tests across settings appears to be dropping in frequency as the roles of psychologists broaden (Groth-Marnat, 2009). Behavioral assessments and session-by-session assessments completed by the client have increased in use over the past several decades to address therapeutic goals and outcomes (see Duncan, Miller, & Sparks, 2004; Hill et al., 1988). Moreover, a counseling psychologist's approach to assessment typically includes ascertaining the client's strengths and assets in personal and interpersonal functioning, a domain tapped by a select subset of assessment devices and procedures.

Assessment Competence

Assessment competency is a fundamental element in Board Certification across psychological specialties. A conference held in 2002 (Kaslow et al., 2004) sought to identify the most critical components

TABLE 5.2 **Ten Most Frequently Utilized Psychological Tests**

Ten Most Frequently Utilized Psychological Tests
Wechsler Intelligence Scales
Minnesota Multiphasic Personality Inventory (MMPI)
Rorschach
Bender-Gestalt
Thematic Apperception Test (TAT)
Other projective drawings (e.g., House Tree Person)
Wechsler Memory Scale (WMS)
Beck Depression Scale
Millon Clinical Multiaxial Inventories (MCMI)
California Personality Inventory (CPI)

Source: From Groth-Marnat (2009).

of psychological assessment. Eight competencies were identified by Krishnamurthy et al. (2004):

1. *A background in the basics of psychometric theory*
2. *Knowledge of the scientific, theoretical, empirical, and contextual bases of psychological assessment*
3. *Knowledge, skill, and techniques to assess the cognitive, affective, behavioral, and personality dimensions of human experience with reference to individuals and systems*
4. *The ability to assess outcomes of treatment/intervention*
5. *The ability to evaluate critically the multiple roles, contexts, and relationships within which clients and psychologists function, and the reciprocal impact of these roles, contexts, and relationships on assessment activity*
6. *The ability to establish, maintain, and understand the collaborative professional relationship that provides a context for all psychological activity, including psychological assessment*
7. *An understanding of the relationship between assessment and intervention, assessment as an intervention, and intervention planning*
8. *Technical assessment skills that include the following:*

   (a) problem and/or goal identification and case conceptualization

   (b) understanding and selection of appropriate assessment methods, including both test and non-test data (e.g., suitable strategies, tools, measures, time lines, and targets)

   (c) effective application of the assessment procedures with clients and the various systems in which they function

   (d) systematic data gathering

   (e) integration of information, inference, and analysis

   (f) communication of findings and development of recommendations to address problems and goals

   (g) provision of feedback that is understandable, useful, and responsive to the client, regardless of whether the client is an individual, group, organization, or referral source. (pp. 732–733)

These competencies form the basis for the assessment portion of the examination for board certification in counseling psychology. Although the competencies imply competence in the culturally appropriate use of psychological assessment, counseling psychologists consider cultural competence to be one of the most critical aspects of psychological assessment.

Diagnostic Classifications as an Aspect of Psychological Assessment

Perhaps the most ubiquitous diagnostic device in use today is the *Diagnostic and Statistical Manual of Mental Disorders* by the Psychiatric Association (*DSM-IV-TR*; American Psychological Association, 2000). *DSM-IV-TR* defines mental illness and details a system for classifying various mental disorders (e.g., personality disorders, psychopathology). *DSM-IV* codes mental disorders on five axes (see Table 5.3), which will likely be reduced in *DSM-V* with the consolidation of Axes I and II.

As of the present writing, a major revision to *DSM-IV-TR* is under way (American Psychological Association, 2012). *DSM-V* will likely embrace a significant shift away from categorical diagnosis and toward the use of scalar or continuous assessment of constructs that cut across diagnostic categories and employs severity ratings (e.g., anxiety, depression suicidal ideation, etc.). Many of these ratings can be based upon assessments provided by the client using simple 5-position Likert scales. In addition, Axis I and Axis II are expected to be consolidated into a single axis of classification. In part, this change is fueled by the realization that there is considerable overlap across categories of disorders or syndromes that makes discrete diagnoses unreliable even for the most skilled of professionals. In addition, clients may have multiple diagnoses complicating any direct link to treatment plans and intervention strategies. The more reliable categorical diagnoses will remain (e.g., borderline personality disorder), but categorical diagnosis of psychopathology has been unreliable across some diagnoses. Dimensional diagnosis is increasingly used with established reliability, as are structured interviews and decision trees developed for *DSM-IV* (Jane, Pagan, Turkheimer, Feidler, & Oltmanns, 2006).

Assessment of Assets and Strengths

The assessment of client strengths and assets has been fundamental to the professional practice of counseling psychology since its inception. Indeed, behavioral assessments containing elements of assets, deficits,

TABLE 5.3 **Five Axes of Mental Disorder**

Axis I: Clinical disorders, including major mental disorders, and learning disorders
Axis II: Personality disorders and mental retardation
Axis III: Acute medical conditions and physical disorders
Axis IV: Psychosocial and environmental factors contributing to the disorder
Axis V: Global Assessment of Functioning (on a behaviorally anchored dimensional scale from 0 to 100)

Source: From *DSM-IV-TR* (American Psychological Association, 2000).

and excesses in a comprehensive assessment have been utilized for several decades (see Kanfer & Saslow, 1969). Moreover, the increasing popularity of positive psychology (Seligman & Csikszentmihalyi, 2000) and constructive, integrative approaches to intervention such as motivational interviewing (Burke, Arkowitz, & Menchola, 2008) underscore the wisdom of strength-based approaches to assessment. A comprehensive model of strength assessment both within the client, and in the environment, proposed by Berg (2009), has four elements: "(a) the client's psychological and behavioral strengths, (b) the client's psychological and behavioral weaknesses, (c) the strengths in the client's environment, and (d) the weaknesses in the client's environment" (p. 10).

Bridging the Gap Between Assessment and Treatment

Although a great deal has been written about assessment and diagnosis, and an equally large body of literature exists in the process and outcome of psychotherapy, very little has been written connecting assessment and treatment (Meier, 2003; Rounds, Tinsley, & Heesacker, 1984). Goldman (1971) introduced the concept of "bridging" both clinical and statistical but was concerned principally with the interpretation of test data for use in predicting behavior in occupational or educational settings. Though useful, Goldman's bridging concept was limited, and it did not address treatment planning and intervention in the comprehensive way in which both are considered in present-day case conceptualization. What is lacking, then, is the link between assessment and case conceptualization, and the subsequent link between case conceptualization and treatment planning (see Fig. 5.1).

The intellectual process by which these links occur is presented in Figure 5.1, which depicts the process that occurs during an assessment interview and leads to a treatment plan and an intervention.

Case Formulation and Conceptualization

Considerable theory and research addresses the process and outcome of psychotherapy and counseling (Gelso & Fretz, 2001). A parallel literature is evident on the diagnosis of client concerns and problems. Very little, in contrast, has been written that bridges assessment and intervention (Goldman, 1971; Meier, 2003). Nonetheless, the formulation and conceptualization of cases is a fundamental and essential aspect of the professional practice of counseling psychology. The scientist-practitioner model presumes, as well, that a counseling psychologist weights the available empirical support for any intervention that derives from the case formulation. This evidentiary approach is a hallmark of counseling psychology.

Case conceptualization can be approached from several perspectives. Cases can be formulated from using a single theoretical approach; using an integrative approach employing one or several theoretical models (Prochaska & Norcross, 2009); from an equity (e.g., feminist) or social justice point of view; from a cultural, family, or systems point of view; or pragmatically using available data from multiple sources, including psychological tests and assessments during a clinical interview. In most cases, as Goldman noted (1971), case formulation is relatively straightforward when practitioners embrace a single theoretical position. When a counseling psychologist adheres closely to a client-centered approach, for example, case formulation involves the assessment of impediments to self-actualization, and therapy is directed toward the creation of therapeutic conditions that promote the integration of emotional experience and the self. In contrast, a practitioner who adheres closely to a cognitive or a cognitive-behavioral approach conceptualizes a case by assessing irrational cognitions and schemata, and refuting, either by logic or evidence, the rationality of such thinking. Although some interplay between assessment, conceptualization, and intervention is required, when a single theoretic approach is utilized, axiomatic guidelines for articulating a clinical approach are, for the most part, quite straightforward.

The past decade or two, however, have evinced significant changes in the theoretical approach of the counseling psychologist. Three related developments have affected how counseling psychologists formulate case conceptualizations: The first is the emergence of integrative theoretical approaches with strong evidential bases beyond cognitive-behavioral models (Lewak & Hogan, 2003), the second is the increasing importance of cultural contexts as considerations in therapeutic intervention, and the third change is the establishment of clear standards for empirically

FIGURE 5.1 **Conceptual map of the link between assessment and intervention.**

Assessment → Case Conceptualization → Treatment Planning → Intervention

supported treatments. These three changes in the field of counseling psychology have influenced case conceptualizations and complicated their connection to interventions. Clear conceptualizations are, thus, not only more difficult but arguably more important than they have been in the past. Although counseling psychologists are conversant with *DSM-IV-TR* (American Psychological Association, 2000), many eschew categorical diagnosis in favor of theoretically or pragmatically derived assessments, a position consistent with Benish et al.'s (2011) meta-analysis of psychotherapeutic interventions with diverse clients. Furthermore, the emerging *DSM-V* revision is moving steadily toward cross-categorical assessment of mental health concerns as explained later (American Psychological Association, 2010).

Board certification in counseling psychology implies a level of sophistication and skill consistent with a mental health professional having 2 years of postlicensure experience. Case conceptualization is a proportionate element in the board certification examination process. Each candidate seeking board certification must present a case and demonstrate case formulation and conceptualization skills that tie logically to interventive strategies and are empirically supportable and implementable with reasonable fidelity given any reality constraints in their current context (Shapiro, 2011).

SYNTHESIZING INFORMATION FROM MULTIPLE SOURCES

Figure 5.2 illustrates the central position of case formulation in the counseling process. Regardless of one's theoretic orientation, case conceptualization in counseling psychology involves an iterative process of weighting and sifting information from multiple sources to arrive at a clear, treatment-relevant view of the client's assets and strengths, presenting issues and concerns, cultural and social contexts, behavior and attitudes, and areas of needed growth. The process of case formulation and conceptualization is a continuous, ongoing process that involves not only the formulation of an overall view of the client's circumstances but also the monitoring and revision of the conceptualization in the face of feedback and progress on the part of the client. The working alliance between the counselor and the client influences the accuracy and direction of the case formulation and, consequently, the treatment plan.

Counseling psychology focuses on normative problems in living. There is an emphasis on clients, not patients, and their adjustment to life circumstances and environments in positive and proactive ways. Counseling psychologists focus on strengths and development even with clients/patients with diagnosable disorders. Counseling psychologists take a holistic perspective and consider broader issues of happiness, well-being, and actualization, rather than an exclusive emphasis on the amelioration of specific disorders, syndromes, and/or behavioral deficits or excesses. Strengths, in the perspective of counseling psychology, then, can be identified and developed to maximize personal and interpersonal functioning. When conceptualizing a client's clinical picture, a counseling psychologist will consider multiple types of information and data from a variety of sources. Figure 5.3 depicts the hierarchical aggregation, described here, of multiple data for use in formulating a clinical picture.

UNDERLYING PROCESSES IN CASE FORMULATION

A counseling psychologist appraises the client's circumstances and conceptualizes cases broadly within a cultural frame and with an emphasis on strengths (Lopez & Edwards, 2008). Although the process may not be the same in each instance, data from multiple sources are aggregated in an inductive-deductive process initially described by Goldman (1971) and later amplified by Millon (1983) and with a connection to intervention by

FIGURE 5.2 **Case conceptualization and formulation process in relation to assessment and intervention.**

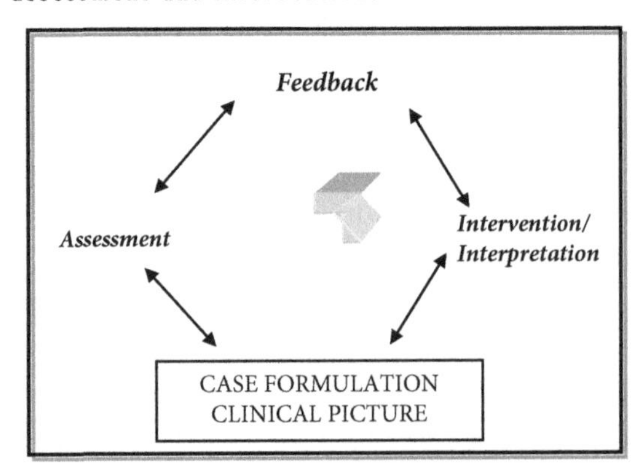

FIGURE 5.3 **General framework of case conceptualization.**

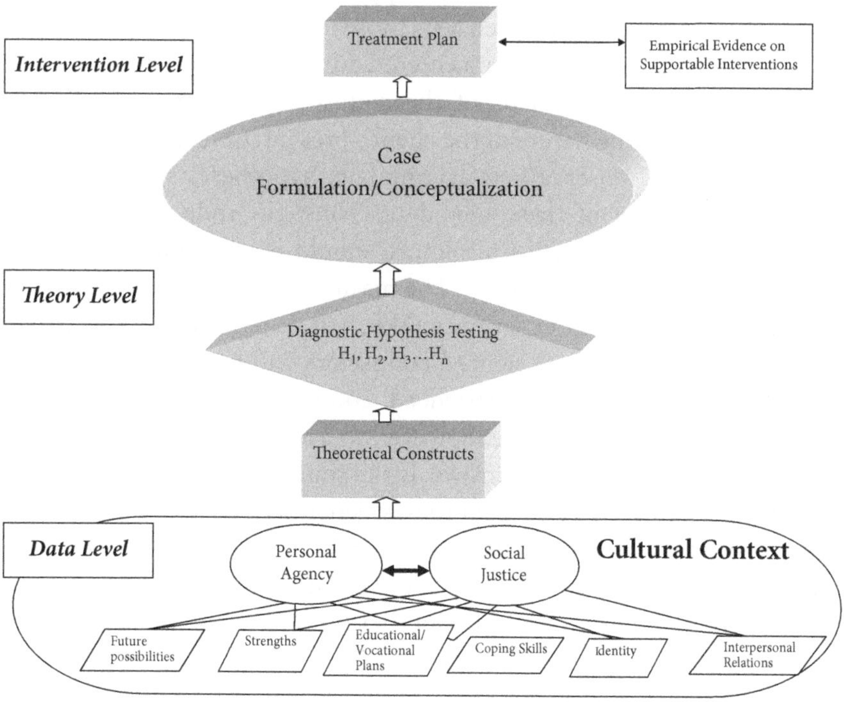

Meier (2003). The data considered in the formulation process depend, in part, upon the theoretical approach of the therapist, and they may vary by presenting circumstances of the client.

Goldman (1971) suggested that there were multiple "bridges" from (test) data to interpretation, the first few of which described the statistical connections between test data and interpretive formulations (e.g., norm bridge, discriminant bridge, regression bridge). While these "statistical" bridges still make sense when psychological tests are used to formulate case conceptualizations, it is Goldman's "clinical" bridge that we discuss in some detail here. "Clinical" refers to the nature of the interpretive progression (e.g., counselor thinking process) rather than to a specialty in psychology (e.g., clinical vs. counseling psychology). The ABCoP oral examination process seeks to examine this inductive-deductive process in the candidate for board certification through discussion of the candidate's assessment and intervention samples and the thinking processes involved in their formulation of the client's clinical picture.

Essentially, however, case formulation follows many of the same rules as scientific research. The counselor appraises the evidence, formulates alternative hypotheses, and then tests those hypotheses against the ongoing counseling process. The data entered during that process are filtered through the therapeutic lens of the counselor to formulate working hypotheses about the nature of the client's presentation and possibilities. As new data and observations accumulate, hypotheses should modify and evolve in light of these new data. Thus, the inductive-deductive processes in creating a clinical picture should not be done hastily and should be open to ongoing input. The mastery of this process appears to improve with time and experience (Skovholt & Jennings, 2004). There is evidence that more experienced counselors will generate many more such hypotheses than inexperienced counselors (McDonald, 1996). The counselor must take care, however, to avoid *confirmatory bias* and "bolstering" in which the counselor is the source of conceptual material and then seeks to confirm hypotheses generated from the counselor's perspective (Haverkamp, 1993). Confirmatory bias may prematurely reduce or inaccurately support preselected hypotheses rather than increase the number of clinical hypotheses under consideration during the counseling process.

Figure 5.3 depicts a general framework that may be used to clarify how a counseling psychologist filters data and observations from client reports, assessment devices, and observations, and filters that information using a theory frame to generate hypotheses that will lead to a case conceptualization and, subsequently, to a treatment plan. Like most therapeutic processes, case conceptualization relies heavily on the clinical skills and judgment of the counselor, but intervention is guided heavily by the base of scientific evidence on the efficacy of various therapeutic methods for the array of client presenting concerns. Because the counseling psychologist considers cultural advantages and constraints and environmental and social justice circumstances to be central in case formulation, observational data are always tempered by sociocultural and ecological considerations. This is a complex thought process that strengthens as the professional counseling psychologist matures (Skovholt & Jennings, 2004) and as the field of counseling psychology evolves.

Writing Reports Based Upon Psychological Assessment

A critical element in psychological assessment is the communication of findings, either in the context of a consultation or in writing to a referral source. Kvaal, Choca, and Groth-Marnet (2003) made five recommendations for improving psychological reports: clearly stating purpose, targeting language to report consumers, readability, addressing referral questions, and providing examples. A specific statement of the reason for the assessment (e.g., to make recommendations for treatment or decisions about ability to work or fitness to stand trial) is crucial to organizing and communicating any assessment findings, as is a clear and specific statement of any recommendations deriving from the assessment. As Kvaal et al. (2003) note, recommendations are typically the weakest aspect of report writing, and they underscore the need to document any recommendations with specific data, behavioral observations or samples, and direct quotes. Also emphasized are clear delineations of the procedure, measures, instrument, and methods employed in the assessment, as well as statements regarding the level of certainty the assessor has about the conclusions stated in the report (Kavaal et al., 2003). It is important to restate that the purpose of the assessment and the nature of the referral dictate, in large measure, the content and format of a psychological report. A forensic report of fitness to stand trial will, of necessity, contain much different information than a consultative recommendation for use in treatment planning. In either case, however, the mental health professional should assume that the client, as well as the referral source, may have access to the report.

Ethical and Appropriate Use of Psychological Assessment in Professional Practice

As implied throughout this chapter, the ethical and appropriate use of psychological assessments is a broad and complex topic area influenced by standards for test construction and use (American Education Research Association, 1999; American Psychological Association 2010), legal precedents, cultural issues, and empirical evidence. This brief discussion highlights several of the critical competencies in the area of ethical and appropriate use of psychological assessment. A psychologist in professional practice:

1. *Understands that psychological assessments are administered and utilized within the context of a professional relationship (Groth-Marnat, 2009).* The client's well-being and protection are paramount in this relationship, and the psychologist is careful to obtain informed consent from the client. The psychologist is clear as to who the client

is and recognizes that the "client" may or may not be the person being assessed; the true client could be a court or agency, and this depends on the setting where the psychologist is working and/or on the nature of the consult or referral source. Despite the distinction in the scenario just described, the psychologist observes the rights of the person being evaluated. The psychologist also understands that the relationship with the client may bias test performance in the positive direction. The psychologist also appreciates that any labeling or diagnostic determination may have effects on the client's future prospects and possibilities (Groth-Marnat, 2009).

2. *Is aware of the effects of culture and acculturation, gender, disability, socioeconomic status, and other potential diversity issues on the client's test performance and ability to absorb and understand information deriving from psychological assessments.* This awareness assumes a thorough understanding of the client's background and consideration of the fact that within-group variations (e.g., variability within Native American culture across tribes, or variability within Hispanic or Asian American culture and across subgroups) may be as important as variability between larger cultural groups.
3. *Is knowledgeable about standards for the development and construction of psychological tests and assessments.* A thorough knowledge of psychometrics, test construction, and validation increases the likelihood that a psychologist will be competent in selecting, interpreting, and evaluating appropriate tests and assessments for a diverse range of clients.
4. *Understands the need to examine any normative data relevant to the use of a psychological assessment with a particular client.* Consulting the technical manual and any relevant empirical studies for normative data that would reflect the client being examined would lessen the likelihood that a psychologist would use a test with a client, group, or subgroup for which no evidence exists regarding whether that test was valid and reliable for that client.
5. *Uses assessments within the purview of his or her training and competence.* Tests are utilized that can be competently administered, scored, and interpreted. When acquiring competence with a new or revised assessment, the psychologist seeks training and/or education and study of that assessment.

6. *Understands the potential therapeutic benefits and pitfalls involved and the nature of the process of communicating assessment findings to the client or the public without misleading the recipient.* Care is taken to convey information at the level that can be understood by the recipient and in a way that minimizes the risk of misinterpretation or inappropriate use of the assessment findings.
7. *Is knowledgeable about what specific information can be communicated without compromising test security.* Amendments to the APA Ethical Principles and Code of Conduct (American Psychological Association, 2010) address the release of test scores (rather than items).

Conclusion

This chapter addressed culturally appropriate competencies in psychological assessment and testing, as well as principles of case conceptualization as a bridge between assessment and intervention. Psychological testing is seen as one subelement of psychological assessment, and it informs the clinical process of case formulation and conceptualization. These essential competencies are fundamental to, and a hallmark of, the professional practice of a counseling psychologist.

SIX

Competence in Intervention

The models of clinical competence found in the literature present competencies that are comprehensive and generic (Belar, 2009; Kaslow et al., 2007), highlighting learning and training expectations and outcomes that cut across professional psychology (Rodolfa et al., 2005). In our review of the relevant literature we did not come across any documents delving into specific competencies in counseling psychology; thus, the aim of this chapter is to discuss clinical competence in intervention and to do so in a way that can be considered as typical of or consistent with the practice of counseling psychology.

The development of generic competencies for professional psychology is an important achievement in the competency movement (Barnett, Doll, Younggren, & Rubin, 2007), and the current models of competence have been developed as consensus statements by teams of professionals that represent various fields of psychology, including clinical, counseling, school, and educational psychology. It should be noted that while the competency models presented here are the product of extensive thinking and hard work on the part of seasoned and devoted clinicians from various domains of professional psychology, they are nonetheless rationally derived statements that have not been linked to the empirical evidence (Lichtenberg et al., 2007; Schulte & Daly, 2009). We do believe that a great deal of evidence is available to support the role of these competencies in effective treatments and outcomes, and that in due time the empirical evidence that supports many aspects of these models will be presented. We also expect that new research will be stimulated by these competency statements, which will undoubtedly lead to modifications and/or extensions of these models.

In our view, there is great overlap in what constitutes professional competence across specialties, and counseling psychologists will employ many of the same interventions that are available to all professional psychologists. Rodolfa et al. (2005) noted in their cube model that "the ways in which specialty education becomes relevant can be visualized through the parameters of practice that differentiates specialties namely: populations served, problems addressed, procedures of theoretical orientation, and settings" (p. 350). As counseling psychologists, we essentially agree with that observation as it applies to intervention since there is great overlap between training programs in professional psychology, including counseling psychology (Fitzgerald & Osipow, 1986). The use of interventions by a counseling psychologist will be a function, to some degree, of the type of client/patient that the professional is treating, the professional's assessment of the client's symptoms and needs, and the type of setting where the professional works (e.g., a hospital vs. a college counseling center, or if the agency provides only brief counseling). Variations in the type or frequency of use of specific interventions by counseling psychologists are likely to be due to the professional's personality, philosophy, and personal approach to treatment and the type of training that he or she received, more so than the fact that the professional is a counseling psychologist versus, say, a clinical psychologist. In our view, the training received by a counseling psychologist and his or her approach to and use of intervention is also heavily influenced by individual faculty members and clinical supervisors, more so than the fact that the program is in counseling psychology. In essence, we believe that there are more appreciable differences in approaches to intervention among counseling psychologists than between them and professional psychologists in other specialties. Highlighting the broad nature of training and of approaches to intervention in the specialty, Goodyear and colleagues (2008) found in their survey of 670 American Psychological Association (APA) member counseling psychologists that the most frequently reported theoretical orientation was eclectic, followed by cognitive, and then psychodynamic orientations.

So where can distinctions be made between counseling psychologists and other professional psychologists? In our view, the philosophical bases of focusing on assets and strengths, on person–environment interactions, on educational and career development, on relatively brief interactions, and our traditional work with intact personalities still characterizes some of the work in counseling psychology, particularly in college counseling centers. These are the aptly discussed five unifying principles of counseling psychology by Gelso and Fretz (2001) and, as they point out, it is the interaction of these principles rather than their individual influence that has characterized the professional identity of the specialty. In this chapter, we extend the notion that these five principles can also be used to describe how intervention is used in our professional specialty.

While counseling psychology can be described and unified in terms of Gelso and Fretz's principles, the ingredients and building blocks of the profession have in fact been derived from theories and knowledge accumulated from every other available discipline in psychology, including individual differences and personality psychology, educational and industrial psychology, developmental and social psychology, psychoanalytic and psychodynamic psychologies, behaviorist, humanistic, and cognitive psychologies, and by postmodern theories such as those of feminism and multicultural psychology. Counseling psychology is a rich and broad specialty, one that has adapted to and assimilated developments in psychology and related disciplines, and one that continues to do so with contemporary trends. For example, intervention in counseling psychology continues to be influenced by psychiatry and the American Psychiatric Association's *Diagnostic and Statistical Manual of Mental Disorders* (*DSM*). The expectations by insurance companies that practitioners document patient psychopathology via *DSM* nomenclature and for practitioners to target the symptoms and problems associated with diagnosis as the basis of treatment have shifted the work of counseling psychologists toward a clinical model (Lichtenberg, Goodyear, & Genther, 2008). Also, the move toward evidence-based practice and toward empirically supported treatments is also beginning to guide the practice and selection of interventions by counseling psychologists, and it will become a stronger influence as evidence-based and empirically supported psychological practice become increasingly the norm and standard in psychological intervention.

Another contemporary trend being assimilated by counseling psychology is the movement toward *strength-based psychotherapy*, inspired by the positive psychology movement brought to national prominence by Martin Seligman. Measures of human strengths have been developed, including the Clifton Strengths Finder (Buckingham & Clifton, 2000; Lopez et al., 2005) and the Values in Action Classification of Strengths (VIA; Paterson & Seligman, 2004), this latter intended to stand in contrast to the *DSM*. Lopez and Edwards (2008) note that therapies are now being developed on the basis of strengths, including manual therapies designed to promote happiness and to treat mental illness, such as depression (see Seligman,

Rashid, & Parks, 2006); each of these therapies has yielded strong empirical evidence of support for their use (Lopez & Edwards, 2008). The positive psychology and positive psychotherapy movements very much parallel the traditional focus of counseling psychology on assets and strengths, and represent an opportunity for counseling psychology to reaffirm its historical stance with respect to intervention and to contribute to the development of positive psychotherapies. Notable recent contributions by counseling psychologists on this topic include *Counseling Psychology and Optimal Human Functioning* (2003) by Bruce Walsh and colleagues and *The Encyclopedia of Positive Psychology* (2009) by Shane Lopez.

Foundational Competencies in Intervention

In the following section we review the models of foundational competence that describe essential knowledge and training in intervention, and we discuss how these relate to practice in counseling psychology.

THE EPPP

As noted in previous chapters, we view the Examination for Professional Practice in Psychology (EPPP) as *the* test of foundational knowledge in professional psychology. There are knowledge areas pertaining to intervention within the EPPP, and Appendix A (ASPPB, 2009) includes an area entitled "Treatment, Intervention, Prevention, and Supervision," which constitutes 14% of the exam. It describes this area as "knowledge of (a) individual, couple, family, group, organizational, or community interventions for specific problems/disorders in diverse populations, (b) intervention and prevention theories, (c) best practices and practice guidelines, (d) consultation and supervision models, and (e) evidence supporting efficacy and effectiveness of interventions" (p. 20). These knowledge bases tested by the exam for treatment, intervention, and prevention are then grouped into 16 clusters, two of which are presented here: The first cluster includes knowledge of "Treatment decision making based on best available data (e.g., matching treatment to assessment/diagnosis, matching client/patient and therapist characteristics, cost and benefit, readiness to change)" (p. 20). The second cluster requires knowledge of "Contemporary theories/models of treatment/intervention and their evidence base" (p. 20). The remaining 10 clusters emphasize knowledge bases that include "treatment techniques/interventions and the evidence for their comparative effectiveness," "career counseling," and "health promotion, risk reduction, resilience and wellness activities and methods" (p. 20). The EPPP is comprehensive in terms of the subject areas that it covers pertaining to intervention and taps essential elements that are foundational to intervention for counseling psychologists. While counseling psychology was strongly influenced in its beginning by the humanism of Carl Rogers and by the vocational rehabilitation movement that followed the end of World War II, since its early days PhD training in the specialty has also been built on the basis of academic psychology, ongoing research on the mind and human behavior, empirical evidence from the broader social sciences, and considerable research on psychotherapy intervention. Our assessment of the EPPP is that it taps essential academic knowledge from the "parent" areas of psychology (Richardson & Patton, 1992) and that it reflects the course work and foundational knowledge bases that underlie counseling psychology.

THE CB MODEL

As noted in previous chapters, the competency benchmarks (CB) model (Fouad et al., 2009) is divided into foundational and functional competencies, which are organized into three developmental levels, that is, readiness for practicum, readiness for internship, and readiness for entry to practice. Each level delineates an "essential component," and specific behavioral anchors or competencies are then delineated for each level. The CB model identifies professionalism, reflective practice/self-assessment/self-care, scientific knowledge and methods, relationships, individual and cultural diversity (ICD), ethics, and interdisciplinary systems as foundational areas of professional competence. In the organization of the current book, we provide individual chapters to ICD and ethics. We also have a chapter on professional competence in interdisciplinary teams, which in our model for this book we view as a functional competence (see Fig. 1.1 in Chapter 1). Thus, in this section we discuss professionalism, reflective practice/self-assessment/self-care, scientific knowledge and methods, and relationships as described in the CB model and as they inform intervention in counseling psychology.

Professionalism

The foundational competency of professionalism is defined in the CB model as "professional values and ethics as evidenced in behavior and comportment that reflects the values and ethics of psychology, integrity, and responsibility" (Fouad et al., 2009, p. S9). The model outlines five domains within this foundational competency: integrity-honesty, deportment, accountability, concern for the welfare of others, and professional identity. The importance of these factors to basic competence as a psychologist may seem as evident to the reader as it is to us, and integrity-honesty, accountability, and concern for the welfare of others also make up key ethical principles of professional behavior for psychologists. Factors that inform and may be informed by counseling psychology may be the concern of the specialty with social justice, with advocacy, and with maintaining a professional identity that reflects the values of the specialty. An effective counseling psychologist has been trained to be attentive to issues of racism and oppression, discrimination, and other environmental and contextual factors (such as poverty) that affect the individual. This would be kept in mind in case conceptualization, in considering whether a diagnosis of psychopathology is warranted, and in planning treatment and interventions that may help the person in offsetting these influences. The competency of concern for the welfare of others may also be associated with advocacy that the therapist may choose to engage in to help the client. For example, a psychologist in a counseling center may help a student arrange to have a new roommate or to transfer to another floor or dorm, if the psychologist believes that racism or intolerance is affecting the client.

Reflective Practice/Self-Assessment/Self-Care

The foundational competency of reflective practice/self-assessment/self-care is defined in the CB model as "practice conducted with personal and professional self-awareness and reflection; with awareness of competencies; with appropriate self-care" (Fouad et al., 2009, p. S10). Counseling psychologists place a high premium on the health and functioning of the therapist, and on being able to attend to the client as a complex and dynamic individual. Training in counseling psychology emphasizes self-knowledge and awareness of self, to others, and to self–other interactions in terms of values, socialization, and worldviews/beliefs. One of the first training experiences for counseling psychology students is a prepracticum course, in which they learn and practice basic helping skills, among them the ability to be fully present and to be empathic in listening. These and other basic helping skills can only be mastered through reflection, personal and professional awareness, and self-care. Reflection, self-assessment, and self-care are crucial throughout professional life, and counseling psychologists are trained to maintain a high level of personal self-care beyond graduate school training.

Scientific Knowledge and Methods

Foundational competence in scientific knowledge and methods is defined in the CB model as "understanding of research, research methodology, techniques of data collection and analysis, biological bases of behavior, cognitive-affective bases of behavior, and development across the lifespan. Respect for scientifically derived knowledge" (Fouad et al., 2009, p. S11). In our view, scientific mindedness in intervention in counseling psychology involves being able to think critically about the circumstances of the client, about the empirical and theoretical knowledge available in intervention, as well as the capacity for the professional to think with complexity. A counseling psychologist who practices scientific mindfulness is able to deconstruct assumptions and beliefs critically and to reconstruct and integrate evidence and ideas into an effective assessment of the client's needs and into an approach to intervention that follows from such an assessment (Critchfield & Knox, 2010). He or she investigates and sifts through possible hypotheses and continually evaluates the viability of data/evidence in order to maintain effectiveness. An example of scientific mindfulness would be evident when a counseling psychologist appropriately questions a core belief of a client that is based on socialization or perhaps internalized racism, and it is evident to the psychologist that such a belief causes distress for the client and is associated with self-defeating behaviors.

Relationships

Foundational competence in relationships is defined as the ability to "relate effectively and meaningfully with individuals, groups, and/or communities" (Fouad et al., 2009, p. S12). Relationship competence is organized around three areas: interpersonal relationships, affective skills, and expressive skills. Counseling psychologists place a very high premium in the therapy relationship as a curative factor in treatment. Training emphasizes the importance of the working relationship in treatment, and the ability of the therapist to work collaboratively with clients in setting goals, establishing tasks, and in building rapport based on trust and liking. Counseling psychologists are also trained to be attentive to the "I/Thou" dimension of interaction with clients (part of what the counseling psychologist Charles Gelso [2011] calls the "real relationship" in therapy), and they are trained through course work and supervision to be attentive to, manage effectively, and solve impasses and ruptures in the therapy relationship.

Functional Competencies in Intervention

THE CB MODEL AND THE NCSPPP MODEL

In the CB model, intervention is described as "interventions designed to alleviate suffering and to promote health and well-being of individuals, groups, and/or organizations" (Fouad et al., 2009, p. S18). There are five functional competency areas in the CB model with respect to intervention: knowledge of interventions, intervention planning, skills, intervention implementation, and progress evaluation. The National Council of Schools and Programs of Professional Psychology (NCSPPP) model (Kenkel & Peterson, 2010) also delineates intervention planning, implementation, and evaluation as core domains, and the NCSPP lists numerous knowledge, skill, and attitude competencies that they deem are essential to each core domain. The NCSPPP model also includes ethics as a domain of intervention competence, which we discuss as a foundation competence in Chapter 3 of this volume. Next, we discuss the relationship between generic intervention—as postulated by these models, namely knowledge, planning, skills, implementation, and evaluation—and intervention in counseling psychology. We discuss these in terms of the CB model, which provides essential components for each domain of intervention. The reader is encouraged to read both models in detail, to better appreciate their considerable overlap and unique contributions to the literature on intervention competence.

Knowledge of Interventions

The CB model describes the essential component of knowledge at the level of readiness for entry to practice as "applies knowledge of evidence-based practice, including empirical bases of intervention strategies, clinical expertise, and client preferences" (Fouad et al., 2009, p. S18). This aptly describes knowledge in intervention in counseling psychology. We would add that a prominent theme in counseling psychology training with respect to intervention revolves around knowledge of human strengths and assets, knowledge of diverse approaches to intervention including gender-aware and multicultural theories of counseling, an appreciation of person–environment interactions and knowledge of the context of the client as essential to understanding his or her problems, knowledge of vocational psychology, and knowledge of psychopathology and of normal development and personality. Knowledge is also conceived in the specialty as the psychologist being highly conversant and comfortable with a theoretical approach to intervention and its associated techniques, including the empirical evidence associated with them as well as their limitations.

Intervention Planning

The essential component of intervention planning at the level of readiness for entry to practice is "independent intervention planning, including conceptualization and intervention planning specific to case and context" (Fouad et al., 2009, p. S19). Intervention in counseling psychology is generally tailored to the individual with an awareness of cultural and environmental factors that affect the individual. Counseling psychologists will certainly direct their attention and interventions at the presenting problem of the client, at reducing his or her symptoms, and helping the person cope and adjust to difficulties. However, the process of intervention also targets the person, his or her broader needs or interests for health, growth, and maturation. Work in treatment generally goes beyond diagnosis or psychopathology and on helping people adjust, cope, and thrive in their environment. A prominent theme in planning is that the work is done in a relatively limited period of time; in counseling centers interventions generally take place within a semester, between 8 and 15 sessions. In most hospitals and clinics the work of psychotherapy dovetails with the customary limits placed by managed care, usually between 8 to a maximum of 25–30 hourly sessions. In private practice the length of the work varies and is determined by the presenting issues of the client and insurance limits, though some counseling psychologists will work with clients as long as needed and make financial arrangements directly with the client.

Skills

The next competency area under intervention in the CB model is skills, and the essential component at the level of readiness for entry to practice is "clinical skills and judgment" (Fouad et al., 2009, p. S19). While counseling psychologists generally receive training that covers the gamut of clinical skills training, a primary skill in counseling psychology is the use of the relationship and the ability of the therapist to identify and integrate into the work the assets and strengths that are evident for the client (e.g., problems-solving ability, work experience, interests and hobbies, and other supportive relationships). Beyond having clarity with respect to his or her theoretical and technical approach to intervention, the effective counseling psychologist is adept at tailoring and applying the approach and the selective use of interventions to the unique circumstances and needs of the client. He or she would approach each case individually with a fresh mind and a respectful attitude and use the therapy relationship to delve deeper into the challenging and difficult phases of the work with the client. Counseling psychologists are trained to "process" with their clients the progress of work (or impasses) and will use effective open-ended questions and the skill of immediacy to evaluate the experience of therapy for the client.

Intervention Implementation

The next competency area under intervention in the CB model is intervention implementation, and the essential component at the level of readiness for entry to practice is "implements interventions with fidelity to empirical models and flexibility to adapt where appropriate" (Fouad et al., 2009, p. S19). The counseling psychologist will build rapport and a working relationship with his or her client by using listening skills, a nonverbal posture that is attentive, respectful, and that invites the client to talk, and will use empathy, unconditional positive regard, and genuineness. These skills set the foundation for the therapist to challenge the client, provide feedback or make interpretations that provide insight, and to prod the client to action with respect to goals and needs that are evident in treatment. Implementation is done in the context of a supportive and respectful relationship. We would add that the concept of "fidelity" noted earlier in the CB model is extended by the effective counseling psychologist to his or her theoretical orientation, beyond empirical models and research evidence, and to his or her experience as a therapist.

Progress Evaluation

The last competency area is called progress evaluation, and the essential component at the level of readiness for entry to practice is "evaluate treatment progress and modify planning as indicated, even in the absence of established outcome measures" (Fouad et al., 2009, p. S19). The effective counseling psychologist will generally evaluate progress with the client as the treatment progresses, and he or she will likely develop further interventions based on reflection about the case, on the process of feedback directly from the client, on supervision or consultation feedback if available, on formal and standardized outcome assessments, and on feedback and comments solicited from the client in the context of a strong working relationship.

THE ABCOP MODEL

The American Board of Counseling Psychology (ABCoP) model represents a higher standard in professional competence than the level of "readiness for entry to practice" delineated in the CB and NCSPPP models. The ABCoP provides board certification in counseling psychology to professionals who have been licensed for at least 2 years, and it remains the only specialty-specific assessment of competence in counseling psychology. This being the case, the ABCoP specifies knowledge and skills sets in intervention that are more integrated and advanced but that would be expected from every counseling psychologist with that level of postdoctoral experience. Certification by the ABCoP is highly desirable and increasingly considered the norm for all counseling psychologists, since it is a review by peers of specialty-specific knowledge and competencies above and beyond generic licensing requirements. The emphasis in the ABCoP model is on the personal integration of theory and technique as expressed in a written self-study and the manifestation of this theoretical stance and techniques in a taped therapy session. The ABCoP will also certify as counseling psychologist professionals who are conversant with scientific and scholarly developments in counseling psychology and can apply them in professional practice. Candidates for certification must be aware of and able to discuss critically the implications and applications of contemporary knowledge in the practice of counseling psychology. This includes knowledge of the integration of theory, research, and practice concerning interpersonal interactions, issues of individual and cultural diversity (e.g., ethnicity, race, gender, age, sexual orientation, disability status, and special populations), ethics and legal foundations, and personal identification.

Science Base and Applications

The ABCoP identifies components of science base and applications that would be evident when the counseling psychologist uses evidence base and theory to inform activities. This requires a definable set of constructs and a theoretical orientation of sufficient complexity. Also, he or she is expected to engage in a critical evaluation of research and of the professional literature and demonstrate a capacity to discuss implication for practice. To be certified in counseling psychology, the psychologist has also made a contribution to the empirical, theoretical, or clinical knowledge base through research, conference presentations, a dissertation, or other writings and professional activities. The psychologist pays attention to interpersonal interactions, individual and cultural diversity, ethics and legal foundations, and is expected to present evidence of a professional identification with counseling psychology as related to the application of and contributions to the science base and practice of counseling psychology.

Examples of passing levels of performance for certification with respect to science base and application include being able to demonstrate awareness of research and other publications relevant to practice. He or she presents a coherent and reasonably comprehensive explanation based on research and theory of client/patient behavior and functioning as a counseling psychologist in each competency domain. The counseling psychologist demonstrates the capacity to thoughtfully evaluate the extant evidence base and to use this assessment to inform practice. In contrast, examples of competence that would not lead to certification would be providing explanations of client/patient behavior that may be accurate but that lack support and/or omit obviously useful theoretical and research constructs. Also unacceptable would be if the psychologist presents as largely unaware of current research or theory or has an inaccurate reading of the pertinent literature. The psychologist would also not be certified if he or she does not understand the contributions of counseling psychology or conveys a general lack of awareness of ways in which interpersonal interactions, individual and cultural diversity, ethical and legal foundations, and professional identification are pertinent to the application of the existing science base.

Intervention

The following components make up the competency area of intervention as defined by the American Board of Counseling Psychology and evaluated via an examination (these can be found at http://www.abpp.org/files/page-specific/3364%20Counseling/02_Candidate_Exam_Manual.pdf): "(1) Intervention contract issues (i.e., client's/patient's goals, boundaries of treatment, payment resources, etc.) are managed responsibly; (2) Intervention procedures chosen are appropriate for the client/patient situation; (3) Interventions are applied with skill and knowledge and appropriate attitude: (4) Attention to interpersonal interactions, individual and cultural diversity, ethics and legal foundations, and professional identification as related to intervention are evident" (American Board of Professional Psychology, 2011, p. 11).

The evaluation of competence for board certification in counseling psychology is done in vivo, where the candidate seeking certification meets examiners from the specialty trained to provide a professional and respectful process. The evaluation of intervention competence usually involves the candidate and examiners viewing together a taped counseling session that the candidate has provided of himself or herself with a client. The candidate is then asked a variety of questions guided by the criteria presented earlier about his or her approach to intervention as manifested in the taped session (see Table 6.1).

Competence in Intervention as Informed by the EBPP and EST Movements

Foundational and functional intervention in counseling psychology are also informed by the current movements toward *evidence-based psychological practice (EBPP)* and *empirically supported treatments (ESTs)*, by the seminal work of a steering committee and task force from Division 29, Psychotherapy, of the American Psychological Association, and by the vast amount of work that has over decades examined the process and outcome of psychotherapy.

We begin this section on the EBPP and EST movements in professional psychology, which are also currently "cultures" in professional psychology, by first discussing the "culture" of counseling psychology. A unique quality about intervention in counseling psychology has been the depth and breadth of focus, which incorporates but goes beyond diagnosis and psychopathology in case conceptualization and attends to but goes beyond the amelioration of symptoms in treatment planning and implementation. Counseling psychologists will often describe their work as helping clients with normal developmental needs, as helping people who have normal problems in living, and will often focus their work on fostering the psychological growth of the individual (Lopez & Edwards, 2008; Packard, 2009). As Gelso and Fretz (2001) point out, even when working with clients who are evidencing significant problems in functioning, counseling psychologists will look for assets and strengths in the individual and will gravitate toward seeing his or her problems in the context of relationships, family, culture, and community. As noted in Chapter 1, several factors—including the development of educational and vocational psychology, the advent of the human potential movement and of humanistic-existential philosophies, specifically Roger's client-centered therapy, and the fact that a primary work setting for counseling psychologists has been the university counseling center—set counseling psychology in its formative years on a path that diverted from models of disease and diagnosis. This early influence explains the ambivalence if not outright resistance in some programs in counseling psychology to the reductionism inherent in diagnosis, and the fear of an unintended dehumanization that can occur when patients are referred to in terms of diagnostic labels or described in terms of their clinical symptoms. In most programs in counseling psychology, the Rogerian ethic of "prizing the client" is still alive and well, and professionals are trained to attend to the person in the client and to their own person as psychologists when interacting with and treating clients. This tradition may also explain the unease that some counseling psychologists experience with respect to using "manualized" treatments and with the movement toward ESTs. The ambivalence is not out of a lack of respect for the rigors of science or out of a lack of appreciation for the need to evolve treatment options that increase quality of care. The ambivalence has more to do with concern about psychological practice where therapist experience and judgment are de-emphasized, and where the client is "fit" to the treatment rather than vice versa. There are also concerns with not attending to the unique individual needs and goals of the client, particularly his or her assets and strengths, context, and values and beliefs. It is important to note that there are professional psychologists in other specialties, including clinical psychology, that on the bases of personal philosophy and training also embrace these sets of beliefs and principles in their work and are also thoughtfully ambivalent about disease models and to the EST movement in psychology.

CORE VALUES FOR COUNSELING PSYCHOLOGY

The counseling psychologist Ted Packard (2009) recently published a set of core values for counseling psychology, which he derived from examining the relevant literature in counseling psychology and from a content analysis he conducted based on interviews with 18 experienced counseling psychology educators (see Table 6.2). True to an ethic in the specialty, he presented these with the caveat that they had been "filtered through (my) biases and assumptions" (p. 610).

These values are presented here because they resonate with the current authors as reflecting our collective experience in the profession, and because they stand in marked contrast with the movement toward identifying ESTs in other domains of professional psychology. It appears that one current distinction between Division 12 (clinical psychology) and Division 17 (counseling psychology) of the APA is each division's stance with respect to ESTs.

CONCERNS WITH EMPIRICALLY SUPPORTED TREATMENTS

The concerns with ESTs have been adequately summarized by Cooper (2008) and include questions as to whether discreet forms of psychological distress exist and whether the effects of empirically supported treatments can be generalized from laboratory studies to diverse clinical settings and to varying populations. There are also arguments that a lack of evidence about many treatments is not the same as counterevidence against their use, and that researcher allegiance effects inflate the evidence of support for certain treatments. Cooper also notes the fact some treatments are much easier to investigate empirically (e.g., cognitive and behavioral therapies, vs. existential approaches and psychoanalysis), which tips the scales in their favor in the published literature. Some, such as the counseling psychologist Bruce Wampold and his colleagues (1997), have also argued that the evidence from meta-analytic studies incorporating thousands of investigations that have examined outcome in psychological practice provide ample support for the efficacy of all bona fide psychotherapies. He and his collaborators have argued for the strong effect of common factors in psychotherapy treatment, in comparison to the unique ingredients of individual therapies, and that the meta-analytic results in support for all bona psychotherapies have in essence provided the empirical evidence for their use as treatments (Ahn & Wampold, 2001; Imel & Wampold, 2008). Lambert (2004) has also proposed that therapies account for about 15% of outcome in treatment, with the remaining 85% of variance in outcome explained by common factors and "nonspecific" factors such as therapist and client factors and relationship and placebo effects.

APPROACHES TOWARD EVIDENCE-BASED PSYCHOLOGICAL PRACTICE

There are counseling psychologists who have been active leaders and critics in the movement toward evidence-based psychological practice (EBPP). The reader is referred to a chapter by Carol D. Goodheart and Jean A. Carter (2008) for a cogent discussion of the evidence-based movement in psychology and its relationship with counseling psychology, and to Wampold, Lichtenberg, and Waehler (2005) for a discussion on the differences between the EBPP and ESTs movements. Goodheart and Carter (2008) note that the APA has not endorsed either evidence-based treatments or empirically supported treatment. What the APA has adopted is "a policy on Evidence-Based Practice in Psychology (EBPP) that is not prescriptive about treatments, which is consistent with the approach taken in the Society of Counseling Psychology's Principles" (Goodheart & Carter, 2008, p. 63). In contrast to clinical psychology, which has sought the "delineation of specific techniques, treatments,

TABLE 6.1 **Examples from the American Board of Counseling Psychology Candidate Exam Manual**

Examples of Passing Levels of Competence in the Area of Intervention

(a) The counseling psychologist ascertains client/patient goals; deals with issues regarding payment arrangements appropriately; defines limits of confidentiality and boundaries of services clearly; conveys availability; and keeps records consistent with existing standards of care.
(b) The counseling psychologist selects interventions that are appropriate to the client's/patient's assessed goals, situation, and resources.
(c) The counseling psychologist implements interventions in a competent fashion.
(d) The counseling psychologist demonstrates attention to interpersonal interactions, individual and cultural diversity, ethics and legal foundations, and professional identification as related to intervention.

Examples of Failing Levels of Competence in the Area of Intervention

(e) The counseling psychologist ignores or does not adequately determine client/patient goals; mishandles payment arrangements.
(f) Fails to address or clearly define limits of confidentiality and boundaries, does not convey information about availability, and fails to maintain acceptable standards of clinical record-keeping.
(g) Selects interventions that are not consistent with the client/patient's goals, situation, or resources.
(h) Fails to consistently provide interventions that are thoughtful and does not adequately communicate about interventions being provided.
(i) Conveys a general lack of awareness of ways in which interpersonal interactions, individual and cultural diversity, ethics and legal foundations, and professional identification are related to intervention.

Source: From American Board of Professional Psychology (2011).

or interventions with demonstrated efficacy and/or effectiveness" (Goodyear & Carter, 2008, p. 48), counseling psychology has advocated for an approach that seeks guidelines or principles for the integration of empirical evidence into clinical practice, and it has adopted this as policy, as have Division 32 (Humanistic Psychology) and Division 29 (Psychotherapy) of the APA (Goodheart & Carter, 2008). As these two authors note, the EBPP is "an integrative approach in which practitioners actively and deliberately use scientific findings to provide effective treatment" (Goodheart & Carter, 2008, p. 47).

Seven principles were developed by a special task group of Division 17 (Society of Counseling Psychology) and were published by Wampold, Lichtenberg, and Waehler in 2002. These principles constitute competencies for psychologists to use in selecting and incorporating accumulated empirical evidence into their psychological practice at varying levels of specificity (and consideration) for activities such as intervention. The first principle is that level of specificity should be considered when evaluating outcomes. Wampold, Lichtenberg, and Waehler (2005) note that there are four levels at which intervention can be identified in the literature, with level 1 being the broadest level, such as supervision, prevention, and guidance, level 2 as modalities of level 1, such as specific therapies or programs, level 3 being specific therapies applied to specific areas or populations, such as the use of CBT therapy with African American clients, and level 4 encompassing specific techniques in specific areas for specific populations, such as the use of CBT therapy for phobic disorders with African American clients. The second principle is that level of specificity should not be restricted to diagnosis but include other client factors such as race, ethnicity, gender, preferences for treatments, motivation, resistance, level of dysfunction, level of premorbid functioning, and so on. The third principle is that scientific evidence needs to be examined in its entirety and aggregated appropriately, meaning that evidence needs to be examined for limitations and flaws, and that equivocal or ambiguous aggregated data be included in assessing the relative strength of effect between evidence and outcome. The fourth principle is that evidence for absolute and relative efficacy needs to be presented, and that treatments not be conceived dualistically as either empirically supported or not, unless the aggregated evidence justifies so convincingly. The fifth principle is that casual attributions for specific ingredients should be made only if the evidence is persuasive, above and beyond the evidence in support for common factors in therapies. The sixth principle is that outcomes should be assessed appropriately and broadly, beyond diagnosis and symptoms and that the measurement of outcome should include factors such as general life functioning, well-being, and costs/benefits. The seventh principle is that outcome evidence should be assessed locally and freedom of choice for psychologists and clients should be recognized. Wampold et al. (2005) sum up the rationale for this principle this way: "science should inform practice, rather than the alternative, science should dictate practice. This principle honors the practitioner and the scientist as an interwoven system. The practitioner, informed by research, trained by scientist/educators, reflective, and continually learning through experience, delivers an intervention ... the scientifically informed practitioner, practicing reflectively, will need to ensure that programs delivered are achieving their objectives" (p. 35). Wampold and his colleagues note that part of the evidence available to psychologists may very well come from research studies examining empirically supported treatments, but they argue for a broader conception of what constitutes evidence and how that evidence is evaluated and by whom for optimal benefit in professional practice.

The Division 29 Task Force on Empirically Supported Therapy Relationships

A consistent finding in the empirical literature has been the substantial effect of the relationship on outcome, explaining up to 30% of the variance in outcome (Asay & Lambert, 1999), and equally important to outcome for relationally oriented therapies as well as non–relationally oriented ones (Elkin, Falconnier, Martinovich, & Mahoney, 2006). A task force comprised of members of Division 29, Psychotherapy, and with representatives of both clinical psychology and counseling psychology, studied the available evidence for specific relational factors and their effect on outcome. On the basis of their review of the empirical literature, the task force distinguished between relational factors that they considered either "demonstrably effective" and those that they considered as "promising and probably effective" (Norcross, 2002). These elements of the therapy relationship are relevant to the current chapter because they highlight specific interventions that based on the empirical evidence are associated with outcome, and that on theoretical and philosophical bases are closely aligned with a core value in counseling psychology. The four interventions classified as "demonstrably effective" were alliance, cohesion in group psychotherapy, empathy, and goal consensus and collaboration. Two additional factors deemed by the task force to be "demonstrably effective" involve client characteristics that need to be accounted for in customizing the therapy relationship: client resistance and level of functional impairment.

Seven interventions were classified as "promising and probably effective" and were as follows: positive regard, congruence/genuineness, feedback, repair of alliance ruptures, self-disclosure, management of countertransference, and quality of relational interpretations. Five additional factors client behaviors and qualities were identified as "promising and probably effective" in customizing the therapy relationship: coping style, stages of change, anaclitic/sociotropic and introjective/autonomous personality styles, expectations, and assimilation of problematic experiences.

The task force did not find sufficient evidence to customize the therapy relationship on the basis of client attachment style, gender, ethnicity, religion and spirituality, preferences, and personality disorders. The reader is referred to Norcross (2002) for detailed reading of chapters that summarize the empirical evidence for each of these relational factors, as well as recommendations of the task force with respect to practice, training, research, and policy. The work of this task force highlights why the relationship in treatment is so important, and which specific therapist interventions make the relationship work. As Norcross (2002) points out, above and beyond the extensive and conclusive evidence that supports the central role of the relationship to outcome is the collective experience of therapists, which tells us that therapy is an intense interpersonal experience that is emotionally involving for clients and to some extent therapists.

Intervention Competence as Informed by Empirical Research and Response Modes

There is a substantial body of empirical research that documents the effectiveness of specific interventions for an array of mental health problems and situations. An entire chapter or book could be written to adequately summarize the evidence that has accumulated over many decades of research, and recently Cooper (2008) provided a cogent summary of this research in his book *Essential Research Findings in Counselling and Psychotherapy: The Facts Are Friendly.* The reader is encouraged to review this important book, as well as Michael J. Lambert's (2004) *Bergin and Garfield's Handbook of Psychotherapy and Behavior Change*, which is considered the authoritative text on psychotherapy research. For purposes of the current chapter, we briefly review what we have determined to be the most salient findings on the effectiveness of interventions, since they bear heavily on the topic of professional psychologist competence. These interventions have been employed to varying degrees by counseling psychologists since their development, and counseling psychologists have contributed significantly to the empirical research in this area.

COGNITIVE-BEHAVIORAL THERAPIES

There are several interventions with substantial empirical support within the class of therapies described as cognitive-behavioral. The interventions with the highest level of empirical support in treating phobias and anxiety disorders/problems are variations of exposure therapy, including in vivo exposure, imaginal exposure, virtual reality, and systematic desensitization (Cooper, 2008). Paradoxical interventions and activity scheduling have also been found to be highly effective interventions of behavior (Orlinsky et al., 2004). These interventions require specific training and supervision and in some instances highly technical training (e.g., virtual reality exposure). Gelso and Fretz (2001) discussed the compatibility between cognitive-behavioral approaches and counseling psychology, and noted the former's consistent focus on uncovering and tapping client strengths and building on them to affect symptom change. They also noted substantial compatibility between these treatments and counseling psychology, in the brevity of treatments, which usually last less than 12 sessions, and the attention given to the person and the environment in shaping and reinforcing thoughts and behavior.

PSYCHODYNAMIC THEORIES

Within psychodynamic theories, the one intervention that has generated the highest level of empirical support is interpretation, which appears to promote insight, awareness, self-understanding, and is of benefit to the development of the working alliance (Allen et al., 1996; Orlinsky et al., 2004). Gelso and Fretz (2001) note that historically psychoanalytic theory was incompatible with counseling psychology, due primarily to the emphasis in psychoanalysis (i.e., traditional drive theory) to long treatments, to finding psychopathology even in fairly normal persons, and an insistence on looking solely at intrapsychic dynamics without attention to the environment. However, Gelso and Fretz (2001) cite developments in psychoanalytic/dynamic therapies that are much more palatable to counseling psychologists, theories such as object relations and self-psychology that now examine normal functioning and development, are focused on psychosocial development and not simply Freudian psychosexual stages, that attend to environmental, social, and cultural factors in development, and that have been refashioned as relative time-limited treatments.

HUMANISTIC/EXPERIENTIAL THERAPIES

With respect to humanistic/experiential therapies, interventions that are most strongly associated with outcome include empathy, focusing (which deepens client experiencing), and two-chair and empty-chair dialogues (Elliott, Greenberg, & Lietaer, 2004). These approaches are deemed deeply compatible with counseling psychology for their focus on the strengths of

TABLE 6.2 **Core Values for Counseling Psychology**

(1) Altruism is our foundation as we strive to enhance the welfare of others.
(2) Positive relationships are a necessary condition for stimulating change in those we seek to help.
(3) The synergistic integration of science and practice is essential to our work and includes use of various methods of inquiry.
(4) We focus on healthy development across the life span, including work and career, and seek to prevent avoidable problems as well as optimize individual and societal growth.
(5) From a holistic frame of reference, we emphasize strengths, resilience, and positive coping in the context of the person's social and cultural environments.
(6) We are committed to respectful treatment for all, inherent human dignity, inclusion rather than exclusion, and accepting and celebrating cultural and individual diversity.
(7) We believe in social justice and the necessity, on occasion, of advocacy for just causes that promote the welfare of others.
(8) We value collaboration, multidisciplinary practice and research, and sharing counseling psychology with colleagues in our own country and around the world.
(9) In our remedial work with dysfunctional clients and systems, whenever possible we focus on strengths and positive coping in the context of a helping relationship.

Source: From Packard (2009, p. 622).

the person and his or her potential for growth and actualization, the focus on intact personalities and normal development, and the use of relatively brief therapy for achieving outcomes (Gelso & Fretz, 2001).

The connection between Rogers's humanism and person-centered therapy with counseling psychology is also evident in the vast amount of research that has accumulated on what are termed helping skills or therapist response modes. This area of psychotherapy is where counseling psychologists have perhaps made their greatest contribution. As Gelso and Fretz (2001) point out, this research goes back to the 1940s when Carl Rogers and Francis P. Robinson were both at Ohio State and started separate but parallel programs of research examining taped counseling sessions. These two researchers began the examination of therapist offered conditions, their verbal and nonverbal behavior, and the content and length of specific speaking turns and their effect on client verbal and nonverbal behavior. This research has led to substantial empirical bases, including research on therapist response modes, process research examining the effect of therapist responses on clients, quality of sessions, and outcome (see Hill, 2001), and research on the therapy relationship, including its manifestation in treatment and its influence on outcome (Gelso, 2011; Gelso & Hayes, 1998, 2007). Cooper (2008) reviewed the empirical evidence on therapist response modes and the research support that has accumulated over the years on their usefulness and effectiveness. These response modes are often the fundamental skills and most often used communication practices by professional psychologists. Response modes of listening, paraphrasing, encouragement, asking questions, guidance and advise, and feedback have been rated by clients as important and helpful within sessions because it helps them feel comfortable and supported by their therapist, and because it facilitates the hard work of reflection, exploration, and action.

Conclusion

In conclusion, while the work of intervention in professional psychology is similar across specialties, we hope that the current chapter has highlighted the way that intervention is used in counseling psychology, including the philosophical attitude of the specialty, its values and parameters, and the relevance of its competency models.

SEVEN

Competence in Career and Vocational Psychology

If there is one specialty and therapeutic function that distinguishes counseling psychology from all other board-certified areas in psychology, it is vocational psychology and career intervention (Blustein, 2008). Career and vocational psychology have been fundamental components of counseling psychology training programs since the inception of the specialty. Much of the research and scholarship in career and vocational psychology centers on the development and validation of career theories that have the potential to explain career-relevant behaviors. Theoretical research and model building are of critical importance to counseling psychology, but the emphasis in this volume is on the practice of counseling psychology as a board-approved specialty. Thus, the focus of this chapter is an overview of specific career and vocational intervention competencies, and the scientific base underlying capabilities in assessment, intervention, and consultation/prevention for work, career, and employment issues. The pursuit of a comprehensive theory of career development that would strengthen the foundations of career intervention and counseling across cultural and subcultural groups will continue as will research that seeks to design and implement more effective career interventions.

As has been the case in prior chapters, the American Board of Counseling Psychology core competencies cut across content areas and are assumed in the career/vocational area as well. Each of the core competencies is assessed during the certification process for a candidate whose certification subarea is identified as career/vocational psychology as well as in general for all applicants. Although career and vocational intervention are considered to be fundamental to all candidates in counseling psychology, those candidates choosing to be examined with a specialty in career and vocational intervention will be expected to be particularly knowledgeable in this area.

The Role of Work in Human Behavior

The ability to work is one of the major social roles across human history and in diverse cultures (Blustein, 2006; Neff, 1985). Work, both as an activity and as a social function, can have pervasive effects upon identity, mental and physical health, social and economic well-being, as well as familial and interpersonal relationships (Juntunen, 2006; Schultheiss, 2006). Two themes typically dominate career and vocational psychology and underlie client presenting problems in professional practice. The first theme is the development and selection of a vocational choice. The second theme is the adaptation and adjustment to work roles in adulthood and within organizations. The inability to work, work inhibition or decrement (Socrardides & Kramer, 1997), and problems adapting or adjusting to work roles can either be a precipitator of mental health problems or be the consequence of an acute or ongoing disorder. Although we once attributed problems in career choice and adjustment to psychogenic sources (i.e., issues of development or personality), we now believe that external or environmental sources of influence may be equally important. Certainly, to illustrate, we know that unemployment has predictably detrimental consequences on mental health and well-being (Paul & Moser, 2009), especially if the period of unemployment exceeds 6 months. We also know that environmental stressors, influences, barriers, and constraints have significant influences on both career development and upon adjustment and adaptation (DeBell, 2006).

More to the point, however, the strengthening of work identity and work roles can have salutary effects on an equally wide range of life variables, and both internal and external influences can have salutary effects on career development. This broad view of the role of work in life (Blustein, 2006) and the integration of career and vocational issues as a core element of therapeutic interventions remains a unique aspect of counseling psychology as compared to other mental health specialties. Finally, counseling psychology's successful globalization (Gerstein, Heppner, Egisdottir, Leung, & Norsworthy, 2010) owes much to career and vocational psychology, which has had an international emphasis for most of its history. Global issues of work are critical for developing nations as well as for industrialized countries.

Assessment as a Critical Competence in Career and Vocational Psychology

The scientific and evidential base of career and vocational counseling covers three major areas: (a) the development and testing of career assessments, (b) the creation and evaluation of models and theories of vocational choice and development, and (c) the implementation and estimation of the efficacy of vocational interventions. The first of these areas, career and vocational assessment, is, and has historically been, the defining element in the identity of career and vocational psychologists.

Many of the foundations of psychological measurement have been derived from vocational instruments—and particularly from interest assessments. Indirect measurement of individual differences (Dawis, 1992), that is, the assessment of psychological dispositions using items not entirely based upon obvious or face-valid content, is one of those foundations. A second is the use of criterion-based scoring and population reference samples in scale development. Simply stated, comparison groups of individuals working in, and satisfied with, a particular occupation are used for construct-specific occupational scales (e.g., a group of accountants). A third contribution of vocational assessment to psychological measurement has been the use and strengthening of factor-analytic techniques for validating the constructs upon which those instruments are based and for detailing structure underlying vocational interests. Factor-analytic techniques have subsequently been widely adopted as a technique for validating psychological inventories (Groth-Marnat, 2009).

The emergence of self-guiding or self-directing vocational inventories and assessments, many based in computer-assisted formats, has advanced contemporary psychology. These self-guiding inventories also provide evidence for the efficacy of psychological inventories as interpretive devices for use in counseling, consultative, and therapeutic interventions. The strongest empirical evidence of the effects of inventory completion and interpretation as therapeutic interventions exists in the vocational arena (Goodyear, 1990; Tinsley & Chu, 1999). Finally, the shift to computer-assisted testing and scoring of patterns of item responses was spearheaded by the field of interest measurement and is now fundamental to much of psychological measurement. The array and sophistication of vocational assessments is remarkable to most observers (Blustein, 2008; Spokane, 1991; Whiston, Brecheisen, & Stephens, 2003). Potential clients and colleagues from related mental health disciplines readily acknowledge the role of vocational assessment in mental health treatment, though few will have specific competencies in the construction and interpretation of these inventories that will result in accurate and clinically valid test use. Counseling psychologists can be expected to possess these skills and to integrate the information derived from vocational assessments into culturally concordant case conceptualizations and treatment strategies for career counseling and intervention, occupational selection and promotion, and education and prevention.

WHAT DO COUNSELING PSYCHOLOGISTS UNDERSTAND ABOUT VOCATIONAL ASSESSMENT?

Although many of the basic competencies in psychological assessment pertain to career and vocational assessment (e.g., test-retest reliability, internal consistency, construct validity, and cultural utility), several specific understandings and psychometric properties of psychological instruments are implied in expertise in career and vocational assessment.

Individual Differences

A counseling psychologist competent in career and vocational psychology understands that individual differences, and the pursuit of work based upon those differences, across social and cultural subgroups can be differentially desirable and/or possible (Dawis, 1992). Consideration of these individual differences is fundamental to accurate assessment of the client's strengths, options, and possibilities. Assessments, therefore, while they are individual in focus should also be multidimensional and contextual in nature. Multiple assessments across measurement domains are desirable so long as the instruments in use have demonstrated validity and cultural utility for the subgroup representing that individual.

Limitations and Uses

Counseling psychologists also understand the cultural, gender, and psychometric limitations of both the construction and the clinical use of assessments based upon these individual differences. In addition, counseling psychologists consider the acculturation level of the client in order to determine the extent to which any cultural influences may be operative in that client's case. In addition to being skilled in career and vocational psychology, a counseling psychologist understands that vocational measurements (with the exception of skills and abilities) typically tap *patterns* of scores, which are then compared to response patterns of criterion groups. They do not necessarily imply *levels* or amounts of a construct such as "interest," nor do they necessarily reflect capability (Tyler, 1961). Thus, a person who scores in the high range on the accountant scale of the SII may have no experience as an accountant and may not necessarily have skill with numbers. Rather, that score reflects a pattern of responses similar to a comparison group of accountants used to validate the scale (criterion-based scoring).

Interrelated Constructs

Interests, personality, and values are intercorrelated constructs that are both stable and malleable. Interests and dispositions are fluid in adolescence, but stabilize in adulthood, and are highly consistent thereafter. There is evidence that interests may "accentuate" or line up with choices made over time and through adulthood. Only about one-third of individuals will have interests that are initially highly congruent with the nature of their choices (Spokane, 1985). Additionally, vocational interests and dispositions may be crystallized and internally consistent, or they may be complex and seemingly incompatible. Either situation can result in a beneficial resolution of vocational choice and adjustment. Thus, a counseling psychologist knowledgeable in career and vocational psychology understands and anticipates the degree to which the client's interests, personality, values, skills, abilities, and particularly his or her cultural background will influence vocational choices and adjustments but also have potential for change and for productive implementation even after relative stabilization is reached.

Scaling Types

Career assessments may involve many different scaling types—frequently within the same inventory. *Direct measures* (i.e., those whose items have readily identifiable content and which tap motivation, current status, and skills) may reflect concurrent and predictive validity more accurately than *indirect measures*. Direct measures may have immediate utility as therapeutic interventions but may reflect knowledge about which the respondent is already aware. In contrast, indirect measures (which, as stated earlier, contain items whose content is not readily connectable to a particular scale or construct, e.g., I like to go to the theater) may tap underlying dispositions, structures, and complexes and may unearth options not presently considered, and have long-term predictive validity. Thus, increasingly, inventories will combine both types of scaling in an effort to reveal more information for the client's use. The complexity of these instruments, their norming, scaling, and validity, is essential knowledge for the career/vocational psychologist because the interpretation of the results of such inventories may not be obvious for the client.

Cross-Dimensional Amalgamations

In addition to multiple scaling types, it is increasingly clear that cross-dimensional amalgamations or clusters of interest, genetic predispositions, values, gender, and culturally specific experiences, skills, and cognitive styles, in combination with external constraints and pressures, determine the choices clients will make. These complexes of qualities (Ackerman & Heggestad, 1997; Armstrong & Rounds, 2010), once clarified and understood, are likely to improve the assessment and intervention process in career counseling. This exciting area of research suggests, for example, that an individual who comes from a culture that values social connectedness, learns skills in interpersonal interaction, and understands complex social situations has an increased likelihood of a career choice that involves high-level transactions with people. In contrast, an individual who comes from a culture that values individual accomplishment, emphasizes detail in language acquisition, or stresses mathematics and science may gravitate away from people-oriented occupations and more toward occupations involving interactions with data or things. Once we understand these processes fully, counseling psychologists can better assist individuals across cultures and backgrounds to either strengthen such complexes or alter them to make choices consistent with their goals and aspirations in the face of barriers and constraints that operate in the labor market in local and global contexts.

WHAT DOES COMPETENCE IN CAREER/ VOCATIONAL INTERVENTION INVOLVE?

In addition to a thorough understanding of vocational assessment, a counseling psychologist specializing in career and vocational psychology understands the nature of structural and labor force limitations to career entry, the organization of the world of work, and the environmental barriers and constraints that act to limit the implementation of desired career aspirations. During the course of intervention the counseling psychologist will consider the client's response to these constraints, as well as any unique cultural influences that may affect response to these barriers. The skilled career psychologist will help the client to anticipate constraints and work realistically to overcome any self-imposed or societally imposed barriers to implementation of the client's career aspirations, especially where these constraints are the result of individual differences in gender, culture, socioeconomic status, disability, or other individual or group differences that may pose inordinately more difficult barriers for the client. Insights derived from vocational theory and research guide such interventions.

The Process and Outcomes of Career Counseling and Intervention

The long history of research on the effectiveness of career counseling (Holland, Magoon, & Spokane, 1981; Swanson, 1995) evinced a major advance with the advent of *meta-analysis* (Brown & Ryan-Krane, 2000; Glass, McGaw, & Smith, 1981: Oliver & Spokane, 1983, 1988). Meta-analysis permitted the aggregation of outcome data across a large body of studies involving thousands of clients and several intervention strategies, and it facilitated general conclusions about the overall effectiveness of career and vocational counseling and intervention. These findings, even when conservatively interpreted, suggest that the average vocational client is better off from an outcome standpoint, between one-third to more than one-half of a standard deviation above study participants who did not receive vocational counseling (Whiston et al., unpublished data; Whiston & Rahardja, 2008).

Meta-analysis also sheds considerable light on the critical or common elements embedded in effective career interventions (Brown & Ryan-Krane, 2000; Holland et al., 1981; Whiston & Rahardja, 2008). One point is clear, counselor-free (i.e., interventions based on the use of computers) career counseling interventions are less effective in comparison to career counseling where a professional person is involved in the process (Whiston, Brecheisen, & Stephens, 2003). Moreover, there are many common elements between general therapeutic approaches and career and vocational interventions, and in specific cases the distinction among effective therapeutic elements is one of therapeutic focus (i.e., the topic of emphasis is work roles and their consequences). Some diagnoses (Rounds & Tinsley, 1984) and contextual aspects of the client's context are unique and involve specific competencies. Those unique aspects are the focus of this chapter. Repeated studies suggest that career and vocational counseling and intervention are empirically supported and have modest to moderate positive outcomes across client populations (Brown & Ryan-Krane, 2000). Several common career therapeutic elements embedded in treatments are associated with successful outcomes. Moreover, the more of these elements that are included in a career intervention, the more successful (larger effect size) that intervention is likely to be (Brown & Ryan-Krane, 2000). Five treatment components increase the likelihood of a positive outcome in career interventions (Brown & Ryan-Krane, 2000). These components, which are discussed in more detail below, include (a) written exercises, (b) individualized interpretation and feedback, (c) information about the structure and possibilities in the world of work, (d) opportunities for modeling and social reinforcement, and (e) a socially supportive network. Although much remains to be done in this area of research, it is likely that the research evidence on the beneficial effects of a strong therapeutic alliance and a highly skilled counselor (Lambert & Vermeersch, 2008) will also add to the success of career counseling outcomes when such studies are conducted. These cross-approach components are important enough to a full understanding of career counseling and intervention that they are each briefly discussed next.

Successful Career Counseling

Career interventions have been practiced and studied in high school and college student populations (i.e., college counseling and/or career development centers), with employed adults in work settings, and in independent practice of psychology. Empirical studies over several decades reveal a number of ingredients that may account for the moderately positive outcomes of career intervention with a diverse array of clients. These ingredients or therapeutic elements are as follows.

FIVE CRITICAL INGREDIENTS

Written Exercises

These written exercises can include a written journal or self-reflection exercises such as career lifelines, goal statements, and so on. They appear to serve as cognitive rehearsal (Holland et al., 1981) or restatement and commitment to aspirations and plans. The clarification and statement of plans has always been a central component of a concept called *career maturity* (Crites & Savickas, 1996) and implies that the client is thinking about and evaluating potential life and career options. The most effective interventions such as semester-long classes or workshops appear to emphasize these exercises (Oliver & Spokane, 1988).

Individualized Interpretations and Feedback

Interpretive feedback can come from multiple sources, but in career counseling it invariably derives from inventories. Skillful collaborative feedback might highlight or clarify options and encourage the client to either incorporate new possibilities or eliminate inappropriate or undesirable options. Increasingly this feedback is computerized or formulated based upon patterns of scores and scales, but it is sufficiently complex that the counselor's perspective and input are valuable in absorbing and utilizing the information provided (Brown & Ryan-Krane, 2000; Whiston &

Rahardja, 2008). Feedback from other sources can also be valuable as an aide in clarifying aspirations. Career counselors encourage clients to discuss, articulate, and verbalize their plans and thinking with others who can provide both a forum for rehearsing such plans, and feedback and perspectives as these plans are articulated. Family members, close friends, mentors, and role models can provide useful feedback to the client.

Information on the World of Work

Many career clients respond that they simply do not know how to go about making and implementing a choice (Osipow, 1999). Much of this difficulty arises because the world of work is both large in terms of the sheer number of possible occupations and complex with respect to the organization and processes by which occupations operate. There are several fine written and online sources of information available for use with clients, including a national and state system of occupational information (O'NET online, 2010). Although the astute career counselor learns as much as possible about these systems, about the organization of the world of work, and about the barriers and constraints that operate in local, state, and national/international labor markets, it is neither possible nor desirable to simply provide such information to the client. Instead, encouraging the client to explore, evaluate, and integrate information about potential occupations is recommended (Spokane, 1991). When the client is positioned within the ongoing flow of information surrounding an occupation, the client can then bring what he or she has learned into the counseling situation for discussion and anticipation of pitfalls, barriers, and ways to handle these problems as they arise.

Modeling

Exposing clients to individuals who have successfully encountered and managed the rigors of implementing a career in a particular field appears to be an important ingredient in successful career and vocational counseling. This step in the counseling process comes later, typically after the client has clarified and narrowed options and seeks a more personal contact or experience with an occupation under consideration. This modeling can be accomplished through shadowing, internships, work-study opportunities, and, increasingly in media, such as film or biography, and, in particular through the Internet via blogs, forums, chat rooms, and so on. Personal contacts on the job site, however, seem particularly powerful experiences for the client both in terms of exploration and modeling.

Social Support and Career Intervention

Clearly, the research literature on career counseling and intervention demonstrates the importance of multiple sources of socially supportive relationships to the effectiveness of career treatments and to the success of career choice and implementation (Brown & Ryan-Krane, 2000; Holland et al., 1981). This support can come from a variety of sources, including counselors, teachers, coaches, clergy, and, most particularly from family, but it appears to address the need to build a supportive network of persons who will assist the client in making and implementing his or her career choice or change. In treatment studies, the research evidence suggests that interventions that involve classes or workshops are particularly effective; individual counseling (i.e., with a counselor) was also more effective than self-directing interventions and was particularly effective on an hour-by-hour basis, though relatively more expensive than group or class interventions (Oliver & Spokane, 1988).

GENERALIZATION AND IMPLEMENTATION

One might reasonably ask the question, Do these critical elements in interventions generalize across cultures, gender, and social class? Such questions are the subject of current research and the competent career counselor will stay up to date on emerging evidence and findings in this area. Although this literature is now too large to review here, one recent article on the role of familial support and efficacy for male and female adolescents in northern and southern Italy (Howard, Ferrari, Nota, Solberg, & Soresi, 2009) is illustrative. Howard et al. found that familial support had direct influence on academic grades and career decidedness for girls in northern Italy, but it was mediated by efficacy more generally for boys and girls in both areas.

These five critical ingredients in career interventions have been shown to exert beneficial effects and are easily embedded either in workshops, groups, or individual counseling. As we understand more about the process of career intervention, other critical elements may emerge. Career interventions may be strengthened by the inclusion of the aforementioned five elements, but as Shapiro (2011) noted, the fields of education and psychology are shifting away from a science of *intervention* in which carefully manualized forms of assistance are carried out in well-controlled conditions and toward a science of *implementation* in which empirically valid interventions are conducted in the field under real-life conditions. The fidelity with which the intervention is implemented is a critical concern for a science of implementation, and adaptations or adjustments for diverse or atypical populations may improve or dilute an intervention previously shown to be effective. Such a move toward a science of *career implementation* is a logical next step for counseling psychology, especially in light of both the socioeconomic and global diversification of psychology's clientele and the urgent need for career assistance in developing countries and following social upheaval. Shapiro's thoughtful paper cites several compelling sources on implementation science.

Consultation With Other Professionals Around Career Issues

Career psychologists are typically called upon to collaborate with other health and mental health professionals when career issues arise. Perhaps the most common instance of consultation occurs when there are distinct career issues in a general therapeutic case, and a referral is made for a career evaluation. Such an evaluation might consist of a battery of inventories and assessments and a summary or recommendations for career intervention. This situation often occurs in professional practice as a result of the specialized knowledge that a counseling psychologist has about vocational assessment and intervention. Similarly, a vocational psychologist may be consulted by business, industry, military, or governmental agencies, when either layoffs are being considered (e.g., transition counseling), for retirement counseling, or for decisions regarding promotion and placement. A related situation may occur when a client or patient has been hospitalized either for a psychiatric disability or perhaps for a physical disability following an illness or an accident, and a counseling psychologist may be called upon to both provide an evaluation and follow the client after release from the hospital. Furthermore, vocational psychologists may conduct psychological evaluations for disability determination and the ability to work or for forensic cases that involve ability to work as an issue in litigation. Most recently, counseling psychologists with knowledge and skills in vocational behavior provide valuable services in postdisaster situations wherein individuals and communities are struggling with recovery and future planning (Spokane, Inman Weatherford, Kaduvettoor-Davidson, & Straw, 2011). Thus, the array and scope of roles and contexts in which a vocationally oriented counseling psychologist might work are substantial indeed.

Integration of Vocational Psychology Into Professional Practice

Susan Whiston and her colleagues (Whiston et al., unpublished data) have proposed six guidelines for the integration of vocational psychology into professional practice. Based on an extensive review and integration of the empirical research and literature, Whiston et al. present a cogent rationale for each guideline along with specific "strategies for implementation." The reader is referred to the original document for detailed in-depth reading, and herein we present only a *very* brief summary of this work.

The first guideline is that "psychologists strive to have an awareness of the pervasive impact of work on an individual's quality of life" (p. 10). Six specific strategies for implementation are presented and, as an example, a portion of one strategy is presented here: "Given the reciprocal relationship between job and life satisfaction, psychologists are encouraged to be aware of factors that may be contributing to the interplay between job and life satisfaction" (p. 16). The second guideline is that "psychologists are encouraged to be aware of the influence work has on mental health as well as the influence of mental health on work" (p. 16). Seven specific strategies for implementation are presented and, as an example, a portion of one strategy is presented here: "Include work satisfaction and workplace stressors in the development of treatment goals" (p. 21). The third guideline is that "psychologists are encouraged to understand the role of work transitions across the lifespan" (p. 22). Six specific strategies for implementation are presented and, as an example, a portion of one strategy is presented here: "Develop direct intervention programs for parents to facilitate their children's vocational development" (p. 27). The fourth guideline is that "psychologists strive to understand how socio-cultural factors, such as gender, ethnicity, socio-economic status, sexual orientation, disability status, and urban/rural residence may influence the pursuit and experience of work" (p. 28). Six specific strategies for implementation are presented and, as an example, a portion of one strategy is presented here: "examine their own contextual factors that may impact their reactions to clients, students, research participants and others from diverse groups" (p. 34). The fifth guideline is that "psychologists strive to understand how the individual negotiates multiple life roles, including that of the worker" (p. 35). Ten specific strategies for implementation are presented and, as an example, a portion of one strategy is presented here: "Assess the meaning of work in people's lives and how it interfaces with family lives" (p. 41). The last guideline is that "psychologists strive to understand how economic and social factors (including labor market, access to education, globalization) impact opportunities for and barriers to employment and subsequently alter the career trajectory" (p. 42). Seven specific strategies for implementation are presented and, as an example, a portion of one strategy is presented here: "Help clients prepare for career transitions in response to changing technology and changing labor force demands" (p.45).

Individual and Cultural Diversity in Career Intervention

Among the fastest growing areas of research and scholarship in vocational behavior and individual and cultural diversity is now an element of most published studies of vocational and career psychology. The critical issues being addressed include the following: (a) Given the steadily changing demographics of the United States, are extant models of vocational and career development valid for underserved and minority groups in the United States (e.g., Hispanic American, African American, Native American)? (b) Can vocational inventories and assessments normed predominantly on Caucasian groups be utilized with minority groups on which they have not been validated? (c) Can, or how, should career and vocational interventions be adapted for nontraditional clients? and (d) Will current research on common therapeutic factors or ingredients apply as well to diverse individuals? Answers to each of these questions are still forthcoming, but one review summarized work in Holland's theory of vocational choice indicating that moderate but reliable differences could be found among minority and majority groups on self-guiding inventories with minority groups scoring higher on social and enterprising scales and lower on investigative scales than majority groups (Soh & Leong, 2001). Cultural group differences appear to lessen somewhat with greater acculturation into the dominant social group. With respect to the counseling process, there appear to be significant group differences in comfort with self-disclosure, expectations for counseling, and transferential issues. Such differences can be very large as counseling psychology extends to underdeveloped and developing nations. Several issues emerge in vocational practice, as they do in other areas of this volume, when constructs, interventions, and assessments are applied in subgroups facing oppression or exclusion, including the following:

- When psychological tests or assessment procedures are utilized that are based in Western or individualistic cultures and are neither culture free nor unbiased, findings from such assessments invariably lead to outcomes that disadvantage individuals from diverse cultures (Sue & Sue, 2007).
- High-stakes testing (e.g., college admission, or job selection or promotion) is particularly dangerous (Padilla & Medina, 1996) and should be conducted with caution.
- Clinical judgments are suspect as well (Groth-Marnat, 2009), but some clinicians are more accurate than others.

Advice to counselors is similar in vocational practice to that in general practice:

- Ask—about background, about family, about level of acculturation.
- Understand the client's worldview—make no assumptions.
- Communicate across cultural lines.
- Structure sessions with clear explanations.
- Pay attention to process.

In sum, questions of individual and cultural diversity have a central place in the professional practice of counseling psychology, and career and vocational psychology share these concerns and inquiries.

Ethical and Legal Considerations in Career and Vocational Psychology

All of the ethical and legal considerations in counseling psychology discussed in Chapter 6 of this volume also apply to career and vocational counseling. In particular, the five foundations of the American Psychological Association (APA) code of ethics (i.e., beneficence, fidelity, integrity, justice, and respect) all apply in career interventions as well. Avoidance of multiple roles, the importance of informed consent, confidentiality, and Health Insurance Portability and Accountability Act conflicts are also relevant. Issues of competence can be particularly important since the proper use and interpretation of vocational inventories requires specific and often unique competencies and understandings such as the use of criterion-based scoring and general reference sample methodology. The inappropriate use of psychological tests is still a frequent source of ethical violations for psychologists. When career and vocational psychologists consult in education, community organizations, business, and industry or become involved in personnel selection, competence in these areas requires additional learning and skills. Also, clarification of multiple roles in organizational consultation may be more complicated as when counseling psychologists consult with educational institutions or with management on the selection, promotion, retention, or even outplacement of employees (O'Neill, 1989). Clear statements about confidentiality and advocacy require special attention when consulting on career issues.

Professional Identification

Career and vocational psychologists identify with several professional organizations. The primary identification at the board-certified level is with Division 17 of the APA—the Society of Counseling Psychology—and a section within Division 17—The Society for Vocational Psychology (http://www.div17.org/vocpsych/), which is devoted to career issues. The Society for Vocational Psychology holds annual meetings at the APA convention and biennial topical conferences on issues of importance to the field, most recently at the University of St. Louis on the role of values in careers. Also, the National Career Development Association (NCDA), a division of the American Counseling Association(see http://association-database.com/aws/NCDA/pt/sp/Home_Page), both publishes a journal and holds annual meetings. Finally, the International Association for Educational and Vocational Guidance (IAEVG; http://www.iaevg.org/iaevg/index.cfm?lang=2) plays an increasingly central role in the field in light of the globalization of career and vocational psychology.

Conclusion

Vocational psychology is an area that is unique to the specialty of counseling psychology, and the current chapter has identified the competencies associated with professional practice within this area. It is clear that the delivery of vocational psychological services is complex, as it incorporates vast information about the individual, his or her development, socialization, and social/historical context, as well as current conditions in the world of work and the economy that are relevant to the client. Adding to the complexity of the work in vocational behavior is the need to attend to the psychological and emotional connections between the world of work and the quality of life for individuals, families, and communities.

EIGHT

Competence in Supervision

Supervision is a relational approach to teaching the highly complex skills of therapeutic practice. Supervision rests on the principles of in situ *learning* (situated learning; Lave, 1991), and it provides a context for the supervisee to reflect on his or her professional practice with a more experienced member of the profession. Ideally, supervisors facilitate a learning alliance that supports and challenges supervisees to critically inquire into their practice and the supervisory process. It is an intense and demanding relationship that requires both participants to be fully engaged and accountable to their respective roles.

Supervision is a method of teaching practice that links the foundational knowledge and skills of the field to professional activities and guides the individual supervisee through the learning progression from neophyte practitioner to entry-level professional. Although the requirement for supervision ends at the completion of the postdoctoral internship in the United States, in the European Union and Australia/New Zealand, consultative supervision is required throughout one's professional career. In this chapter, the focus is on *training*, those practice hours that are required to be supervised by a licensed psychologist in order to complete training for professional psychology licensure. *Consultative supervision*, which refers to those supervisory relationships post minimal requirements for licensure, is not required by licensure or professional organizations in the United States and thus will not be covered in this review.

The Centrality of Supervision to Professional Psychology

Supervised practice has been a component of training counseling psychologists since 1947 when the American Psychological Association (APA)

Committee on Training in Clinical Psychology required supervised experience in their training guidelines (1947, 1965a, 1965b). Supervision has continued to be acknowledged as a significant competency in professional training by numerous professional psychology organizations and accrediting bodies—for example, National Council of Schools and Programs in Professional Psychology (Peterson, Peterson, Abrams, & Stricker, 1997), the National Conference on Scientist-Practitioner Education and Training (Belar & Perry, 1992), and the Association of Psychology Postdoctoral and Internship Centers (APPIC). Furthermore, the ethical principles of psychologists (American Psychological Association, 2002) state that psychologists who are engaged in supervisory practice have an ethical responsibility to acquire competence in supervision. Most psychologists in their professional careers will provide supervision; in fact, it continues to be within the top five activities on which psychologists spend their time (Norcross, Hedges, & Castle, 2002). The trainees and supervisors have rated supervision as highly instrumental in increasing both self- and therapeutic awareness (Bernard & Goodyear, 2004; Orlinsky, Botermans, & Ronnestad, 2001), as well as professional competency and skill development (Steven, Goodyear, & Robertson, 1998).

By the mid-1990s it was argued by numerous accreditation bodies (Association of Counselor Education and Supervision; Borders et al., 1991; and the American Psychological Association, 1996) and leaders in supervision research that supervision should be identified as a practice competency for psychologists (Dye & Borders, 1990; Holloway & Neufeldt, 1995; Peterson et al., 1997). In the early part of the 21st century, professional psychology organizations that establish guidelines for education and training of professional psychologists have shifted training objectives into the language of professional competencies; supervision has been a salient component of this movement because of its role in clinical training (Falender & Shrafranske, 2004). Yet the majority of supervisors continue to have very inadequate or no supervision training at all (Kavanagh et al., 2003; Scott, Ingram, Vitanza, & Smith, 2000). There is an obvious discrepancy between viewing supervision as a highly demanded professional activity, supposedly central to successfully training counseling psychologists, and the lack of systematic training in supervision.

The Role of Counseling Psychology in Supervision

Counseling psychology has been prominent in building a scientist-practitioner model of supervision. This is evidenced in the definition used by The Society for Counseling Psychology of the APA and referenced in defining the specialty area of counseling psychology by the American Board of Professional Psychology (ABPP) to determine whether applicants have been functioning as counseling psychologists. Note the inclusion of *supervision* as a recognized service.

> A Counseling Psychologist facilitates personal and interpersonal functioning across the life span with a focus on individual, group, and community interventions for emotional, behavioral, vocational, and mental health problems using preventative, developmental, and remedial approaches, and in the assessment, diagnosis, and treatment of psychopathology. Counseling Psychologists participate in a range of activities including psychotherapy, assessment, teaching, research, supervision (author's italics), career development and consultation. They employ a variety of methods closely tied to theory and research to help individuals, groups and organizations function optimally as well as to remediate dysfunction. (http://www.abpp.org/i4a/pages/index.cfm?pageid=3424)

Supervision is an evolving area for certification with ABPP. Although only a handful of counseling psychologists have chosen supervision as a practice exemplar in the examination process, at the time of this writing, the American Board of Counseling Psychology is developing a set of criteria for the assessment of supervision practice as an option for the practice example in the diplomate examination process. This initiative may serve as a catalyst and encouragement for supervision to be identified as a practice proficiency.

MODELS AND RESEARCH IN SUPERVISION

It is widely recognized that research in the field of counseling and counseling psychology has prominently figured in the development of models and research efforts in supervision (Falender et al., 2004). Over the last two decades there have been excellent reviews on the research of supervision by authors in counseling psychology (Borders, 2005; Constantine, 2008; Ellis & Ladany, 1997; Freitas, 2002; Holloway, 1992; Inman & Ladany, 2008) and the reader is referred to these authors for a comprehensive discussion of research findings. The most recent of these reviews (Constantine et al., 2008; Inman & Ladany, 2008) provide an overview of the critical findings regarding the variables related to the supervision process (e.g., the supervisory relationship, evaluation, conflictual situations, and parallel process), the supervisor (e.g., development, countertransference, and self-disclosure), and the supervisee (e.g., development and nondisclosure). Inman and Ladany conclude "the complex and interrelated roles of the supervisor, supervisee, and client challenge researchers' ability to assess the relevant issues that influence the supervision process and outcomes in psychotherapy. This certainly highlights the disconnect that exists in theory, research, and practice" (2008, p. 511). Although research related to the client of the supervisee is reviewed, there is scant literature on *client outcomes* as related to supervision variables. As client outcome research presents a significant challenge to researchers and is a concern of increasing importance in the competency-based literature, this topic will be reviewed in detail later in this chapter.

Counseling psychologists have also focused on the practice of supervision and have developed numerous heuristic models to guide the supervisor in finding effective strategies for teaching psychotherapy. Early models of supervision in counseling psychology were viewed as analogous to the practice of counseling. In 1983 *The Counseling Psychologist* published an issue on models of supervision (Bartlett, Goodyear, & Bradley, 1983). The majority of these approaches were named after their counseling counterparts—Rational Emotive Supervision, Client-Centered Supervision, Social Learning, and Working Alliance (Goodyear, Bradley, & Bartlett, 1983). These models were built on the assumption that the method of teaching a specific approach to practice must mirror the counseling approach being taught. At the time, this was a reasonable assumption given the traditional psychoanalytic approach to training was entering into analysis and learning by being the patient. Despite the prominence of these counseling-based approaches, there were murmurings from a minority of scholars in counseling psychology that the practice of supervision must be considered as a *praxis* that involved competencies and skills distinct from counseling (Holloway, 1984; Kagan & Kagan, 1990; Loganbill, Hardy, & Delworth, 1982). Holloway and her colleagues (Holloway, 1982; Holloway, Freund, Gardner, Nelson, & Walker, 1989; Holloway & Poulin, 1995; Holloway & Wolleat, 1981, 1994) and Ladany and associates (Ladany & Friedlander, 1995; Ladany, Inman, Constantine, & Hofheinz, 1997; Ladany & Lehrman-Waterman, 1999) published a persuasive body of research in the 1980s and 1990s that corroborated this contention.

DEVELOPMENT OF CURRICULUM IN SUPERVISION

The increase in research in supervision as a field of inquiry separate from counseling and psychotherapy led to the development of a curriculum in supervision theory and research as well as establishing supervised practicum of supervision (Scott et al., 2000) in many counseling psychology programs. Partly in response to these efforts, in 1996 the APA's Committee on Accreditation (now a "Commission on Accreditation") no longer assumed that having competency in professional practice meant competency in teaching professional practice in supervision and stated in their accreditation guidelines that supervision become a part of the curriculum (American Psychological Association, 1996). Supervision was finally considered a necessary and required part of professional training, but the specific skills and competencies needed by the supervisor were left undefined within professional psychology practice. The extent and manner to which supervision was integrated into professional psychology curriculum and internship sites was largely left to the interpretation of individual programs. With the exception of the work by the American Association of Counselor Education and Supervision that created standards for counseling supervisors (Dye & Borders, 1990), a curriculum guide for supervisor training (Borders et al., 1991), and ethical guidelines specific to supervision (Hart, Borders, Nance, & Paradise, 1995).

COMPETENCY MOVEMENT AND SUPERVISION

In 1998 the focus on "competence" in psychology training ushered in a new era for professional psychology policy, curriculum, and research. A concerted effort to articulate and delineate the core competencies in professional psychology including supervision as a core domain of a psychologist's activities (Dienst & Armstong, 1998; Summerall, Lopez, & Oehlert, 2000) has dominated the bandwidth over the last decade. The "competencies" conference cosponsored by APPIC in 2002 culminated in a consensus statement that identified "five supra-ordinate factors that are not only essential, but permeate all aspects of professional development ... Each contributes a key component to the practice of supervision and requires consideration within education and training and as a subject for systematic empirical investigation" (Falender et al., 2004, p. 775). The five factors are listed in Table 8.1.

This consensus statement on the areas of competency for supervision led to new models and language in the discourse of supervision in the United States, the United Kingdom, and Australia. By 2004 the zeitgeist of supervision discourse was "competency-based training" for supervisors. In this movement, Falender and Shrafranske (2004; Falender & Shrafranske, 2006) have been prominent scholars in the development of models for competency-based supervision. However, the profession as a whole has promoted the competency movement through professional conferences that have resulted in a series of papers that specify professional competencies, methods for the education of and training of these competencies, and the assessment of competencies. The details of each of these landmark events have been described in detail in Chapter 1. The salience of competencies in professional psychology to the practice of supervision will be the focus of this chapter's discussion.

Competency-Based Supervision Practice

Supervision is a method of teaching practice and assessing the preparedness of the trainee at the practicum, internship, and entry-level professional stages of his or her development. *The Assessment of Competency Benchmarks Workgroup* (Fouad et al., 2009) updated the *cube model* (Rodolfa et al., 2005) and identified behavioral and benchmark descriptors for the foundational and functional competencies over the education and training programs of a professional psychologist. Benchmarks are "the behavioral indicators associated with each domain that provide descriptions and examples of expected performance at each developmental stage, and are standards for measurement of performance that can be used for comparison, to identify where needs for improvement exist, and to determine if a given competency has been achieved" (Kaslow et al., 2009, p. S34). Supervision as a primary teaching method in practice is implicated in the competency movement, not only as a functional competency itself but also as a primary or secondary method of teaching the foundational competencies. Within the functional competency in supervision six essential elements for practice are named: expectations and roles, processes and procedures, skills development, awareness of the factors affecting quality, participation process, and ethical and legal issues. Supervision occurs across all development levels as it is employed at practicum, internship, and entry-level professional training periods. Furthermore, the supervisor is charged with the responsibilities of formative and summative evaluation of the trainee. Thus, the articulation of best practices for assessment of each of the benchmarks becomes a critical component of the supervisor's education.

Kaslow et al. (2009) have used the benchmarks as the foundation for the creation of a tool kit of assessment devices that might best be used with each of the benchmarks. Assessment methods deemed relevant to supervisory functioning included the following: annual review, regular case reviews, rating forms, consumer surveys, objective structured clinical examinations, ratings of performance, self-assessment, simulations/role plays, standard patient interviews, standard oral exams, and 360-degree feedback. It is evident from this list that supervisors must be well versed in formative and summative assessment methods as well as specific tools that might best be applied at each stage of trainees' learning progression. Up until the identification of assessment tools, supervisors have largely used methods of assessment that have been developed locally and adapted by training programs and service delivery centers. There has been little standardization of tools across the profession, although there is commonality of approaches found among supervisors as evaluation forms and processes are often taught in supervision courses and training center orientations. The tool kit of assessment resources should include relevant research that can test the utility and psychometric characteristics of these assessment approaches for specific competencies at different levels of a trainee's experience (Kenkel & Peterson, 2010).

The Role of Supervision in Foundational Competencies of the Psychologist

An examination of the benchmarks assessment methods reveals that supervisors are listed as a primary agent in evaluating the foundational competencies of reflective practice-self-assessment, relationships, ethical-legal standards, and individual-cultural diversity at the readiness for internship and readiness for entry into practice levels (Assessment of Competency Benchmarks Workgroup, 2007). Many of these behaviors are experienced and catalogued during supervised practice. Intrapersonal awareness and interpersonal competence are essential components of a psychologist's foundational competencies and professional functioning as well as critical elements of development of multicultural awareness and competence (Constantine, 2008). Forrest, Miller, and Elman (2008) have written extensively on the salience in having strong and clear evaluation processes for this domain of practice. This kind of assessment has long been a source of frustration for educators. It is not an uncommon occurrence to have a student who performs very well on conventional academic standards and yet exhibits behaviors that are not consistent with the interpersonal or emotional behavior expected of a psychologist. For example, this type of student might engage in disruptive or toxic interpersonal behaviors with staff and colleagues, demonstrate a lack of integrity or unwillingness to engage in appropriate self-care, exhibit stereotypical and prejudicial attitudes and behaviors toward disadvantaged and particular racial and ethnic

TABLE 8.1 Five Factors Essential to Professional Development

(a) Recognition that acquiring supervision competencies is a lifelong pursuit
(b) Recognition that attention to diversity is an integral component of competent supervision practice
(c) Recognition that knowledge and decision-making skills in legal and ethical issues are essential
(d) Recognition that the delivery of supervision is influenced by professional and personal factors such as values, beliefs, and interpersonal biases
(e) Recognition that self- and peer assessment are critical processes in developing and maintaining effective supervisory practice.

Source: From Falender et al. (2004, p. 775).

groups, or be highly dysfunctional in a therapeutic and professional environment. Because supervision is an intense, dyadic relationship, these problematic behaviors are quite likely to surface in the supervisory process. Frequently, the supervisor is on the front line in identifying and ameliorating these behaviors with a trainee and if he or she is unsuccessful in helping the trainee change these dysfunctional behaviors, the supervisor may refer the student to therapy or seek to terminate his or her practice experience. It is a difficult and time-consuming process to pursue the termination of a trainee based on interpersonal dysfunction; and it has only been in the last 5 years that competency requirements for interpersonal behavior have been explicitly named as a requirement for professional practice. Donovan and Ponce (2009) point out the need for a sharper focus on these "soft" domains of competence in refining the benchmarks tool kit resources. However, without effective assessment approaches, evaluation of intrapersonal and interpersonal competence as related to therapeutic and multicultural competence has historically been exceedingly difficult, especially when the student has been successful in the more conventional academically oriented assessments (as is often the case).

Benchmarks and Therapist Competence

The establishment of benchmarks, evaluation resources, and assessment tools for the training of professional psychologists has identified the supervisor as a primary agent in both delivering and assessing the trainee's competence. Supervision is named across all developmental levels of practice and is heavily weighted in determining internship and professional entry-level readiness. In fact, supervisors hold significant responsibility in providing summative evaluations and being gatekeepers to entry-level practice. Thus, it is imperative that the functional competencies of supervision be delineated to guide the education and training of supervisors, who in turn enhance the learning and assessment of the trainee. The essential components of learning domains, behavioral anchors, and assessment methods for supervisors were outlined by the *Assessment of Competency Benchmarks Work Group* (Fouad et al., 2009) and the reader is referred to the original for a full description of the benchmarks.

These benchmarks and learning activities are a useful guide for educators of supervision to program the inclusion of various learning experiences in the education of the supervisor. However, the listing of coursework in supervision, consultation on supervision practice, reflection and self-assessment, case method teaching approaches, ethical and legal knowledge, relational intervention techniques, and formative and summative evaluation processes have been standard in teaching and practicing supervision since its inclusion in APA's Committee on Accreditation core functions of professional psychologists (1996). The inclusion of assessment methods of the supervisor's competency and effects of supervision is a relatively new but important addition. The specification of assessment methods is lacking because it relies on self-evaluation, peer observation, trainee evaluation of supervisor, coursework completion, and comprehensive examinations. An examination of the Benchmark Tool Kit (Kaslow, 2009) provides a more refined articulation of assessment of competent supervision. The tool kit includes a number of assessment approaches that can be applied to the supervision competency area. Assessment tools that address both formative and summative evaluation are useful in encouraging the development of the supervisor's expertise, for example, in providing objective structured clinical reviews of supervision process, in fostering interpersonal competence in creating a facilitative learning environment for the supervisee, and in enhancing the delivery of case-relevant clinical knowledge to the supervisee based on current empirical knowledge.

While these methods of assessment can be useful, they still fail to address the impact of supervision on improved client functioning, which is referred to by Ellis and Ladany (1997) as the "acid test" of supervision—Does supervision impact client outcome? In the next section, the scant literature available that examines the linkages between supervisor and therapist interventions as related to client outcome will be reviewed.

Supervision and Client Outcome

Critical to the definition of "competence" in supervision practice is the question of the effects of supervision on client outcome. In 2000, Bambling and King reported that there had been 32 published reviews of empirical studies of clinical supervision and counselor training (Bambling & King, 2000). Reviews of supervision efficacy concluded that although a substantial number of studies had examined the process and characteristics of supervision (Ellis & Ladany, 1997; Holloway, 1992; Holloway & Neufeldt, 1995; Stein & Lambert, 1995; Wampold & Holloway, 1997), there was little research on the effect of supervision on client outcome. In large part, supervision efficacy has been inferred from supervisees' reports of the effects of supervision on their professional development and their skill with client concerns. Across the last 20 years, the findings of many studies, based on supervisees' perceptions have concluded that supervision was beneficial because it enhanced skill development, increased confidence, provided support for emotional insight, and benefited the counseling relationship. Supervisors' judgments of the efficacy of supervision have typically been strongly related to supervisees' engagement in the relationship. Holloway and Neufeldt (1995) in their review of supervision outcomes related to psychotherapy concluded, "it is disconcerting that supervisors, who have the responsibility to insure the therapist's competent practice with clients, are perhaps more influenced by the trainee's interpersonal involvement in supervision than their effectiveness with the client" (p. 211).

In the last 10 years, a comprehensive review of psychotherapy supervision appeared in *Psychotherapy supervision: Theory, research, and practice* (Hess, 2008). The book's authors and the research cited within the chapters are testament to the significant leadership of counseling psychology in supervision research. Consistently these reviews have remarked on the need for research that addresses key supervision processes that are operationalized and related to key factors for the supervisee and the client (Gonsalvez, 2008; Wheeler & Richards, 2007). Finally, research on the efficacy of supervision in relation to client change has begun in earnest in the last decade with the rise of evidence-based therapy (EBT) in psychotherapy. Targeted reviews have narrowed in on the empirical evidence regarding the measureable clinical outcomes for clients (Freitas, 2002; Gonsalvez, 2008; Neufeldt, 2004; Wheeler & Richards, 2007).

LINKING SUPERVISION TO CLIENT OUTCOME

Linking the impact of supervision to client outcome has been very difficult to investigate empirically for a number of reasons. Because supervision must necessarily be linked to the psychotherapeutic process, any outcome study of the relationship of supervision to client change must be able to specify relevant variables in both supervisory and psychotherapeutic contexts. Wampold and Holloway (1997) point out the necessity of complex methodological considerations in any study that examines the potential causality between supervision and client outcome. The most proximal effect of supervision (and one that has been a favorite of researchers since the 1980s) is the change in therapist attitudes, behaviors, and skills as related to the supervision process. The next causal effect, between the most proximal and distal, is the therapist's behavior in the therapeutic relationship, in other words, the transfer of learning from supervision to the practice of psychotherapy. Finally, the most distal outcome is the impact of supervision on client outcome that is assumed to be mediated through the therapist's behavior in the causal model. The latter of these variables, client outcomes, has become of significant importance in the push for competency models in professional education and training. If supervision is to take an empirically validated role in professional psychology training, then its efficacy in relation to client outcome must be validated. Up to this point, the significance of supervision as a core component of therapeutic training has largely relied on very subjective supervisees' report of its value in their learning and to a lesser degree the therapist's behavior in psychotherapy as related to supervisory process (Orlinsky et al., 2001). Thus, in any consideration of supervisory practice, actions taken by the supervisor in the supervisory relationship must ultimately be assessed by observing the therapist's behavior in the counseling relationship and the client's progress. In a latter section, the program of research by Lambert and associates will be discussed as a beginning to establishing a method for designing an assessment process that takes into account the distal outcomes of supervision.

The focus on EBTs and the role of supervision in manualized training has witnessed a resurgence of empirical interest in the specific skills and competencies that constitute effective supervision (Freitas, 2002; Gonsalvez, 2008; Pelling, Barletta, & Armstong, 2009). In the late 1990s the rise of EBT in psychology resulted ultimately in the scrutiny of supervision as a method of teaching best practice models (Gonsalvez, 2008). Supervision has been acknowledged in EBTs as the primary educational component in training a specific set of skills, monitoring fidelity in treatment delivery, and preventing therapist burnout by enhancing therapist satisfaction in treatment delivery (Pelling, Barletta, & Armstong, 2009). However, despite the inclusion of supervision in training and monitoring EBT, there has been considerable debate over the years on the efficacy of supervision on client outcomes (Bambling & King, 2000; Ellis, Ladany, Krengel, & Schult, 1996; Holloway & Gonzalez-Doupe, 1999; Holloway & Neufeldt, 1995). Counseling psychologists Nicholas Ladany, Michael Ellis, and Myrna Friedlander (1999) have concluded that there are four primary findings in the supervision literature that *suggest* that supervision has the *potential* to affect client symptom outcome (p. 318):

- A positive supervisory relationship increases supervisee tendency to model and accommodate observed supervisor therapeutic skills and may enhance supervisees' demonstration of the same therapeutic skills in client work (Pierce & Schauble, 1971; Schacht, Howe, & Berman, 1989).
- Supervision reduces supervisee anxiety and role ambiguity and enhances confidence in counseling practice (Friedlander, Keller, Peca-Baker, & Olk, 1986; Kennard, Stewart, & Gluck, 1987).
- Supervision contributes to the development of basic counseling skills, although its impact on the development of more complex counseling skills is unclear (Lambert & Ogles, 1997).
- Supervision may assist therapists to manage working alliance and resolve therapeutic impasses (Alpher, 1991; Patton & Kivlighan, 1997).

The research supporting these four primary findings in the supervision literature was largely conducted by counseling psychologists on counseling psychology graduate students. Counseling psychologists might now pursue how research findings such as these could be translated into competency benchmarks in supervision practice.

STUDIES ON SUPERVISION/CLIENT OUTCOME

At this stage of our knowledge, the extrapolation of findings to competencies is necessary because studies that explicitly examine the causal relationships between supervisory factors and client outcome are rare. In several reviews of the literature that focused on the impact of supervision on client outcome, there were less than a dozen studies that fell into this category prior to 2001 (Freitas, 2002). And many of these had questionable methodological rigor and only tentative connections to improved client outcome. More recently with advances in psychotherapy outcome studies, there has been a better opportunity and clearer path to evaluate the effects of supervisory variables on specific psychotherapeutic factors. In an extensive review of the empirical literature in supervision from 1980 to early 2006, Wheeler and Richards (2007) identified three studies that met the criteria for supervision/client outcome investigations. Milne, Pilkington, Gracie, and James (2003) focused on the effectiveness of cognitive-behavioral therapy supervision on the supervisee and her client. He discovered that there was a thematic transference of material from supervision to therapy; however, he pointed out that does not necessarily constitute effective therapy for the client. In a qualitative study, Vallance (2005) investigated counselors' perceptions of the impact of supervision on their work with clients. She concluded that supervision, which provided emotional support, directly impacted the therapist's ability to remain focused on the client and not be distracted by his or her own emotional material. Although she did not access clients' perceptions of the counseling experience, she did ask supervisees to connect specific processes and experiences in supervision with their actions as a counselor. However, there still remains the issue of the dependence on the therapists' reports of client improvement rather than reports acquired directly from the clients regarding not only their therapeutic experience with a given therapist but, more important, their symptom reduction and perception of improvement of well-being. This is particularly problematic given the considerable volume of findings that have revealed therapists and supervisors are more generous in their assessment of client improvement and underestimate clients' deterioration when compared to client reports (Worthen & Lambert, 2007). If therapists are not able to determine when treatment interventions are failing, then their reports to supervisors will be overly optimistic and not trigger the supervisor to guide the therapist to a more effective course of treatment. Furthermore, clinicians, including supervisors, are inclined to devalue actuarial/statistical data in preference for their own subjective impression. Thus, even if supervisors are using direct observation or video/audiotapes of the therapeutic sessions, they may still be overly influenced by their self-fulfilling observations of treatment efficacy.

Worthen and Lambert (2007) have developed a client feedback approach that systematically sends client feedback to the therapist after each session. This feedback is gathered through the use of an Outcome Questionaire-45 (OQ-45; Lambert et al., 2004) completed by the client for each session. The OQ-45 assesses symptoms, interpersonal problems, social role functioning, and well-being. Modeling procedures are used to determine whether the client is "on track" for a positive therapeutic outcome or is "not on track" and will decline or remain at status quo (Finch, Lambert, & Schaalje, 2001). A unique four-level, color coding scheme, indicating the outcome trajectories, is used to give the client feedback to therapists. The trajectories represent a continuum from the client is making expected progress with a predicted positive outcome to the client is not making change with a predicted negative outcome. Studies (Hawkins, Lambert, Vemeersch, Slade, & Tuttle, 2004; Lambert et al., 2002; Lambert & Hawkins, 2001; Whipple et al., 2003) that have investigated the effects of this feedback model have demonstrated that "the difference between providing feedback and withholding it was not only statistically significant, but produced effect sizes around" (Worthen & Lambert, 2007, p. 50). Effect sizes were greater for clients who were "off-track" than for those clients whose trajectories showed them "on track" (Lambert, Harmon, Slade, Whipple, & Hawkins, 2005). Although these studies link the receipt of client progress feedback to the therapist, the researchers discovered that the "not-on-track (NOT)" clients were not improving even when feedback was provided. Ergo, therapists did not know how to intervene to change the downward clinical path. To assist therapists in determining an intervention that would effectively put the client back "on track," Lambert and his associates (Lambert et al., 2004) developed a manual of clinical support tools (CSTs) that operationalized the interventions that would address therapeutic alliance, motivation to engage in therapy, the clients' social support network, maladaptive perfectionist attitudes, use or change of medication, and alternative therapeutic modalities. Relevant psychological inventories were employed to assess these constructs and this feedback was again provided to the therapist. Research on the effects of using the CST manual, including training therapists on the decision tree (it identifies problematic areas based on the assessment data and incorporates appropriate treatments to address these areas), indicated that "in a client population of 1,000 NOT clients, recovered/improved clients would increase from 250 to 490 and clients that deteriorate would decrease from 190 to 80" (Worthen & Lambert, 2007, p. 51).

Although the provision of client progress data was only supplied to the therapist in these studies, the compelling evidence for change in the NOT clients led to the investigation of supervisors' and supervisees' receptivity to using such data in supervision. Supervisors were not overly positive about the use of client outcome data in the early stages of this program of research (not surprising given the history and studies that demonstrate clinicians prefer to rely on their intuitive clinical knowledge). However, as the utility of the client progress data became more persuasive, they used this information to focus supervisory discussions. These studies did not directly measure supervisory interventions with client outcome, but rather examined supervisors' receptivity to include client outcome data in their thinking and direction of the supervisory practice. The evidence that client progress and outcome trajectory data can significantly affect client improvement by influencing the therapist's intervention strategies is a strong argument to have supervisors utilize such client outcome information to guide their supervisory strategies. As Worthen and Lambert conclude, "We believe the use of (client-monitoring) feedback (system) ... will significantly assist our mandate as supervisors to monitor client welfare and through supervision, enhance client outcomes. Thus, outcome oriented supervision can help facilitate the two primary aims of supervision, enhanced practice and improved client outcomes" (2007, p. 53).

The Competent Supervisor

The final link that connects supervision efficacy to client outcome has yet to be demonstrated conclusively. Supervision, at all development levels of training, is involved in training psychologists to engage in competent practice. To date, we have strong indications that the provision of client progress feedback to the therapist is effective in realigning the therapeutic process for those clients at risk and producing better client outcomes. We also have initial evidence that therapists and supervisors find client outcome data useful in planning effective interventions that impact client outcome. The next step in the education and training of competent supervisors is the connection between supervisory instructional delivery and tools that assist the therapist in making the appropriate changes in therapy that in turn enhance client outcome. Benchmarks identify the knowledge base and practice experiences that supervisors need at each of the three developmental stages; however, benchmarks do not specifically name those supervisory practices that might be used to engage supervisees and increase their knowledge and skill level at each of the developmental levels. In other words, how do we match supervision strategies with the learning tasks, therapeutic interventions, and developmental level of the supervisee?

As discussed earlier, the competency tool kit, which operationalized the Assessment of Competency Benchmarks, identified a number of formative and summative assessment tools that supervisors might use to determine whether trainees were gaining the appropriate competence in specified areas of practice at each developmental level. Some of these same tools are useful in the assessment of supervisor competencies, particularly at the readiness for internship and entry-level stages of development when skills in the practice of supervision are expected. However, the identification of tools to assess the supervisor's practice does not identify the actual processes in which supervisors must engage to be effective. Inman and Ladany's (2008) review of supervision research identified only eight studies from 1980 to 2007 that examined constructs related to supervisor strategies and/or competence, such as development, countertransference, and self-disclosure. Although the developmentally oriented studies are often confounded by experience level, Steven et al. (1998) found that experience alone does not influence supervisor development; however, "the type of training that supervisors receive does influence the stance they take in supervision" (e.g., more supportive, less critical and dogmatic as cited in Inman and Ladany, 2008, p. 507). Countertransference, in the supervisory dyad, has been known as *supertransference*. Teitelbaum (1990) and Ladany et al. (2000) found that supervisor countertransference did occur in response to unresolved personal issues on the supervisor's part and were triggered by the trainee's interpersonal style, trainee–client interactions, or factors relevant to the environment in which the work took place. Such reactions did appear to influence supervision outcome as related to the trainee. Finally, Ladany and Walker (2003) and Ladany and Lehrman-Waterman (1999) found that different types of supervisor self-disclosure as well as nondisclosure impacted to varying degrees shifts in the supervisory working alliance, supervisee disclosure, and supervisee ability to learn.

The research on supervisor constructs that impact supervision process is a beginning in the identification and linkage of these processes to outcomes in supervision. We now have sufficient evidence from empirical investigations of supervision to construct competencies of the supervisor that include the proximal and distal outcomes. For example, supervisors need to be competent in identifying "supertransference" processes, making use of opportunities for appropriate self-disclosure, developing and maintaining a strong supervisory working alliance, and incorporating client progress into the design of effective interventions. Ultimately, it is the connection between the proximal outcomes of supervision—supervisor behavior and therapist behavior—with client progress that will validate not only the efficacy of supervision but also empirically identify competencies to guide the teaching of supervision.

Conclusion

Studies of supervision competence must move beyond the delineation of knowledge, skills, and values and examine empirically the impact of competent (and incompetent) supervisors on supervisory outcomes that are both proximal—therapist response to supervision and learning alliance in supervision—and distal—therapist behavior in therapeutic encounter, working alliance of therapy, and client outcome. Although the empirical literature has adequately examined the numerous variables related to the supervisor, the supervisee, and the supervisory relationship, the validation of supervision impact on client symptoms has been elusive. Pelling, Barletta, and Armstrong (2009) noted that from January 2000 to May 2008 the majority of papers published worldwide on supervision were discussion and review papers rather than research-based reports. Unfortunately, for all its definitional and modeling efforts, the competency-based literature of supervision has not yet been empirically validated. It is imperative that these types of investigation be pursued in earnest given the significant efforts being expended on competency-based efforts in curriculum, training, and evaluation dependent on supervisory practice. Unfortunately, we cannot yet verify a path from supervisory intervention to therapist skill in practice to client outcome. However, it is imperative that this be done in order to establish an evidence-based practice of supervision and to secure its position as a central instructional method in the training of professional psychologists.

NINE

Competence in Consultation

Consulting psychology is the practice of psychology that focuses on "consultation to, with, or for individuals and organizations at individual, group, and organizational/system-wide levels rooted in multiple areas of substantive expertise" (American Psychological Association, 2007). Professional psychologists engage in consultation and training activities in a variety of settings such as community mental health centers, medical centers, educational institutions, and business and industry. "Consultation and teaching activities will continue to expand as the field of professional psychology becomes more diverse, relevant in an increasing array of settings, and at the same time more specialized" (Illback, Maher, & Kopplin, 1992). Since Illback et al.'s predication, the consultation literature in psychology has become increasingly more differentiated around setting as psychologists have ventured into new areas of consultation practice such as environmental and sports psychology. Broadly speaking, there are three primary areas of consultation practice relevant to counseling psychology: mental health, education, and business organizational consultation. The Society of Consulting Psychology, Division 13 of the American Psychological Association (APA), embraces all areas of psychological consultation in their membership, and their flagship journal, *Consulting Psychology Journal: Practice and Theory*, publishes papers relevant to a broad array of practice settings. The last decade has witnessed substantial progress in the definition of psychological consultation as a unique set of skills and proficiencies culminating in APA adopting *Guidelines for Education and Training at the Doctoral and Postdoctoral Levels in Consulting Psychology/Organizational Consulting Psychology*[1] (American Psychological Association, 2007). The guidelines are drawn for application of organizational consulting psychology (OCP) in a wide range of organizational settings; however, they are embedded in the foundational competencies of professional psychology, including the specialties of counseling, clinical, school, and industrial/organizational. In this chapter, we will focus on OCP as a competency-based practice within the specialty of counseling psychology.

Consultation Activities of Counseling Psychologists

Counseling psychologists have long been involved in the delivery of consultation services in mental health, higher education, and industrial and organizational settings (Shullman, 2002). As early as 1976 Nutt reported that *Society of Counseling Psychology,* Division 17 members overall spent 15% of their time in consultative activities and with those members employed outside of academic settings reporting a mean of 22% in consultation practice (Nutt, 1977). Since the 1970s there have been several reports on the demographic, educational, employment, and professional affiliations of counseling psychologists (Kurpius, Fuqua, Gibson, Kurpius, & Froehle, 1995; Munley, Pate, William, & Duncan, 2008; Toomer, 1982; Watkins, Lopez, Campbell, & Himmell, 1986). Not surprisingly, each of these surveys confirmed the general sentiment that counseling psychology is a broad field of practice that finds application in a wide variety of settings with the majority of counseling psychologists reporting that their primary activity was in health and mental health services (Munley et al., 2008). However, consultation emerged consistently as a secondary component of professional activities with a large majority of counseling psychologists.

In 1982, Toomer reported from a survey of clinical, counseling, and I/O psychologists registered in APA Divisions 12, 14, and 17 that only 7.85% of counseling psychologists considered consulting, either with individuals or firms, as their primary work setting. However, when asked the question, "How interested would you be in expanding the application of your professional skills into the following other work settings?" Counseling psychologists, in particular, indicated a high level of interest in business/industry and health care settings.

Six years after Toomer's survey, Watkins et al. (1986) included consultation as a designated activity in his survey of all Division 17 members. Findings indicated that again psychotherapy was the most prevalent activity across counseling psychologists, occupying 27.5% of their time, but consultation was the second most endorsed activity (60.9% of sample), occupying 7.3% of professional activities.

Surveys completed by Division 13, Society of Consulting Psychology, add to our knowledge of the prevalence of consulting activities and the specific areas of those activities of counseling psychologists. Kurpius et al. (1995) surveyed all members of Division 13 to explore the training and education characteristics of members as well as the clients and settings in which they performed consultation services. Of particular interest to this discussion were inclusion of data on the four specialties of professional psychology, most influential type of education and training received, and the current parameters of their consulting practice. The largest psychology specialization represented in Division 13 was clinical/community psychology; with 31.1% of members, however, counseling psychology and counselor education graduates represented 22.2% of those who responded and were members of Division 13. Kurpius et al. found that a large number of academicians report involvement in consultation given the typical 1-day release allowed by most universities. This finding corroborates Watkins et al.'s (1986) survey of members of Division 17 where the role of consultant was identified by 19.9% of the respondents as the second highest secondary professional identification after clinical practitioner. The representation of specialties in these surveys is consistent with the 2009 Division 13 membership roster (American Psychological Association, 2009) in which 11.9% of members identified counseling psychology as a subfield to consulting psychology, the second largest specialty group in Division 13. Of Division 13 members, 7.5% also had membership in Division 17, Counseling Psychology. In 1995 the composite profile of a Division 13 consulting psychologist was depicted as "an older White male who graduated from an APA-approved training program approximately 20 years ago and is currently a certified/licensed psychologist. Providing consultation on a part-time basis, the majority of consulting psychologists either work in a college/university setting or are engaged in private practice" (Kurpius et al., 1995, p. 79). This profile has changed in the last 15 years with greater racial, ethnic, and gender diversity in the younger ranks of professional psychologists.

Historical Development of Consultation in Counseling Psychology

The consideration of consultation in *The Counseling Psychologist,* a Division 17 flagship journal that publishes articles of timely and relevant concerns to the profession, has spoken loudly to the significance of consultation as a professional activity. Mary Leonard (1977) wrote enthusiastically about the role of the organizational consultant as presenting new possibilities for the counseling psychologist. Although the foundational training of counseling psychologists was a strong basis for working in organizational settings, she named additional training areas needed to work effectively in the organizational setting:

> course work to augment system and organizational theory; advanced study in career and adult development; and theories and models of consultation. Methodological skills would include survey development, opinion polling, interview techniques for assessment, and analytic processes to render this information relevant to organizational needs. Finally, the inclusion of practicum and internship in organizational settings such as health care, education, and industry would provide trainees with the apprenticeship necessary to transform knowledge into reflective practice. In years to come we will undoubtedly see increased demand for the knowledge and skills of counseling psychologists who can function as well with organizational systems as with the individuals within those systems. (p. 76)

Early evidence of the field's interest in organizational consultation continued into the 1980s. There were five major contributions on the topic of consultation between 1982 and 1985. These discussions considered consultation practice in business and industry (Osipow, 1982), research (Meade, Hamilton, & Yuen, 1982), conceptual models (Gallessich, 1985), interventions (Kurpius, 1985), training and supervision (Brown, 1985), and ethics (Robinson & Gross, 1985).

The Counseling Psychologist published a special issue on *Counseling Psychology: Applications in the World of Work*. In a major contribution to this issue, Osipow (1982) argued for counseling psychologists to utilize their foundational skills in vocational psychology and career development in business and industry. His focus of application is less related to the system of an organization and more focused on the application of these skills on an individual consultation basis to professional staff and managers in issues of leader succession, retirement, and career development. He spoke to the connection between mental health, "healthy" organizational environments, and employees' work satisfaction and overall well-being. He used the concept of "hygiology" to describe counseling psychologists' growth development and facilitation. Responses to Osipow's article brought on much head nodding and concerns around how counseling psychologists can enter into the business world and develop competencies that will prepare them with the knowledge and skills needed in the large, dynamic systems of organizations.

Ridley and Stark (1982) claimed that the naming of work as "counseling" in the organization be replaced by the word "consulting"; the idea of "talking with a counselor" connotes a discussion in which an individual client is potentially weak, inept, or highly vulnerable. Thus, individuals in positions of decision making who are expected to be competent and achieving would find it difficult to seek out the "counselor," whereas the label of "consultant" suggests that a fully functioning client is seeking out "an individual of circumscribed expertise" (p. 53) in an area where knowledge and guidance is needed by the client. Forecasting a collaboration that would happen decades later, Ridley and Stark recommended that Division 17 and Division 13 both legitimize the term "consulting" as a professional designation.

Osipow, with astute prescience, commented in his 1982 treatise on counseling psychology in the world of work:

> Thus, industry has tended to take a different view of employees. It sees employees as serving the institution rather than the other way around. However as industry comes to see employees as important resources and assets needing periodic "maintenance, repair and improvement," then counseling will be accepted not on an abstract philosophical, humanitarian basis, but rather in terms of profit statements and productivity. (p. 19)

MOVE TOWARD MENTAL HEALTH DIRECT SERVICES

In the late 1980s and 1990s as pressure increased within the profession to qualify counseling psychologists for state licensure and eligibility for third-party payments, the profession moved away from its origins in vocational and occupational psychology toward direct service and remedial interventions. In turn, educational curriculum and supervised practice became more focused on direct delivery of mental health services. As counseling psychology curricula became filled with accreditation requirements related to mental health, it became less and less feasible for trainees to take courses, practica, and internships in OCP. The culmination of this trend in the profession is evidenced in mental health direct service as the primary professional activity in every survey of counseling psychologists since 1986 (see earlier discussion).

This movement toward mental health dampened the fledgling attempts in the 1980s to transfer counseling psychology's historical interest in vocational and occupational psychology into organizational consultation pursuits. In a bibliographic search of counseling psychology's flagship journals few articles on consultation were found.[2] All records available in PychInfo and Ebsco electronic databases that used some form of the term "consult*" in the title or abstract were identified for the *Journal of Counseling Psychology (JCP)* and *The Counseling Psychologist (TCP).* The *Journal of Counseling Psychology* published five articles that addressed consultation in the years 1961, 1974, 1977, 1980, and 1982. The *Counseling Psychologist* fared better with 32 references, the earliest in 1977 and the latest in 1994. All but six of these 32 references were in the special issues on consultation in 1982 and 1985. We considered the possibility that counseling psychologists working in consultation may find a better audience for their work in journals such as *Journal of Consulting and Clinical Psychology, Consultation: An International Journal,* and *The Consulting Psychology Journal: Practice and Theory (CPJ).* This led to an author affiliation search of all three journals from their inception to 2010 for all authors that listed counseling psychology, counselor education, school of education, and/or educational psychology and NOT school psychology in their affiliation. The first two of these journals yielded none and one counseling psychology authors, respectively. However, the search of *CPJ,* a flagship journal of Division 13, resulted in 27 articles between 1992 and 2009 and within this group of authors were many of the counseling psychologists that are referenced in this chapter and who have contributed substantially to the literature and leadership in consulting psychology—Robert Bradford, Stewart Cooper, Dale Fuqua, Dewayne Kurpius, Sharon Robinson Kurpius, Jodie Newman, and Thomas Froehle. It appears that the *CPJ* may be a viable outlet for counseling psychologists interested in the research and practice of consultation; however, representation of counseling psychologists' authorship is small in comparison to the large number of articles published. Overall, it may be concluded that consultation almost disappeared from the radar screen of scholars in counseling psychology from the mid-1980s through the turn of the century. Despite the lackluster attention given to consultation in counseling psychology scholarship, it remains that consultation is a professional activity that approximately 50% of counseling psychologists report as being approximately 13%–15% of their practice (see earlier discussion).

PROBLEMS AND OPPORTUNITIES IN THE 21ST CENTURY

The 21st century ushered in a new set of problems for mental health providers as decreased compensation for mental health services, increasing regulation of psychologists by health maintenance organizations, and government-regulated cost accounting made independent practice in counseling and psychotherapy less attractive. Professional psychologists began to look at more viable markets for consulting psychology in business and industry. In concert, over the last decade, business and industry has become increasingly aware of the significance and impact of workplace well-being to the financial bottom line. True to Osipow's prediction, there are now numerous books and research articles on the importance of respectful engagement in the workplace (Kusy & Holloway, 2009), the cost of bad behavior at work (Pearson & Porath, 2009), and the significance of treating employees with personalized care and healthy environments (Sisodia, Wolfe, & Sheth, 2007). The "Time Has Come, The Walrus Said" as Meade et al. (1982), so aptly put almost 30 years ago; and yes, still the question remains whether counseling psychology programs will invest in the creation of curriculum and training that will develop knowledgeable and competent *consulting counseling psychologists.*

Consulting Psychology as a Competency-Based Specialty

The Cube Model for competency development in professional psychology includes consultation as a *functional competency* defined as "the ability to provide expert guidance or professional assistance in response to a client's needs or goals" (Rodolfa et al., 2005, p. 351). In the model it is assumed that each functional competency will be informed by the foundational competencies of (a) reflective practice and self-assessment, (b) scientific knowledge-methods, (c) relationships, (d) ethical-legal standards-policy, (e) individual-cultural diversity, and (f) interdisciplinary systems. The development of the functional competency will occur at all five levels of professional development: doctoral education, doctoral internship, post-doctoral supervision, residency/fellowship, and continuing education. However, consultation has lagged behind other competencies in the development of common educational curriculum and evidence-based practice. The Society for Consulting Psychology, Division 13 of the APA, has played a major role in identifying consulting psychology as a "special proficiency" within clinical, counseling, and school psychology programs. Until this time, "consultation" or "consulting practice" was a term rather loosely used by psychologists to describe many different types of activities that employed their knowledge and expertise as psychologists and did not refer to direct service delivery in mental health. There were no programs reported in psychology that gave a doctoral degree in *consulting psychology*, school psychology was most likely to offer courses on consultation, and those psychologists with counseling and clinical specialties engaged in postdoctoral practice and workshops to gain expertise (Hellkamp, Zins, Ferguson, & Hodge, 1998). Despite counseling psychology's history in vocational counseling and workplace environments, most consultation knowledge and experience came during practica and internship experiences largely in university and college environments (Morrill, Oetting, & Hurst, 1974). By 2002, the Education and Training Committee of Division 13 had published a comprehensive document that outlined the competencies for doctoral or postdoctoral training in consulting psychology. Their purpose was to ground consulting practice in well-defined and distinct domains of knowledge and skills that would add to existing professional psychology specialties and would guide faculty in designing curriculum that were competency based (Lowman et al., 2002).

Consultation and interprofessional collaboration competency-based training were addressed in a coordinated series of publications from 2002 through 2010—Society of Consulting Psychology, Division 13 (2002), the Workgroup on Consultation and Interprofessional Collaboration (Arredondo, Shealy, Neale, & Winfrey, 2004), the Guidelines for Competency-Based Training in CP/OCP (American Psychological Association, 2007), and *Competency-Based Education for Professional Psychology* (Kenkel & Peterson, 2010).

CURRICULUM AND CONSULTATION

Stanton (2010) pointed out that curriculum in competency-based practice in consultation and education lagged behind other functional competencies—only 78% of all schools of psychology require a course in consultation and education, 18% offer an elective course in this competency, and it ranks the lowest in emphasis among all competencies in the curriculum. Consider these statistics given the prevalence of consultation among psychologists; Paskiewicz et al. (2006) reported over 60% of faculty respondents engaged in external consultation, the third most frequent faculty scholarship activity. Thus, given faculty's involvement in the practice of consultation, one might presume that faculty in psychology have the experience and knowledge to teach consultation and education; however, in Stanton's survey of all NCSPP member schools most programs offered one combined course in consultation and supervision. Even in these courses, education and management content appeared to be underemphasized, whereas supervision was more prominently represented. Notwithstanding, APA accreditation requires that consultation and education competency be addressed to complete the mandatory specified content areas of psychology. Furthermore, satisfactory fulfillment of this requirement cannot be simply a course or course content but must represent a systematic progression of learning at each developmental level (Arredondo et al., 2004).

CONSULTING PSYCHOLOGY CLUSTERS

By 2010 the competencies in consulting psychology had been organized around five skill clusters (see Table 9.1) that are described by knowledge, skill, and attitude for each of the three developmental levels: begin practicum, begin internship, and complete doctoral degree.

These broad clusters are consistent with other specialty areas of professional psychology and only in a detailed content analysis of the meaning of these clusters to the teaching and training of consulting psychology would a distinctive competency specialty emerge. The APA (2007) confirmed the importance of distinguishing CP/OCP from the other specialties by articulating the specific knowledge base and practice approaches needed to effectively intervene in organizations, systems, groups, and individual systems that emerge in organizational settings. These domain-specific competencies to consulting psychology as embedded in the five clusters of knowledge and training are represented in Figure 9.1.

In the next section, we will discuss the fit between consultation competencies and the specialty of counseling psychology.

Overlap of Consulting Competencies and Counseling Psychology

Important to our discussion of consulting *counseling* psychologists is the recognition that doctoral training in industrial/organizational, counseling, and clinical psychology "can provide considerable training that is relevant for the practice of consulting psychology" (Arredondo et al., 2004, p. 213). The Consultation and Interdisciplinary Relationships

TABLE 9.1 **Skill Clusters for Competencies in Consulting Psychology**

- Knowledge of evidence-based theories, models, and interventions
- Relationship skills
- Diversity and cross-cultural competency in consultation
- Problem-solving and implementation skills
- Ethical and professional practice skills

Source: From the American Psychological Association (2007).

Workgroup (Arredondo et al., 2004) pointed out that their group was made up of members from all four primary specialties in professional psychology—clinical, counseling, school, and I/O—and that "since consultation and interprofessional collaboration embody skills applied in unique and common ways by practitioners across the four specialty areas... Discussions yielded many points of commonality and preferred practice approaches based upon respective specialties" (pp. 798–799). The overlap of competencies for all four traditional specialty areas with consulting psychology is evident from the report. The 2007 report by the APA, *Guidelines for Education and Training at the Doctoral and Postdoctoral Levels in Consulting Psychology/Organizational Consulting Psychology*, sought to reinforce and strengthen previous efforts in standardization of "the quality of teaching and learning in the area of the practice of CP (*Consulting Psychology*), especially OCP (*Organizational Consulting Psychology*), within the scientific discipline and professional of psychology" (American Psychological Association, 2007, p. 980). The standards adhere to the overarching principles and 10 general areas of learning for professional psychology while identifying three areas considered to be domain specific to consulting psychology: individual-level interventions, group-level interventions, and organizational/systems-level interventions (American Psychological Association, 2007). The report lists competencies and bibliographies that relate to each of these levels of intervention and ethical conduct guidelines for consultation practice.

Each of the domain specific areas of expertise as pictured in the center of Figure 9.1 (individual, group, and organizational/systems) has competencies such as assessment, relationship, process skills, and multicultural competency (Stanton, 2010). Each of these interacting competencies within the domains resonates with the benchmarks for competent practice for a counseling psychologist. Shullman (2002) argues counseling psychology adequately prepares one for consultation. Drawing from a comparison of Gelso and Fretz's (1992) five unifying principles in counseling psychology and three core roles of counseling psychologists (Heppner, Casas, Carter, & Stone, 2000), she concludes:

> Putting together the five historical themes and three roles, counseling psychology has principally focused on helping essentially intact people and groups in organizational entities remediate and prevent problems and enhance and develop their capacities. This is done primarily through shorter term interventions that take into

> consideration the contextual impact of the environments in which people live, work, and learn. Such a conceptualization seems most consistent with much of what is proposed as the core of consulting psychology education and training endeavors, especially at the individual and group levels. (Shullman, 2002, p. 244)

Shullman buttresses her claim to historical and theoretical grounding of consultation in counseling psychology with the Morrill, Oetting, and Hurst (1974) seminal article that organized the functional work of a counseling psychologist in a three-dimensional cube named "The Thirty-Six Faces of Counseling." One of the methods of interventions was consultation and training for individuals, groups, institutions, and communities at the remedial, preventative, and developmental levels. Although Morrill et al.'s work was specifically relevant to campus and university systems, the genesis of the more generically applied, 21st century Cube Model (Rodolfa et al., 2005) of competency-based professional psychology is evident in this early model. Foley and Redfering (1987) and Gerstein and Shullman's (1992) comparisons of counseling psychologists' roles to other helping professions in business and organizational settings demonstrated the breadth of functions in which counseling psychologists were engaged, including human resources, training, organizational dynamics, career development, equal employment opportunity programs, labor relations (sexual harassment), and community outreach. The prevalence of counseling psychologists in organizations and business has increased, according to Shullman (2002). As greater opportunities for professional services such as coaching have increased, career and leadership development activities have become more recognized as viable market alternatives for counseling psychologists (Shullman, 2002).

Despite the historical precedents of counseling psychologists as consultants in organizational settings and business, Gerstein and Shullman (1992) found "that only 21% (of counseling psychology) had programs with their own subspecialty in business and organizational practice, whereas 17% had subspecialties elsewhere available in the university, 10% had access only to business classes as options, and 52% had no program focus on training students for business and organizational settings" (p. 245). These figures are largely substantiated in more recent surveys of curricular training in counseling psychology programs (Hellkamp et al., 1998; Paskiewicz et al., 2006). It would appear that most counseling psychologists are not receiving training in consulting practice until internship or postdoctoral work.

GENERAL COMPETENCIES

The counseling psychologist who chooses to engage in organizational consultation will have been prepared in the scientist-practitioner model with attention to the 10 general competency areas common to applied psychology. The 10 competencies areas, which circle the domain-specific areas of *I-G-O (individual-, group-, organization-level interventions)* in Figure 9.1, warrant further examination for comparing counseling preparation with consultation proficiencies. In a number of the 10 listed general competencies, counseling psychologists have made substantial contributions in education, training, and research for the overall profession of psychology. For example, in the areas of self-awareness/self-management and relationship development, counseling psychology has been prominent in the scholarship and practice of supervision (Sullivan, 2009), in studying the role of reflective practice in psychotherapy training (Neufeldt, Karno, & Nelson, 1996), and in seeking standards for trainees' interpersonal competence with fellow professionals and peers as well as in the delivery of therapeutic services (Forrest, Miller, & Elman, 2008; Mangione & Nadkarni, 2010). Furthermore, as evidenced in this volume, counseling psychologists have played a major role in the development, research, and application of (a) assessment inventories especially related to vocational interests, aptitudes, and career placement; (b) knowledge in racial and ethnic identity; and (c) multicultural awareness skills. Substantial contributions on process and outcome research strategies for individual and group interventions have been made by the field of counseling psychology and are strongly emphasized in the curriculum.

Nonetheless, there are several of the 10 general competencies that must be more specifically developed within the counseling psychology curriculum to successfully prepare the consulting counseling psychologist for organizational work. These include (a) process consultation and action research; (b) knowledge of organizational and leadership theory; (c) case studies, empirical research applications, and evaluation methods; (d) business operations, legal and industry regulations, technological advances; and (e) professional ethics and standards.

Process Consultation and Action Research

Process consultation, action research, and evaluation are important OCP competencies in each of the I-G-O domains (see Fig. 9.1). Schein (1989) identified the principles behind process consultation and these principles are familiar to the counseling psychology perspective, but they may not be studied specifically in the context of organizational interventions: "many

Figure 9.1 Overview of consulting psychology/organizational psychology guidelines: general principles.

Reprinted from the American Psychological Association (2007). Guidelines for Education and Training at the Doctoral and Postdoctoral Levels in Consulting Psychology/Organizational Consulting Psychology, *American Psychologist, 62*, p. 981.

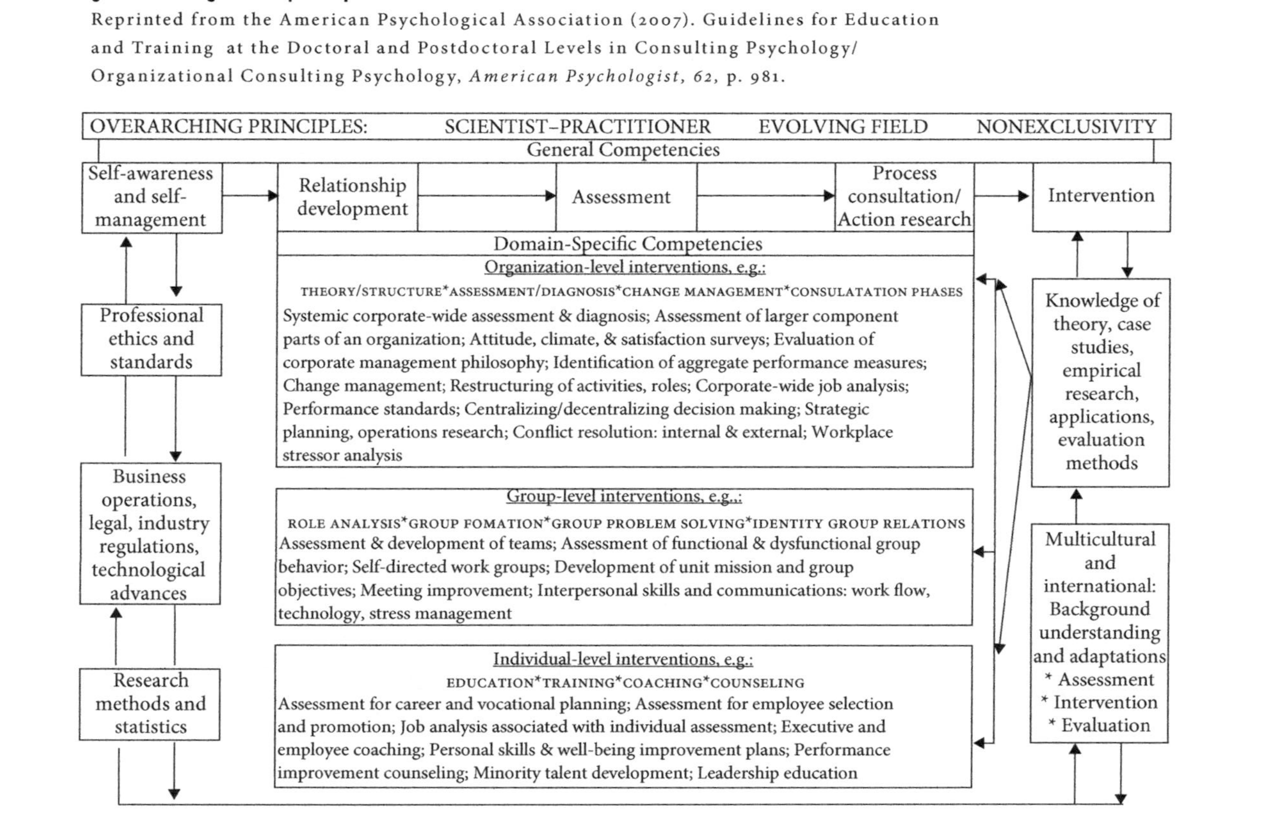

of the problems in human systems are such that clients... would benefit from participation in the process of making the diagnosis... only clients know what form of remedial intervention will really work because only they know their personalities and what will work in their group or organizational cultures" (p. 5).

The iterative process of consultation, intervention, evaluation, consultation, and so on is the same process that is engaged in *action research*, a particularly useful approach to investigating the effectiveness of programmatic interventions in organizational settings. Action research, too often considered a second-class methodological approach in psychology programs, is typically ignored in favor of the more traditional research designs that support quasi-experimental and correlational methods. Meade et al. (1982) remarked on the complexity from a methodological and political perspective of doing research in organizational settings and the contribution research designs that adapt to these field conditions can make:

> The most useful overriding constructs for conducting outcome research seem to be *evaluation* and *action research.* Taking the latter first, there can be no doubt that we must begin to integrate research efforts into actions efforts... Doing this, making the research effort a first step in the consultation, and the making the *results* of that research effort the basis for, or beginning of, the action, serves the dual purpose of sound social science methodology and effective intervention. (p. 47)

Case Studies

Organizational and business researchers have made excellent use of case study designs in their investigations of effective change processes. Blanton (2010) in her survey of members of the Society of Consulting Psychology (SCP) discovered that *Harvard Business Review (HBR)* was rated higher than management journals, human resource journals, and other psychological journals as most popularly read and useful to their consultation practice. Although clinical case studies are an integral component of practice training for individual-level interventions, students are not schooled in case study research methods that are both more sophisticated (Yin, 2009) and traditionally applied in business cases as frequently featured in *HBR*.

Business Operation

The significance of a solid understanding of business operation is a competency needed at all levels of intervention in OCP. Whether providing coaching consultation services to an executive-level client, working with a team leader, or engaging in a large-scale organizational intervention, understanding the legal constraints, industry-wide regulations, human resource policies, and technological interfaces is essential to compete with the business management consultants. More important, to intervene successfully at the systems level, knowledge of systems that operate on clients' functioning and welfare is a critical element of designing the intervention at all levels of the organization (Lowman et al., 2002).

Ethics and Standards

Ethics and professional standards are a pervasive, general competency across all specialties of professional psychology. Ethical guidelines and the complexity of ethics within organizational setting has been the subject of great consternation for counseling psychologists since Robinson and Gross's 1985 major contribution to *The Counseling Psychologist* (1985). Shullman (2002) commented that the 1992 APA Ethical Principles were insufficient in their guidance for consultation practice particularly around issues of corporate values that may be in direct conflict with the ethical or moral code of professional psychologists. In the most recent editing of APA *Ethical Principles of Psychologists and Code of Conduct* (American Psychological Association, 2002) ethical dilemmas that consulting psychologists face in general and specifically in organizational settings have been addressed with greater specificity. However, in his address at the 2005 APA Convention, Bradt (2005) commented that the ethical principles must go further in providing guidance and knowledge on knotty issues that frequently emerge in consultation practice. For example, in the current climate of corporate downsizing, management exiting, mergers, and acquisitions, consultants are often called to resolve conflict and shepherd significant change. Consultants may discover in these highly charged situations with significant financial repercussions that their personal values are in conflict with the leadership actions in the treatment of staff. When these conflicts arise, they must decide whether and how to continue the provision of the contracted service. Psychologists trained in the ethical dilemmas typically found in mental health delivery are not prepared to recognize the ethical and moral issues that can emerge within complex, multifaceted systems. As early as 1985, Gallessich, a counseling psychologist, outlined the ethical questions that the consulting psychologist faces. These ethical issues continued to be raised throughout the next two decades by other consulting counseling psychologists (Crego, 1985; Fuqua & Newman, 2002; Newman, 1993; Newman & Robinson, 1991). The culmination of these efforts is reflected in the final note in the APA 2007

Guidelines for ethical competencies for the consulting psychologist and is reproduced here (see Table 9.2) in entirety because of the salience of these issues for consultation practice in complex organizational systems and rarely present in direct service of mental health.

DOMAIN-SPECIFIC COMPETENCIES

The overarching principle of "nonexclusivity" in the *Guidelines* (American Psychological Association, 2007; see Fig. 9.1) recognizes the different routes that a consulting psychologist might take in becoming competent in his or her practice. Thus, academic education and training taken from any of the four primary specialties of professional psychology I/O, clinical, counseling, or school could provide relevant knowledge and practice for the CP/OCP. However, as a part of the professional psychology training programs or through postdoctoral education, the consulting psychologist would be expected to gain proficiency in the three domains of competence, I-G-O, that distinguish CP/OCP practice. Figure 9.1 describes the meaning of each of these domains within the specific context of consulting psychology. Note that within each domain there is a specification of a skill set deemed necessary to effectively perform a variety of intervention within that level of the system. Within each domain all 10 general competencies are brought to bear on the design of the intervention to lesser

TABLE 9.2 Ethical Questions for the Consulting Psychologist

Who is my client? The organization? The manager? The individual employee?
What are the parameters of confidentiality in the client's expectation? Are they acceptable to me?
Are the goals of the organization and consulting contract congruent with my personal and professional values and ethics?
What rights, power, and freedom does each individual participant in the consultation process have? Are these acceptable to me?
How do I balance the task dimension and the human dimension of my work with this organization?
What control do I have over the use and dissemination of information I gather as a consultant?
What are the parameters of my accountability? Are they acceptable to me?
Do I have the skills to be an effective and efficient consultant to this organization and for this concern?
How do I bridge the gap between maintaining the high standards of my profession and the profit motive that permeates consultation?
How do I maintain objectivity and independence and avoid being used by one faction of the organization?

Source: From the American Psychological Association (2007, p. 990).

or greater degrees dependent on the problem at hand. Further multilayer interventions should create a coherent intervention approach to ensure a "whole systems" design consistent with the theoretical foundation of consultation (e.g., Fuqua & Newman, 2002; Stanton, 2010). *Systems theory* is a way of thinking, understanding, and organizing one's approach to intervening in complex human behaviors. A system might be defined as "an ordered and comprehensive assemblage of facts, principles, doctrines... in a particular field of knowledge or thought" (*Random House Dictionary*, 1967, p. 1444). Counseling psychologists are well suited to take a "systems" approach to assessing and designing intervention strategies within each domain. The significance of Lewin's (1951) person–environment interaction, a precedent to more contemporary system theorists, has long been a part of counseling psychology given its historical emergence from vocational psychology. The relevance of counseling psychology's training in systems theory has oftentimes been ignored in contexts larger than small groups and therefore not actively considered in formulating assessment and interventions in larger organizational entities (Gallessich, 1985a; Gerstein & Shullman, 1992; Shullman, 2002).

Development of Curricula and Training in Consulting Psychology

The domain-specific competencies of consulting psychology are not intended to conflict or usurp those competencies established in clinical, counseling, school, or I/O specialties. Rather, the I-G-O model has been developed to guide the conceptualization and development of curricula that will support and integrate the 10 general competencies of professional psychology, as they are specifically relevant to the consultation practice in work and organizational settings.

BRIEF HISTORY OF PROGRESS

Since 1977 counseling psychologists have discussed the relevance of current counseling psychology curricula to consultation and recommended specific course and practice opportunities needed to create a well-prepared and knowledgeable consulting counseling psychologist (Foley & Redfering, 1987; Gallessich, 1985; Gerstein & Shullman, 1992; Leonard, 1977; Meade et al., 1982; Osipow, 1982). These early suggestions were efforts to encourage counseling psychologists to recognize the relevance and potential extension of their curriculum to open up market opportunities in workplace contexts. Twenty-five years later Shullman

(2002) and Fuqua and Newman (2002) responded as counseling psychologists to the Division 13's published account of expected competencies for consulting psychologists. Ironically, their remarks and recommendations reflect some of the same issues raised in previous decades. The crux of the dilemma that has inhibited the design of a curriculum for consulting psychology is twofold: (a) the debate regarding the degree to which consulting psychology represents a unique professional specialty, and (b) the lack of doctoral programs designed specifically to prepare consulting psychologists. The APA *Guidelines* (2007) have wrestled with both of these dilemmas and emerged with a resolution that allows multiple paths of professional psychology training toward proficiency in consulting psychology. Thus, they did not raise consulting psychology to the level of a professional specialty but carefully delineated the unique domains of practice competencies within the context of the general competencies of professional psychology. Nonetheless, there remains the translation of these unique competencies into a coherent curriculum design in order to be an option during doctoral training in professional psychology or in postdoctoral work. The challenges of designing specific coursework and practicum experiences to meet these competencies remain at this writing. However, significant contributions have been made toward this goal and have been reported through a series of papers since 2002 (American Psychological Association, 2007; Arredondo et al., 2004; Cooper, 2002; Fuqua & Newman, 2002; Sears, Rudisill, & Mason-Sears, 2006; Shullman, 2002; Stanton, 2010). There is a high level of agreement across these authors' recommendations for necessary skill sets in a consultation proficiency built on top of the foundation of a professional psychology specialty. The progression of competency acquisition across each developmental level is outlined in Stanton's report in the *Competency-Based Education for Professional Psychology* (Kenkel & Peterson, 2010).

There has also been progress on the identification of resources that contribute to foundational knowledge in consultation. DeWayne Kurpius, during his tenure as Education and Training Committee chair for SCP, created a consulting psychology reading list, which is published in the bibliography of the 2007 APA *Guidelines*. The bibliography includes seminal texts that are relevant to each of the I-G-O domain-specific competencies in consulting psychology. In 2007 O'Roark, "as a part of the SCP 1999 survey of 'the best of the century' reported the names of psychologists with the greatest influence on contemporary consulting psychologists" (American Psychological Association, 2007, p. 982). A perusal of the chapter listings for the *Handbook of Consulting Psychology* (Lowman et al., 2002) and *Consultation Skills for Mental Health Professionals* (Sears, Rudisill, & Mason-Sears, 2006) provides a comprehensive list of topics that are relevant to the teaching of consultation competencies. A comprehensive curriculum plan is not yet widely available. Although professional psychology programs have provided training in these areas for decades, we are now faced with developing courses, practica, internship, and postdoctoral experiences that are well articulated, delivered by knowledgeable faculty, and culminate in competent practice.

CURRENT OBSTACLES

There are significant obstacles to integrating consultation competencies into the training and education of professional psychologists in each of the specialties. Stanton (2010) identified the difficulties as follows:

> 1. Competition in the curriculum from other established core competencies
> 2. Lack formal academic coursework and high level of mastery in consultation practice of NCSPP faculty
> 3. Inadequate number of training sites for supervised consultation practice
> 4. Internship selection bias puts students with primarily consultation rather than mental health experience at a competitive disadvantage. (pp. 152–153)

The first step to overcoming these barriers is to provide incentives for faculty to incorporate consultation knowledge, attitudes, and skills in existing courses or to recognize the increasing viability of consultation practice in the marketplace. Counseling psychology programs would find a satisfying coherence between historical roots in the workplace, vocational counseling, strength-based counseling, and systems thinking, and consultation theory and practice. Considerable work is needed in the development of practice sites in which well-trained supervisors and mentors are available to guide the learning through the required developmental achievements. At the internship level, potential sites that emphasize consultation and training roles over provision of mental health services need to be considered viable alternatives to more traditional sites and be encouraged to seek APA internship accreditation. Students cannot be asked to jeopardize their potential for licensure or certification because they follow consultation proficiency within their specialty. There has been tremendous progress in defining consulting psychology within the larger context of professional psychology over the last decade. Competencies have been conceptualized, organized, and defined, making the development of curriculum a logical extension of this work. Even with these achievements, the question remains whether consultation practice is evidence based.

Evidence-Based Practice

The APA *Guidelines* (2007) for consultation competency adhere to the scientist-practitioner model of training, thus endorsing the view that the science of psychology must guide the consultant's choice of interventions and assessment methodologies. It is expected that consulting psychologists will use empirical data to determine the best match between the identified goal, client characteristics, and intervention approach. In their 2002 critique of the competency principles recommended by SCP, Fuqua and Newman posed the question, "Is consulting psychology a science-based practice or the application of experience-based judgments?" (p. 228).

META-ANALYTIC REVIEWS

As early as 1991, Gibson and Froehle reviewed the empirical literature in consultation and concluded that there was empirical literature to substantiate organizational interventions. Subsequently, there have been a number of meta-analytic reviews that offer cumulative evidence for different types of consultation practices, for example, mental health consultation (Gibson, 1991; Gibson & Chard, 1994), organization development (Baer, 2004; Neuman, Edwards, & Raju, 1989), and leadership development programs (Collins & Holton, 2004). In a meta-analytic study of 1,643 consultation outcomes, Gibson and Chard (1994) found a moderate effect size of .562. Their review included studies on typical consultation interventions such as mental health consultation, organizational development, participative decision making, problem-solving interventions, team-building interventions, training and development, management by objective (MBO), and goal setting. Neuman et al. (1989) concluded from their analysis of 126 studies that multifaceted interventions have been more effective in modifying satisfaction and attitudes of workers than was the use of singular techniques. In fact, team building and lab training were the most effective in changing attitudes and creating satisfaction. Collins and Holton (2004) studied 83 studies from 1982 to 2001 that used formal training interventions. They examined the effects of these programs on performance, knowledge, and expertise at the individual, team, and organizational levels. They concluded from the data that practitioners can make substantial improvements in both the knowledge and skills of leaders *if* sufficient assessment is conducted to make the right developmental fit between the program offered and the leaders to whom it is offered.

These are only a few examples of the meta-analytic studies that are available in the organizational and human resource development literature. However, they represent a total of approximately 1,900 studies in consultation that have been published between 1982 and 2004 that contribute to substantial effect size in meta-analytic studies. However, despite sufficient evidence upon which to base some types of interventions, Blanton (2010) found that research played a relatively minor role in practitioners' design and implementation of intervention strategies. Consultants use discussions with colleagues, professional judgment, and experience to determine a course of action. She points out that consulting psychologists could profit from viewing evidence-based practice as not merely applying research findings to any situation, but rather using the research to discover general truths and through dialectic exchange with others in the local field of practice discerning a specific application that has a high probability of success.

METHODS

Blanton (2010), former president of Division 13, has called for increased diversity of methods that responds to real-time concerns of consultants in the field. Over the last 30 years there have been relatively few counseling psychologists who have contributed to the research literature in the field of consultation (Shullman, 2002). However, with the increasing defection of counseling psychologists from direct delivery of mental health services and movement into consultation environments whether in education or corporate organizations, there is an excellent opportunity for counseling psychologists to use their diverse methodological skills and content expertise to contribute to the empirical literature. As evidenced in this volume, counseling psychologists are experienced investigators of process and outcome studies, diversity in the workplace, vocational assessment, career counseling in workplace environments, and supervisory practice. As important, counseling psychologists have a history of embracing innovative methodologies that accommodate the complexity of the phenomenon being studied. Qualitative methods have become more prevalent in the counseling psychology literature since the mid-1990s and are being regularly taught in the curriculum of accredited programs. The use of evaluation, action research, and sophisticated multiple case study designs are all well suited to the study of consultation practice. New qualitative methods such as situational analysis (a postmodern approach to grounded theory; Clarke, 2005) and narrative methods for organizational and communication research (Boje, 2001) offer tools that can add clarity and organization to the complexity and dynamic unfolding of consultative practice.

Conclusion

The practice of consultation whether in mental health, education, or corporations is already part of the counseling psychologist's professional activity. As health maintenance organizations continue to use masters-level practitioners to deliver direct services and constrict the type and length of services in the marketplace, counseling psychologists will look to other avenues to utilize their knowledge and training. In the 1970s and 1980s prior to the push for licensure to receive third-party payments, counseling psychologists were recognizing the potential value and market in business and organizational contexts for their skills. The historical development of the field in vocational counseling and the workplace, the strength-based approach to maximize human development within the context in which clients work and live, and the process-oriented approach to understanding change are all strengths of counseling psychology relevant to consulting. Counseling psychologists have already made important contributions to the development of a competency-based proficiency in consulting; however, there is a great deal left to do in curriculum development, evaluation of competencies in the field, supervised practice settings, and research methodologies that contribute to evidence-based practice. Counseling psychology can add substantially to this burgeoning professional field and promote a growing class of *consulting counseling psychologists.*

Notes

1. Heretofore referred to as *Guidelines.*
2. The authors would like to express their gratitude to Graduate Reference Librarian Deborah Baldwin for her assistance in creating the bibliographic searches for Chapters 8 and 9.

TEN

Competence in Research

In this chapter we review the literature on professional competencies in research and then discuss this competence in relation to counseling psychology. As has been noted throughout this book, the competencies that have been published about professional practice in psychology are generic in scope, and this is true with respect to the competencies outlined for research, which are designed to cut across all specialties of professional psychology. Here we present brief examples of the research competencies that have been proposed for professional competence, and we discuss research in a way that is consistent with the scope of professional practice and inquiry in counseling psychology. We point to areas in counseling psychology where research activity has been particularly strong, and we review methodologies that have been used by counseling psychologists in research over the past several decades. The reader will note that counseling psychologists have used virtually every method available to psychologists to conduct research, and that in some areas counseling psychology has made notable contributions to the literature, both in terms of the knowledge advanced in professional psychology and in the methods devised for such research.

Research Competency Models

THE CB MODEL

The competencies benchmarks (CB; Fouad et al., 2009) model treats competence in research as a functional competence, though the foundational area called "scientific knowledge and methods" covers some of the content inherent in knowing how to use and conduct research in professional psychology. For example, scientific knowledge and methods includes the ability to evaluate the methodology of studies and the scientific basis of findings. This is essential to effective practice, given our professional responsibility to keep up with advances in knowledge and techniques in professional psychology. Likewise, the functional area of research notes the need for competence in "understanding of research methods and techniques of data analysis" (Fouad et al., 2009, p. S21). The overlap, close association, and interplay between what is foundational and functional in professional psychology are evident in the professional area of research. In our minds this is such a close relationship that making the distinction between foundation and function in research is more of an academic exercise than a practical reality in professional practice. Without foundational knowledge in research methods and design, as well as some basic but sound understanding of statistics, functional competence in research is impossible.

Two additional foundational competency areas that seem relevant to functional competence in research are ethics and individual and cultural diversity. Ethics is very important because there are very clear and enforceable guidelines published by the American Psychological Association for conducting research and for protecting human participants. These guidelines also reflect federal laws, for example, the Health Insurance Portability and Accountability Act, which was enacted by the US Congress to ensure the security and privacy of patients' health information. The CB model (Fouad et al., 2009) delineates the following three competency areas in ethics: (a) knowledge of ethical, legal, and professional standards and guidelines; (b) awareness and application of ethical decision making; and (c) ethical conduct. Each of these domains contains benchmarks organized by developmental level, which are readiness for practicum, readiness for internship, and readiness for entry to practice. For example, in area "b" called awareness and application of ethical decision making, at the level of readiness for entry to practice, the following competency is noted: "applies applicable ethics concepts in research design and subject treatment" (Fouad et al., 2009, p. S15). Likewise, the American Psychological Association's (APA) Ethical Principles of Psychologists and Code of Conduct delineate several standards of ethical behavior that are specific to research. These standards include the following: (a) receiving institutional approval; (b) obtaining informed consent after clarifying to participants risks, rights, and limitations; (c) protecting prospective participants from adverse consequences of declining or withdrawing from participation; (d) when research participation is a course requirement or an opportunity for extra credit, the prospective participant is given the choice of equitable alternative activities; (e) offering reasonable and appropriate inducements to potential participants; and (f) debriefing participants. Counseling psychologists are trained to meet these standards in conducting research and are assessed of this knowledge via course, comprehensive examinations, and as part of their thesis and dissertation projects.

The CB model (Fouad et al., 2009) includes individual and cultural diversity as a foundational area, and in 2003 the American Psychological Association published guidelines for professional psychologists who work with multicultural populations. We believe that these two documents are relevant to research competence in several ways. The APA guidelines state the following: "culturally sensitive psychological researchers are encouraged to recognize the importance of conducting culture-centered and ethical psychological research among persons from ethnic/linguistic and racial minority backgrounds" (p. 388). In these guidelines, researchers are to include theoretical frameworks that address cultural diversity and to devise research questions and designs that are consistent with and appropriate given the populations under study. Researchers are also encouraged to conduct assessments using measures with psychometric properties that are appropriate given the samples/populations included in the studies and to make informed analyses and interpretations that are sensitive to the cultural phenomena and to the experience of the participants in the research. The CB model encourages professionals to develop awareness of themselves, others, and of their professional interactions as shaped by racial and cultural diversity. This awareness seems particularly relevant to how persons are approached, prepared, and treated by researchers, and consistent with the APA guidelines listed earlier, with how research questions and hypotheses are formulated, investigated, and discussed. All these efforts require that researchers be knowledgeable about and sensitive to cultural factors and to the special needs of the populations/participants that they include in research. Given the traditional focus of counseling psychology on person–environment interactions and on multicultural counseling, these guidelines are particularly relevant to the specialty.

Another foundational area of competence identified by the CB model (Fouad et al., 2009) involves work in interdisciplinary systems. This is certainly relevant to much of the research that counseling psychologists conduct, and it is also relevant to their work in evaluation. The CB model defines interdisciplinary systems as "knowledge of key issues and concepts in related disciplines. Identify and interact with professionals in multiple disciplines" (p. S15). The four domains for this area are as follows: (a) knowledge of the shared and distinctive contributions of other professions, (b) functioning in multidisciplinary and interdisciplinary contexts, (c) understanding how participation in interdisciplinary collaboration/consultation enhances outcomes, and (d) respectful and productive relationships with individuals from other professions. These competency areas are applicable to researchers in counseling psychology since we tend to work in teams across departments and universities as well as with members of other professions, including medicine, nursing, clinical psychology, school counseling, and with administrators from various agencies.

THE EPPP

For its part, the Examination for Professional Practice in Psychology (EPPP) from the Association of State and Provincial Psychology Boards includes approximately 14 items (8%) that pertain specifically to research methods and statistics. As mentioned in previous chapters, we see the EPPP as a good measure of foundational competence in professional psychology. The section on research methods and statistics in the EPPP is described as "knowledge of (a) research design, methodology, and program evaluation, (b) instrument selection and validation, (c) statistical models, assumptions, and procedures, and (d) dissemination methods" (Association of State and Provincial Psychology Boards, 2009, p. 20). There are eight subdomains listed, including knowledge of "Sampling and data collection... Design of case studies, correlational, quasi-experimental and experimental studies... Analytic methods: qualitative (e.g., thematic, phenomenological)...and critical appraisal and application of research findings" (pp. 20–21). These areas represent foundational (and in our view also functional) knowledge that is consistent with the professional preparation of counseling psychologists. When these content areas are properly assimilated, they lead to professional competence in scientific thinking, in the critical use of evidence dictated by the movement toward evidence-based professional practice, and to general competence in areas such as therapy, supervision, research, and consultation in counseling psychology.

THE NCSPP MODEL

The research competencies outlined by Trierweiler, Stricker, and Peterson (2010) for the National Council of Schools and Programs of Professional Psychology (NCSPP) practitioner-scholar model of training include the following three competency domains: (a) critical evaluation of research, (b) conducting and using research in applied settings, and (c) ethics and professional competence. Each domain is organized into three developmental levels: begin practicum, begin internship, complete doctoral degree; and the competencies are organized into skills, knowledge, and attitudes. A sample skill at the level of complete doctoral degree in the critical evaluation of research domain is the "ability to critically evaluate research literature in terms of applicability to specific clinical questions" (p. 127). A sample knowledge competency at the level of complete doctoral degree in conducting and using research in applied settings is "understanding of how to build new practice methods and adjust interventions based on new evidence" (p. 127). A sample attitude competency at the level of complete doctoral degree in the ethics and professional competence domain is "commitment to the importance of research and evaluation in ongoing inquiry and lifelong learning" (p. 129).

The NCSPP model identifies competence in research in the form of the local clinical scientist model/concept. Trierweiler et al. (2010) note that this model helps the clinician focus on the relevant scientific issues in a specific (i.e., local) domain of practice. They note that going beyond the application of science (as in the scientist-practitioner model), the local clinical scientist model promotes complexity, critical thinking, and scientific inquiry. They note that this model provides a "bridge" between science and practice, and add that "in keeping with the helping goal that is intrinsic to the professional practice, the local clinical scientist model demands that the empirical truths of particular cases in particular clinical settings provide the ultimate criteria for the success of professional inquiry" (p. 126). It is difficult for us to argue with the value of this particular line of reasoning, but we would argue that the scientist-practitioner model as practiced in counseling psychology provides the kind of competence that these authors mention, particularly the capacity for scientific and critical thinking, the ability to consume and extend knowledge and research, and how to use and apply findings in the context of specific cases. This line of reasoning is also highly consistent with the principles developed by Wampold et al., (2002), and discussed in Chapter 6, to guide counseling psychologists in the practice of evidence-based professional practice (e.g., that the selection of treatments and their effectiveness should be assessed locally and freedom of choice for psychologists and clients should be recognized). The better contrast to the local clinical scientist model may be the empirically supported movement within clinical psychology, which eschews the local "empirical truths" inherent in clinical cases, and that greatly diminishes the role of clinician judgment and experience, as well as client needs/expectations/strengths, the clinical relationship, and other relevant factors in the process and outcome of treatment. It seems important at this point in the chapter to discuss the model of research training in counseling psychology, including the developmental nature of training and the content covered in most programs.

Training in Research in Counseling Psychology

THE PHD AND THE PSYD

In discussing research competence in counseling psychology, it is important to highlight the underlying philosophical framework that constitutes training in the specialty and that, at least in theory, links research with practice. It is essential to the work of the counseling psychologist that he or she has an understanding of the knowledge bases of practice and their associated empirical evidence. The scientist-practitioner model of training dictates the systematic evaluation and thoughtful analysis of human behavior and experience, the thoughtful application of knowledge available, and the evaluation of outcome and of the effectiveness of the knowledge applied (Meara et al., 1988). The scientist-practitioner model prepares and demands from psychologists the use of empirical evidence in selecting and using assessments and interventions across professional activities, as well as the advancement and refinement of knowledge of relevance to practice through the conduct and accumulation of rigorous research. The competence of a scientist-practitioner can be characterized as having the ability to think and practice scientifically, critically, and reflectively (Gelso, 1979; Goodyear & Benton, 1986; Pepinsky & Pepinsky, 1954). Given that most graduates of counseling psychology programs conduct very little to no research after receiving their PhD, there has been some debate about the practical value of the scientist-practitioner model of training (Heppner, Kivlighan, & Wampold, 2008) and alternative models have been adopted. In 1973, the American Psychological Association endorsed the PsyD model (practitioner scholar) as appropriate to train individuals less interested in conducting research and more intent on working exclusively in the direct delivery of professional services. The PsyD model has been adopted by a handful of counseling psychology programs in the United States and by the National Council of Schools and Programs of Professional Psychology (NCSPP). Despite the advent of this model and its popularity among PsyD clinical psychology programs, the overwhelming majority of counseling psychology programs still adhere to the PhD degree and continue to follow the guidelines of the scientist-practitioner model. In essence, the belief in these programs is that the scientist-practitioner model promotes the best possible training for students who wish to learn about and conduct research, and to use research findings to advance their clinical work. As professionals, this model trains students to think critically, scientifically, and with complexity.

TRAINING IN STATISTICS

We have noted the overlap between foundational and functional competence in research. There is also a developmental/incremental sequence in scientific research training in counseling psychology that becomes increasingly complex and applied. Doctoral students in counseling psychology are generally expected to have, upon graduation, knowledge competence in fundamental areas of statistics. Basic training in the foundations of statistics includes knowledge of probability theory, measures of central tendency, and descriptive statistics, including variance, standard deviation, and standard error of measurement and standard error of estimate (Betz & Fassinger, 2012). Intermediate training would include knowledge of inferential statistics, including sum of squares, the t-test, confidence intervals and effect sizes, and analysis of variance. More advanced training would include knowledge of effect sizes, correlation, and multivariate statistics, including regression, multivariate analysis of variance, discriminant analysis, and factor analysis. Sound training, to the comfort of students, would begin at a basic foundational level, and with proper feedback and evaluation would progress to fairly advanced levels of statistical sophistication. The reader is referred to a chapter by the counseling psychologists Nancy E. Betz and Ruth E. Fassinger (2012) for a thoughtful and helpful description of research design and statistics covered in doctoral training and used in professional practice in counseling psychology research.

Parenthetically, we note that in the last 10 years or so it has become routine for research published in the *Journal of Counseling Psychology* and in *The Counseling Psychologist* to include analyses of multilevel models that examine casual models and analyses of moderation and mediation variables with powerful techniques such as structural equation modeling (SEM), multilevel modeling (MLM), and latent growth curve modeling (LGM). Indeed, the level of statistical analyses that has become common place in training and in use in counseling psychology research has evolved considerably in just a decade or so, and it has become so advanced that many of us who graduated from counseling psychology programs 15 or 20 years ago have had to seek further training to keep up with these advances, not only as researchers but as consumers of the research being advanced by more recently trained counseling psychologists.

TRAINING IN RESEARCH DESIGN

Academic training in research design is complex and, to many students, a challenging aspect of their training. Doctoral students in counseling psychology are generally expected to have, upon graduation, knowledge competence in several areas of design. Knowledge areas covered and assessed include the ethics of conducting research, how to derive research questions and hypotheses, how to identify and formulate scientific research questions, how to conduct probability sampling and randomization of participants, knowledge about threats to validity (including internal, external, putative cause and effects, and statistical conclusion validity), and the mechanisms as well as strengths and limitations of various designs, including full experiments and quasi-experimental designs, correlational/passive research designs, and single-subject and time series designs. The most commonly used text on this topic in counseling psychology is *Research Design in Counseling*, by the counseling psychologists P. Paul Heppner, Dennis M. Kivlighan Jr., and Bruce Wampold (2008).

DEVELOPMENTAL TRAINING IN RESEARCH

As highlighted by Heppner et al. and in the Model Training Program (MTP) in counseling psychology (Murdock, Alcorn, Heesacker, & Stoltenberg, 1998), the practical "how to" training in research competence in counseling psychology is ideally developmental in that students begin their training and learning with simple assignments as part of research teams being directed and supervised by faculty in the program. Such "simple" assignments include survey coding, data entry, conducting library and Internet searches for literature, and collection of data or "running of subjects" to use a more historical term in psychology. More advanced participation involves students in designing research questions and hypotheses, preparing documents for institutional review boards, selecting measures and scales with which to collect data, collecting data in sensitive situations such as before or after counseling sessions, collecting data in the laboratory (e.g., in counseling analog designs), or collecting data from participants in interviews or related qualitative methodologies. A yet more advanced level of participation would include assisting and receiving supervision with data analysis, content analysis of "word data" as in qualitative research, and participating in writing and in the preparation of manuscripts based on research. Thus, at the end of training, counseling psychology graduates not only possess a great deal of knowledge about statistics and research design but also a sophisticated skill level in conducting and evaluating research.

EVALUATIONS FOR COMPETENCE IN RESEARCH

In most programs in counseling psychology students are required to demonstrate competence in research via course examinations evaluated with letter grades. They are also evaluated on knowledge via a comprehensive examination that is often comprised of a broad essay question or an assignment where students critically evaluate research articles and propose ways to advance the studies reviewed (e.g., quantitatively, qualitatively, or both) or improve the research design and analysis of the articles examined. Competence in research training is also established and evaluated via a masters-level thesis or some equivalent research competency project that is guided by a faculty advisor and evaluated by a faculty committee. The culminating research competence project in graduate training in counseling psychology is the completion of a doctoral dissertation prior to graduation. This research study is undertaken by the graduate student working independently but with the support and guidance of a faculty member, and it is required to be of such depth and scope that it represents an original contribution to the knowledge base in counseling psychology. We add then that two competencies that are expected of a PhD graduate in counseling psychology would be the ability to conduct independent research that is of sufficient quality to contribute to the knowledge base in the specialty, and the ability to evaluate research critically, to the point of being able to identify flaws and strengths in any study in the specialty.

MAXIMIZING TRAINING, COMPETENCE, AND PRODUCTIVITY

After discussing the normal challenges associated with research training in graduate programs, Heppner, Kivlighan, and Wampold (2007) cite Gelso's (1979, 2006) compilation of observations on factors that maximize training and competence in counseling psychology. While including the entire list of observations here is prohibitive, we would like to note some of these gems as they reflect skills, knowledge, and attitude competencies that can enhance research training. These include having training programs

> organize early and minimally threatening involvement in research training, uncouple the artificial connection between research

> and statistics, teach students to integrate their own experiences with the findings in the research literature to facilitate involvement and thinking, provide more explicit training on how science and practice can be wedded, emphasize the suitability of multiple research methodologies for different research questions, develop more social activities within the research enterprise, such as research teams, and continually emphasize the role of scientific thinking in graduate training.
>
> (Heppner, Kivlighan, & Wampold, 2007, p. 27, citing Gelso, 1979, 2006)

Gelso and Fretz (2001) make similar recommendations, leading us to observe that a unique quality and aim in research training in counseling psychology is the social, developmental, nonthreatening approach that emphasizes logic and design to investigating phenomena that are personally interesting and meaningful to students.

In terms of empirical evidence on the topic of research training, competence, and productivity, Mallinckrodt and Gelso (2002) examined longitudinal data from 325 counseling psychology graduates who had participated in an earlier study that examined predictors of research productivity (Royalty, Gelso, Mallinckrodt, & Garrett, 1986). Mallinckrodt and Gelso (2002) found that two specific factors in the research training environment (RTE) were associated with productivity for male graduates, namely their faculty modeling appropriate scientific behavior, and these students having been shown that science can be a social experience (e.g., through advising and the student–advisor relationship, and by participation in research teams). For women, the only RTE factor marginally associated with research productivity was the untying of statistics from research and the reinforcement of the logic of science and of research. Mallinckrodt and Gelso also found that the Holland Investigative personality type was slightly associated with productivity for both men and women, but that better distinctions could be discerned between the highly productive and low productive programs. Training programs from which highly productive students graduated were more likely to emphasize faculty modeling of research and scientific behavior, to reinforce students' scientific behavior, and to provide early involvement in research. Mallinckrodt and Gelso (2002) conclude that faculty modeling, early involvement, positive reinforcement, and observational learning in a social context appear to be the best predictors of research activity and productivity in counseling psychology training. These predictors represent small effect sizes and thus are marginal, leading us to conclude that, while all students graduating from PhD programs can be considered competent to conduct research at a fairly sophisticated level, the factors associated with productivity of research remain largely unknown, clearly go beyond competence and the research training environment, and involve a personality dimension and career orientation goal that has yet to be uncovered.

RIGOR VERSUS RELEVANCE

As noted in previous chapters, Charles J. Gelso and Bruce Fretz (2001) have written what many consider to be the authoritative text about counseling psychology. In their book, they discuss an interesting dichotomy in research that is irresolvable and represents a decision point for any professional psychologist conducting research. The issue is one of inevitable tension between the *rigor* versus *relevance* of research. We note this because we feel that knowledge about the limitations of all research designs, and knowledge that all research is flawed in some way, is a fact of scholarly life and a basic knowledge and attitude competence with which we all have to come to terms in our scientific work. As Gelso and Fretz point out, to the extent to which the researcher attends to questions of *internal validity*, for example, by conducting carefully controlled research in the laboratory using experimental or quasi-experimental designs, he or she inevitably compromises on the *external validity* or "relevance" of the research. That is, by attending to questions of internal validity, the extent to which the research can be generalized to practice in the field is compromised. There is an inverse relationship between internal validity and external validity, and a skill competence on the part of the counseling psychologist is being able to select research designs that address the most salient and important questions in the area of inquiry being investigated. We would add that while researchers in counseling psychology have been leaning in favor of external validity considerations for some time, they have been publishing research with relevance to practice that is nonetheless of high *scientific rigor*. They are doing so by deriving complex and elegant research questions, by using sound procedures and measures with strong psychometric properties, and by using powerful statistical analyses. Thus, while the rigor of carefully calibrated laboratory studies and analog experiments has been de-emphasized in counseling psychology research in the last two decades, the scientific rigor of field research with relevance to practice has not only not diminished but in our view has increased significantly in that time.

Qualitative Methodology and Counseling Psychology

Concomitant with the increasing use of complex and sophisticated statistical analyses that have become commonplace in published research in counseling psychology, counseling psychologists have also made greater use of what are termed *qualitative designs* in their research. The trends toward sophistication and alternative methodologies were already evident two decades ago and identified by Gelso and Fassinger (1990) in their *Annual Review of Psychology* paper as an unequivocal trend in counseling psychology research. Qualitative designs are approaches to investigation that do not follow the scientific method but represent serious, sophisticated, and challenging approaches to inquiry. As Gelso and Fassinger noted, qualitative methods are often used to examine practice in the field (e.g., examining in-session events in counseling), to foster the development of theory and to augment training practices, and in some instances to move areas of inquiry forward where there are equivocal results accumulated from traditional quantitative designs or when research in certain areas has stagnated. Much of what qualitative researchers examine in counseling psychology is directed at professional practice to explain and demonstrate how, why, and when assessments and interventions work in professional practice, and to provide the description and understanding that is often missing from numbers and tables generated by traditional scientific research. Another laudable goal of qualitative research in counseling psychology is to stimulate further quantitative inquiry that follows from its discoveries.

CONTRIBUTIONS OF COUNSELING PSYCHOLOGISTS TO QUALITATIVE RESEARCH

Counseling psychologists have without a doubt conducted a significant amount of qualitative research in the last 20 years, and in some cases they have led the field of psychology in using qualitative designs and by devising new methodologies. A primary example of this kind of contribution is the development of *Consensual Qualitative Research (CQR)*, a descriptive, inductive methodology created by the counseling psychologist Clara E. Hill and her colleagues based on other qualitative approaches, including grounded theory (Strauss & Corbin, 1998), phenomenology (Giorgi, 1985), and comprehensive process analysis (Elliott, 1989). While CQR was developed for use with interview data, Hill has now modified the approach for use with short, simple data (CQR-M) and for use with case studies (CQR-C). The reader is referred to Hill (2011) for an easy-to-read description of how CQR studies are conducted and for a description of several studies already published using this methodology. Betz and Fassinger (2012) also present an excellent discussion of paradigmatic bases and epistemological stances of qualitative research in counseling psychology, including *positivist* and *postpositivist, constructivists-interpretivist,* and *critical-ideological paradigms.* These authors also present easy-to-read descriptions of the following qualitative research methods: *grounded theory method, narratology* (Murray, 2003), *ethnography* (Patton, 2002), *phenomenology,* and *participatory action research* (Kidd & Kral, 2005). They also present criteria that can be used to evaluate qualitative research, which centers on the trustworthiness or credibility of the endeavor (Morrow, 2005). Betz and Fassinger cite the criteria developed by Morrow (2005), which includes the social validity or social value of the study, the subjectivity of the findings as reflecting the data in the project and not the opinions of the researcher, and the adequacy or informative value of the data.

CONSENSUS ON METHODOLOGICAL PLURALISM

Having noted the increasing use and popularity of CQR and qualitative methodology, we believe that at the present time there is a consensus in counseling psychology that quantitative, qualitative, and mixed-methods designs are needed, valued, and should be further promoted for use by researchers in the specialty. While there are strong opinions in the specialty about the merits and limitations of both quantitative and qualitative designs, there is a palpable sense in counseling psychology about the need for flexibility and triangulation in research, since contemporary research questions about professional practice dictate the use of various methods and approaches of inquiry (Betz & Fassinger, 2012). Whether that viewpoint in the specialty persists over the long term remains to be seen. We believe that the premium placed on methodological pluralism will continue to have merit and will be maintained in the years ahead.

Sample Research Published by Counseling Psychologists

Turning now to the content of the research published by counseling psychologists, Buboltz, Deemer, and Hoffman (2010) recently published a content analysis of articles published in the *Journal of Counseling Psychology* (*JCP*) between 1999 and 2009. In their analysis they included 514 articles, and consistent with the methodology used for a similar analysis conducted

TABLE 10.1 Categories of Articles Published in the *Journal of Counseling Psychology*

Outcome research	Process research	Process and outcome research
Counselor training and supervision	Research on attitudes and beliefs about counselors	Multiculturalism and/or diversity
Personality and adjustment research	Academic achievement	Research on vocational behavior
Research on the development and evaluation of tests and measures	Research methods and statistics	Research reviews
Theoretical articles	Interpersonal and/or social support and/or attachment	Miscellaneous

Source: From Buboltz, Deemer, and Hoffman (2010).

in 1999 (Buboltz, Miller, & Williams), organized them into 15 categories (see Table 10.1).

These categories are included here to provide the reader with an overview of the content areas examined by researchers published in the most prestigious journal in counseling psychology. Buboltz et al. (2010) found for the 10-year period examined the five primary areas that made up 57% of all the articles published were the following: (1) multiculturalism and/or diversity, (2) research on development and evaluation of tests and measures, (3) personality and adjustment, (4) outcome research, and (5) interpersonal and/or social support and/or attachment. Buboltz et al. noted the marked decrease in process and outcome research from their review published in 1999, covering the period between 1973 and 1988; it was ranked first in 1999 and tenth in 2010. They explained the increase in the quantity of research published in the area of multiculturalism/diversity as consistent with the mission of *JCP* and the increased globalization and diversification of counseling psychology. Buboltz et al. also noted that perhaps the decrease in psychotherapy research published in *JCP* was due to a decrease in the quality of psychotherapy research being conducted in counseling psychology coupled with the very high standards for publication in place at *JCP*. They also speculated that perhaps more counseling psychologists interested in psychotherapy have gravitated to Division 29 of the APA (Psychotherapy) and its journal *Psychotherapy: Theory, Research, Practice, and Training*, and to the Society for Psychotherapy and its journal, *Psychotherapy Research*. Buboltz et al. (2010) also reported that the largest group of participants across the categories was college students (i.e., 40% of the total number of participants).

Scheel and colleagues (2011) also conducted a search and content analysis of all articles published from 1978 to 2008 in the two most important journals for counseling psychologists, *The Counseling Psychologist* and *JCP*. They examined the number and percentages of articles published that were counseling related. Like Buboltz et al. (2010), Scheel et al. uncovered a stark decline in the number of articles dealing with counseling/psychotherapy published in both journals, particularly in *JCP*. The authors lamented this decrease since as they note, counseling psychologists have reported consistently over decades up to the present that their primary activity of work is counseling/psychotherapy. Indeed, the title of the Scheel et al. paper is "Whatever Happened to Counseling in Counseling Psychology?" They offer four explanations for the observed decrease. Like Buboltz et al. (2010), Scheel and his colleagues posit that perhaps the quality of the research in studies of counseling and psychotherapy has not kept up with the very high expectations for sophisticated designs and statistical analyses in *JCP*. They also note that counseling psychologists have been increasingly active and publishing in the psychotherapy journals of Division 29 and of the Society for Psychotherapy Research. Scheel et al. also suggest that the fascination in counseling psychology with multiculturalism, diversity, and social justice might have supplanted the interest of researchers who might otherwise study psychotherapy. They further suggest that Bruce Wampold's meta-analytic findings about the equivalency of treatments may have stifled interest and further research about psychotherapy process and outcome. While we concur with many of the observations made by Scheel et al., our collective experience is that publishing in the psychotherapy journals is as challenging and rigorous as in *JCP*; however, more and more counseling psychologists have moved addresses and made Division 29 and SPR their intellectual homes, given the exclusive focus of these organizations to studying counseling and psychotherapy. The first author of this book has been recognized as a leading multicultural researcher in the United States, and yet he laments that not enough research is being conducted linking multiculturalism with counseling and psychotherapy. This is clearly an opportunity for counseling psychologists to explore in future research.

THEMES FROM THE JOURNAL *PSYCHOTHERAPY*

The counseling psychologist Charles J. Gelso (2011) recently reflected on his 6 years as editor of the journal *Psychotherapy: Theory, Research, Practice, and Training* and noted the prevalence of six themes or trends in the research published in the journal during his tenure as editor. These trends are important to note since they present us with an indication of where the research and practice of psychotherapy is heading but also because they denote the type of knowledge, skills, and attitudes that will be required by researchers, including counseling psychologists, if these trends are to be sustained. The first theme is the increasing integration in research of specific therapy techniques with the therapeutic relationship; Gelso sees techniques and the relationship as dependent on one another, and their interplay has gained increasing attention in research designs and hypotheses tested. Gelso also notes the increasing focus on theoretical integration, which has come about from the proliferation of various therapies and from attempts by theoreticians to weave a parsimonious nomological net from the various theories and techniques in the literature. Another theme is increasing efforts at research-practice integration, spurred by researchers using a wider arrange of scientific approaches with closer relevance to clinical practice, including qualitative approaches. The fourth trend observed is the increases in more specific, integrative reviews of theory and technique, which Gelso values because such reviews highlight what we know and do not know about psychotherapy and treatment (and these reviews are now more and more data-based and use the standard index of an effect size to better guide the reader). The integration of biological, neuroscience understandings is the fifth trend, which Gelso summarizes by noting "the newest neurobiological evidence not only demonstrates how neurobiology affects intrapsychic events and behavior, but how experiences, including the psychotherapy relationship, affect and change the structure of the brain" (p. 16). The final theme is the integration of diversity and cultural considerations into psychotherapy, with increasing emphasis on examining cultural factors in process and outcome in treatment. He discusses each in terms of its impact on the field of psychotherapy and their implications for where the field of psychotherapy is heading. Clearly the operative word is integration, not the blending in or mixing of various factors but their assemblage as parts that seems to hold promise for enhanced service delivery in assessment and intervention in psychotherapy. The ability for counseling psychology researchers to think critically, to be able to take the proverbial architectural "exploded" view of parts and structures, to examine their qualities and potential for interaction with other parts and structures, and then to be able to assemble them into an integrated and parsimonious whole, in our case the integration of psychotherapy parts and components to enhance service delivery, seems increasingly important and necessary.

REVIEW OF *HANDBOOK OF COUNSELING PSYCHOLOGY*

Another good source for examining the type of research and scientific thinking engaging counseling psychologists is Brown and Lent's *Handbook of Counseling Psychology*, which is now in its fourth edition. In examining the third (2000) and fourth editions (2008), it is apparent that the basic organization of the handbook has remained highly similar. There are broad sections on professional and scientific issues, on career and vocational psychology, on counseling interventions, and on development and prevention. In the fourth edition, a fifth section was added, entitled "diversity and multicultural psychology." Consistent with the observations mentioned earlier by Buboltz et al. (2010) and Scheel et al. (in press), multiculturalism has made a substantial gain in the field of counseling psychology, and the fourth edition of the handbook allots 10 chapters (out of a total of 34) on this topic, including chapters on multicultural competence, social class and classism, gender, sexual orientation, disability, race and culture in counseling and psychotherapy, social justice, and the growing internationalization of counseling psychology. The third edition included 4 chapters on the topic, out of a total of 25. Thus, while the handbook continues to address traditional topics in counseling psychology, such as prevention, counseling process and outcome, and career/vocational psychology, the area with the fastest rate of growth as reflected in the handbook is multiculturalism, broadly defined. This evolution is highly consistent with the mission of Division 17, the Society of Counseling Psychology, and is also consistent with the development of other helping professions within psychology and in medicine. In behavioral medicine, for example, it is now essential that service delivery models incorporate or address biology, psychology, sociology, and culture in the person/patient. We would also note that in terms of content, counseling psychologists have also made significant contributions in the knowledge base in some of the areas covered as chapters in the current book, particularly vocational psychology, supervision, and consultation. Perhaps the most significant contribution made by counseling psychologists in the area of counseling and psychotherapy (as noted in Chapter 6) has been the now five decades of pioneering research on therapist interventions or response modes, and the work that evolved from that research into the examination of the process of therapy (see Hill & Williams, 2000; Hill, 2011).

Epilogue

Writing this book has provided us, the authors, with an overview of the specialty and an affirmation of the values and depth that continue to characterize counseling psychology. We certainly hope that we have provided the reader with an overview and an appreciation for the science, values, and depth of counseling psychology. While the models of professional competency reviewed in this book are intended to be generic to professional psychology practice across specialties, it is clear to us that these models reflect professional practice in the specialty of counseling psychology. And this is as it should be. Counseling psychologists such as Nadya Fouad have been instrumental in devising these professional competencies; moreover, as noted in this book, there has been an evolution in the practice of counseling psychology such that the specialty is now in many ways similar to clinical psychology. Nonetheless, counseling psychology remains distinct as a professional specialty, with its own history, traditions, and characteristics shaped by historical, empirical, and philosophical frameworks of psychology. While the current practice of counseling psychology adheres to the standards of professional practice from state licensing boards and accrediting agencies like the American Psychological Association, the specialty can still be described in terms of its history, philosophical flavor, and Gelso and Fretz's (2001) unifying principles discussed throughout this book, that is, its focus mainly on strengths and assets of fairly normal persons, its attention to person–environment interactions and the phenomenology and socialization of the individual, its particular focus on career and vocational problems, and its characteristic parameters of fairly brief interventions.

Counseling psychology continues to advance knowledge in psychology in areas such as helping skills, the process and outcome of treatment, the proper use of evidence-based professional practice, vocational psychology, multiculturalism, supervision, and consultation. As presented in this book, the research conducted in the specialty over five decades is of very high quality and has pioneered or made use of varied methodological approaches, from laboratory analog studies to new qualitative methodologies. Clearly, the specialty has made contributions and continues to thrive as an important area of professional psychology, not just within Division 17 (Counseling Psychology) of the American Psychological Association (APA) but across divisions of the APA and particularly within Divisions 29 (Psychotherapy) and 42 (Psychologists in Private Practice). However, the current movements in evidence-based professional practice and the movement toward competency-based training and practice will pose new challenges to the specialty, primarily in establishing a balance between its traditions and the pressure to align its practices even more along the lines of these new movements in professional psychology.

One of the primary challenges for the profession will be in maintaining its unique identity when the field of professional psychology increasingly demands uniformity in the types of interventions and activities that are considered "competent." Although the intent of the competency-based professional practice movement is not to blur distinctions between professional specialties (namely counseling and clinical psychology), the end result of this new movement may well be one where distinguishing between specialties is even more difficult than it is today. We hope that this book has argued successfully on behalf of counseling psychology's distinctiveness in terms of its philosophy and practice, and on behalf of the unique contributions that the specialty has made over its many years of existence. It is evident to us that counseling psychologists will need to continue to evolve the profession's identity in a manner consistent with the broader agenda of professional psychology. We strongly believe that this evolution will be fruitful, as the specialty has proven particularly adept at assimilating new developments and overcoming challenges throughout its history. Counseling psychologists are capable of undertaking the next phase in the competency-based training and practice movement, which to us appears to be the empirical examination of these standards in professional practice. A central question that needs to be investigated is whether training and practice as defined by the competency models actually improve training and practice, above and beyond what we already do as a specialty. Another question to be empirically investigated is whether these competencies and the movement toward evidence-based psychological practice address a specific problem in training or practice that is currently not properly addressed by the scientist-practitioner or scholar-practitioner models of professional training. In the current book we have begun to address the relationship between the current models of competence and counseling psychology, and we have also identified competency areas and practices that are characteristic of professional practice in the various domains of the specialty.

Another movement that is of interest to psychology in general and counseling psychology in particular is the movement toward positive psychology and positive psychotherapy. As noted in our work, we believe that counseling psychologists have been positive psychologists from the very early days of the specialty. One only need to examine Super's (1953) theory of life-span career development to appreciate the historical focus of counseling psychology on development, adjustment, maturation, and lifelong functioning and fulfillment. In fact, prominent counseling psychologists have been involved in the recent movement toward positive psychology, but we believe that this movement can still be better harnessed by counseling psychologists to fit with our goals for evolving the specialty. Simply put, there is the potential for counseling psychology and positive psychology to further inform one another and for collaboration in developing a psychology based on human strengths, possibilities, and the integration of the healthy self in matters of health, adjustment, work, and life fulfillment. A particularly promising venue is to examine the treatment of psychopathology in all its forms from the perspective of positive psychology. For example, effective and efficacious treatments might be developed where the focus shifts from the elimination or reduction of symptoms to the enhancement of the person's strengths, assets, and sources of support in overcoming psychopathology and in adjusting to the world of human relationships and fulfilling work.

Given the evidence that has accumulated about the emergence of multiculturalism in the writing and research being conducted in counseling psychology, we conclude with some brief observations about why we believe that multiculturalism represents great potential for counseling psychology in addressing some of the most important behavioral-psychological issues currently evident in the United States. If demography is indeed destiny, as the old adage goes, then the demographic changes that are now taking place and are expected to accelerate in the United States will certainly make matters of diversity and the relevance of multiculturalism in education and health care a top priority. These matters are already of critical importance and include the educational gaps at the school and college level that are evident within communities that are primarily African American and Hispanic. Also of importance is the unequivocal evidence of outcome disparities in mental health care and medical care, affecting in disproportionate rates African American, Hispanic, and immigrant and refugee populations. There is also evidence that these groups are affected by disproportionate rates of violence, chemical dependence, and teenage pregnancy. While many of these problems can be explained as a function of poverty, racism, and the underappreciated challenge of acculturation, they are nonetheless serious problems that have the potential to magnify in scope. And this is where counseling psychologists could offer significant expertise in helping develop effective psychological and multicultural programs and interventions, with our constant sensitivity to person–environment interactions, along with our mastery of both quantitative and qualitative methodologies. The specific competencies of counseling psychologists—in developing psychoeducational interventions, in vocational and career development, in development and prevention, in short-term yet effective interventions—can still be better integrated and harnessed more directly and effectively at addressing human development and growth, as well as some of the problems contained within the realm of psychopathology, poverty, acculturation, and oppression.

REFERENCES

Ackerman, P. L., & Heggestad, E. D. (1997). Intelligence, personality, and interests: Evidence for overlapping traits. *Psychological Bulletin, 121*, 219–245.

Ahn, H., & Wampold, B. E. (2001). Where oh where are the specific ingredients? A meta-analysis of component studies in counseling and psychotherapy. *Journal of Counseling Psychology, 48*, 251–257.

Allen, J. G., Coyne, L., Colson, D. B., Horwitz, L., Gabbard, G. O., Frieswyk, S. H., ... Newson, G. (1996). Patterns of therapist interventions associated with patient collaboration. *Psychotherapy, 33*, 254–261.

Alpher, V. S. (1991). Interdependence and parallel processes: A case study of structural analysis of social behavior in supervision and short-term dynamic psychotherapy. *Psychotherapy: Theory, Research, Practice, Training, 28*(2), 218–231.

American Board of Professional Psychology. (2007). *Periodic comprehensive review (PRC) of the American Board of Counseling Psychology*. Retrieved January 2012 from http://www.abpp.org/i4a/pages/index.cfm?pageid=3285

American Board of Professional Psychology. (2011). *Candidate examination manual for board certification in counseling psychology for the American Board of Professional Psychology*. Retrieved January 2012, from http://www.abpp.org/files/page-specific/3364%20Counseling/02_Candidate_Exam_Manual.pdf

American Education Research Association. (1999). *Standards for educational and psychological testing* (2nd ed., rev.). Washington, DC: Author.

American Psychiatric Association. (2000). *Diagnostic and statistical manual of mental disorders* (4th ed., text rev.). Washington, DC: Author.

American Psychiatric Association. (2012). *DSM-V: The future of psychiatric assessment*. Retrieved April 2012, from http://www.dsm5.org/Pages/Default.aspx

American Psychological Association. (1952). Recommended standards for training counseling psychologists at the doctorate level. *American Psychologist, 7*, 175–181.

American Psychological Association. (1996). *Office of program consultation and accreditation guidelines and principles for accreditation of programs in professional psychology*. Washington, DC: Author.

American Psychological Association. (2002). Ethical principles of psychologists and code of conduct. *American Psychologist, 57*, 1060–1073.

American Psychological Association. (2003). Guidelines on multicultural education, training, research, practice, and organizational change for psychologists. *American Psychologist, 58*, 377–402.

American Psychological Association. (2005). *Presidential Task Force on Evidence-Based Practice*. Retrieved November 2010, from http://www.apa.org/practice/ebpreport.pdf

American Psychological Association. (2007). Guidelines for education and training at the doctoral and postdoctoral levels in consulting psychology/organizational consulting psychology. *American Psychologist, 62*(9), 980–992.

American Psychological Association. (2008). Report of the Ethics Committee, 2008. *American Psychologist, 64*, 464–473.

American Psychological Association. (2011, January 20). *Demographic characteristics of Division 13 members 2009*. Retrieved May 2012, from http://www.apa.org/about/division/div13-2009.aspx

American Psychological Association. (2011). *The ethical principles of psychologists and code of conduct*. Retrieved in January 2011, from http://www.apa.org/ethics/code/index.aspx

Anglin, D. M., & Wade, J. C. (2007). Racial socialization, racial identity, and Black students' adjustment to college. *Cultural Diversity and Ethnic Minority Psychology, 13*, 207–215.

Antony, M. M., & Barlow, D. H. (Eds.). (2002). *Handbook of assessment and treatment planning for psychological disorders*. New York: Guilford Press.

APA Insurance Trust. (2002). *Getting ready for HIPAA: A primer for psychologists*. Rockville, MD: The Trust.

Armstrong, P. I., & Rounds, J. (2010). Integrating individual differences in career assessment: The Atlas Model of Individual Differences and the Strong Ring. *Career Development Quarterly, 59*,143–153.

Arredondo, P., Shealy, C., Neale, M., & Winfrey, L. L. (2004). Consultation and interprofessional collaboration: Modeling for the future. *Journal of Clinical Psychology, 60*(7), 787–800.

Arthur, N. (2000, April). *Predictive characteristics of multicultural counseling competence*. Paper presented at the Annual Conference of the American Educational Research Association, New Orleans, LA.

Asay, T. P., & Lambert, M. J. (1999). The empirical case for the common factors in therapy: Quantitative findings. In M. A. Hubble, B. L. Duncan, & S. D. Miller, *The heart and soul of change: What works for whom in therapy*. Washington, DC: American Psychological Association.

Assessment of Competency Benchmarks Workgroup. (2007). *A developmental model for the defining and measuring competence in professional psychology* (Issue Brief APA Board of Professional Affairs, Washington DC: American Psychological Association).

Association of Psychology Postdoctoral and Internship Centers. (2002). *Competencies conference 2002: Future directions in education and credentialing in professional psychology*. Retrieved November 2010, from http://appic.org/news

Association of State and Provincial Psychology Boards. (2009). *ASPPB information for candidates. Examination for Professional Practice in Psychology (EPPP)*. Montgomery, AL: Association for State and Provincial Boards of Psychology.

Baer, D. M. (2004). Program evaluation: Arduous, impossible, and political. In T. L. Rzepnicki (Ed.), *Using evidence in social work practice: Behavioral perspectives*. (pp. 310–322). Chicago, IL: Lyceum Books.

Baker, D. B., & Subich, L. M. (2008). Counseling psychology: Historical perspectives. In W. B. Walsh (Ed.), *Biennial review of counseling psychology* (pp. 1–26). New York: Routledge.

Bambling, M., & King, R. (2000). Supervision and the development of counselor competency. *Psychotherapy in Australia, 6*, 4.

Bartlett, W. E., Goodyear, R. K., & Bradley, F. O. (1983). Guest editors' introduction. *The Counseling Psychologist, 11*(1), 7–7.

Barnett, J. E., Doll, B., Younggren, J. N., & Rubin, N. J. (2007). Clinical competence for practicing psychologists: Clearly a work in progress. *Professional Psychology: Research and Practice, 38*, 510–517.

Belar, C. D. (1992). Education and training conferences in graduate education. In A. E. Puente, J. R. Mathews, & C. L. Brewer (Eds.), *Teaching psychology in America: A history* (pp. 285–299). Washington, DC: American Psychological Association.

Belar, C. D. (2009). Advancing the culture of competence. *Training and Education in Professional Psychology, 3*, S63–S65.

Belar, C. D., & Perry, N. W. (1992). National conference on scientist-practitioner education and training for the professional practice of psychology. *American Psychologist, 41*(1), 71–75.

Benish, S. G., Quintana, S. & Wampold, B. E. (2011). Culturally adapted psychotherapy and the legitimacy of myth: A direct comparison meta-analysis. *Journal of Counseling Psychology, 58*, 279–289.

Bennett, B. E., Bricklin, P. M., Harris, E., Knapp, S., VandeCreek, L., & Younggren, J. N. (2006). *Assessing and managing risk in psychological practice: An individualized approach*. Rockville, MD: The Trust.

Berg, C.J. (2009). A comprehensive framework for conducting client assessments: Highlighting strengths, environmental factors and hope. *Journal of Practical Consulting, 3*, 9–13.

Bernal, M. E., Sirolli, A. A., Weisser, S. K., Ruiz, J. A., Chamberlain, V. J., & Knight, G. P. (1999). Relevance of multicultural training to students' applications to clinical psychology programs. *Cultural Diversity and Ethnic Minority Psychology, 5*, 43–55.

Bernard, J. M., & Goodyear, R. K. (2004). *Fundamentals of clinical supervision*. Boston, MA: Pearson Education.

Betz, N. E., & Fassinger, R. E. (2012). Methodologies. In J. C. Hansen & E. M. Altmaier (Eds.), *Handbook of counseling psychology* (pp. 237–269). New York: Oxford University Press.

Blanton, J. S. (2010). Why consultants don't apply psychological research. *Consulting Psychology Journal: Practice and Research, 52*(4), 235–247.

Blustein, D. L. (2006). *The psychology of working: A new perspective for career development, counseling, and public policy*. Mahwah, NJ: Erlbaum.

Blustein, D. L. (2008). The role of work in psychological health and well-being. A conceptual, historical, and public policy perspective. *American Psychologist, 63*, 228–240.

Boje, D. M. (2001). *Narrative methods for organizational and communication research*. Thousand Oaks, CA: Sage.

Bond, T. G., & Fox, C. M. (2001). Applying the Rasch Model: Fundamental measurement in the human sciences. Mahwah, NJ: Erlbaum.

Borders, L. D. (2005). Snapshot of clinical supervision in counseling and counselor education: A five-year review. *The Clinical Supervisor, 24*(1–2), 69–113.

Borders, L. D., Bernard, J. M., Dye, H. A., Fong, M. L., Henderson, P., & Nance, D. W. (1991). Curriculum guide for training counseling supervisors: Rationale, development and implementation. *Counselor Education and Supervision, 31*, 58–82.

Bradt, K. H. (2005). *Values, ethics, and politics: Dilemmas for the consulting psychologist.* Society for Consulting Psychology Fellows Invited Address at the 113th Annual Convention of the American Psychological Association, Washington, DC.

Brown, D. (1985). The preservice training and supervision of consultants. *The Counseling Psychologist, 13*(3), 410–425.

Brown, S. D., & Lent, R. W. (2000). *Handbook of counseling psychology* (3rd ed.). New Jersey: Wiley.

Brown, S. D., & Lent, R. W. (2008). *Handbook of counseling psychology* (4th ed.). Hoboken, NJ: Wiley.

Brown, S. D., & Ryan-Krane, N. E. (2000). Four (or five) sessions and a cloud of dust: Old assumptions and new observations about career counseling. In S. D. Brown & R. W. Lent (Eds.). *Handbook of counseling psychology* (3rd ed., pp. 740–766). New York: Wiley.

Bryant, A., & LaFromboise, T. D. (2005). The racial identity and cultural orientation of Lumbee American Indian high school students. *Cultural Diversity and Ethnic Minority Psychology, 11*, 82–89.

Bordin, E. S. (1984). Psychodynamic model of career choice. In D. Brown & L. Brooks (Eds.), *Career choice and development* (pp. 94–136). San Francisco, CA: Jossey-Bass.

Blocher, D. H. (2000). *The evolution of counseling psychology.* New York: Springer.

Bourg, E., Bent, R. J., McHolland, J., Stricker, G. (1989). Standards and evaluation in the education and training of professional psychologists: The National Council of Schools of Professional Psychology Mission Bay Conference. *American Psychologist, 44*, 66–72.

Buboltz, W., Deemer, E., & Hoffman, R. (2010). Content analysis of the Journal of Counseling Psychology: Buboltz, Miller, and Williams (1999) 11 years later. *Journal of Counseling Psychology, 57*, 368–375.

Buboltz, W., Miller, M., & Williams, D. J. (1999). Content analysis of research in the Journal of Counseling Psychology (1973–1988). *Journal of Counseling Psychology, 46*, 496–503.

Buckingham, M., & Clifton, D. O. (2000). *Now, discover your strengths.* New York: Free Press.

Burke, B. L., Arkowitz, H., & Menchola, M. (2008). The efficacy of motivational Interviewing: A meta-analysis of controlled clinical trials. *Journal of Consulting and Clinical Psychology, 7*, 843–861.

Carter, R. T., Helms, J. E., & Juby, H. L. (2004). The relationship between racism and racial identity for White Americans: A profile analysis. *Journal of Multicultural Counseling and Development, 32*, 2–17.

Chen, G. A., LePhuoc, P., Guzman, M. R., Rude, S. S., & Dodd, B. G. (2006). Exploring Asian American racial identity. *Cultural Diversity and Ethnic Minority Psychology, 12*, 461–476.

Clarke, A. (2005). *Situational analysis: Grounded theory after the postmodern turn.* Thousand Oaks, CA: Sage.

Collins, D. B., & Holton, E. F. (2004). The effectiveness of managerial leadership development programs: A meta-analysis of studies from 1982 to 2001. *Human Resource Development Quarterly, 15*(2), 217–248.

Constantine, M. G. (2002). Predictors of satisfaction with counseling: Racial and ethnic minority clients' attitudes toward counseling and ratings of their counselors' general and multicultural competence. *Journal of Counseling Psychology, 49*, 255–263.

Constantine, M. G., Fuertes, J. N., Roysircar, G., & Kindachi, M. M. (2008). Multicultural competence: Clinical practice, training and supervision, and research. In W. B. Walsh (Ed.), *Biennial review of counseling psychology* (Vol. 1, pp. 97–128). New York: Routledge.

Constantine, M. G., Juby, H. L., & Liang, J. J-C. (2001). Examining multicultural counseling competence and race-related attitudes among white marital and family therapists. *Journal of Marital and Family Therapy, 27*, 353–362.

Constantine, M. G., Ladany, N., Inman, A. G., & Ponterotto, J. G. (1996). Students' perceptions of multicultural training in counseling psychology programs. *Journal of Multicultural Counseling and Development, 24*, 241–253.

Constantine, M. G., Warren, A. K., & Miville, M. L. (2005). White racial identity dyadic interactions in supervision: Implications for supervisees' multicultural counseling competence. *Journal of Counseling Psychology, 52*, 490–496.

Cooper, M. (2008). *Essential research findings in counselling and psychotherapy: The facts are friendly.* Los Angeles, CA: Sage.

Cooper, S. E. (2002). Foreword: Perspectives and reactions to the principles for education and training in organizational consulting psychology. *Consulting Psychology Journal: Practice and Research, 54*(4), 211–212.

Corsini, R. J., & Wedding, D. (2008). *Current psychotherapies.* Belmont, CA: Brooks/Cole.

Council of Counseling Psychology Training Programs and the Society of Counseling Psychology. (2005). *Model Training Program in Counseling Psychology.* Counseling Psychology Education and Training Guidelines. http://cospp.org/guidelines

Crego, C. A. (1985). Ethics: The need for improved consultation training. *The Counseling Psychologist, 13*(3), 473–476.

Critchfield, K. L., & Knox, S. (2010). Conceptual skills needed for evidenced-based practice of psychotherapy; A few recommendations. *Psychotherapy Bulletin, 45*(2), Retrieved May 2012, from http://www.divisionofpsychotherapy.org/conceptual-skills-needed-for-evidence-based-practice-of-psychotherapy/

Crites, J. O., & Savickas, M. L. (1996).Revision of the Career Maturity Inventory. *Journal of Career Assessment, 4*, 131–138.

Cumming-McCann, A., & Accordino, M. P. (2005). An investigation of rehabilitation counselor characteristics, white racial attitudes, and self-reported multicultural counseling competencies. *Rehabilitation Counseling Bulletin, 48*, 167–176.

Dawes, R. M., Faust, D., & Meehl, P. E. (1989). Clinical versus actuarial judgment. *Science, 243*, 1668–1674.

Dawis, R. V. (1992). The individual differences tradition in counseling psychology. *Journal of Counseling Psychology, 39*, 7–19.

DeBell, C. (2006). What all applied psychologists should know about work. *Professional Psychology: Research and Practice, 37*, 325–333.

Department of Health and Human Services. (2001). *Mental health: Culture, race, and ethnicity: A supplement to mental health: A report of the Surgeon General.* Retrieved September 2008, from http://mentalhealth. samhsa.gov/cre/ch2_ racism_ discrimination_and_mental_health.asp

Dienst, E. R., & Armstong, P. M. (1998). Evaluation of students' clinical competence. *Professional Psychology: Research and Practice, 19*, 339–341.

Donovan, R. A., & Ponce, A. N. (2009). Identification and measurement of core competencies in professional psychology: Areas for consideration. *Training and Education in Professional Psychology, 3*(4 Suppl.), S46–S49.

Duncan, B. L., Miller, S. D., & Sparks, J. A. (2004). *The heroic client: A revolutionary way to improve effectiveness through client-directed outcome-informed therapy.* San Francisco, CA: Jossey Bass.

Dye, H. A., & Borders, L. D. (1990). Counseling supervisors: Standards for preparation and practice. *Journal of Counseling and Development, 69*, 27–32.

Ebbinghaus, H. (1911). *Psychology: An elementary text-book.* (M. Meyer, Trans.). Boston, MA: D.C. Heath. (Original work published 1908).

Egan, G. (2010). *The skilled helper* (9th ed.). Belmont, CA: Brooks/Cole.

Elkin, L, Falconnier, L., Martinovich, Z., & Mahoney, C. (2006). Therapist effects in the National Institute of Mental Health Treatment of Depression Collaborative Research Program. *Psychotherapy Research, 16*, 144–160.

Elliott, R. (1989). Comprehensive process analysis: Understanding change process in significant therapy events. In M. J. Packer & R. B. Addison (Eds.), *Entering the circle: Hermeneutic investigations in psychology* (pp. 165–184). Albany, NY: SUNY Press.

Elliott, R., Greenberg, L. S., & Lieter, G. (2004). Research on experiential psychotherapies. In M. Lambert (Ed.), *Bergin and Garfield's handbook of psychotherapy and behavior change* (6th ed., pp 493–530). New York: Wiley.

Ellis, M. V., & Ladany, N. (1997). Inferences concerning supervisees and clients in clinical supervision: An integrative review. In C. E. Watkins, Jr. (Ed.), *Handbook of psychotherapy supervision* (pp. 447–507). New York: Wiley.

Ellis, M. V., Ladany, N., Krengel, M., & Schult, D. (1996). Clinical supervision research from 1981 to 1993: A methodological critique. *Journal of Counseling Psychology, 43*, 35–50.

Falender, C. A., Erickson Cornish, J. A., Goodyear, R., Hatcher, R., Kaslow, N. J., Leventhal, G., ... Grus, C. (2004). Defining competencies in psychology supervision: A consensus statement. *Journal of Clinical Psychology, 60*, 771–785.

Falender, C. A., & Shrafranske, E. P. (2004). *Clinical supervision: A competency-based approach.* Washington, DC: American Psychological Association.

Falender, C. A., & Shrafranske, E. P. (2006). *A casebook for clinical supervision: A competency-based approach.* Washington, DC: American Psychological Association.

Finch, A. E., Lambert, M. J., & Schaalje, B. G. (2001). Psychotherapy quality control: The statistical generation of expected recovery curves for integration into an early warning system. *Clinical Psychology and Psychotherapy, 8*, 231–242.

Fitzgerald, L. F., & Osipow, S. H. (1986). An occupational analysis of counseling psychology: How special is the specialty? *American Psychologist, 41*, 535–544.

Foley, R. J., & Redfering, D. L. (1987). Bridging the gap between counseling psychologists and organization development consultants. *Journal of Business and Psychology, 2*(2), 160–170.

Forrest, L. M., Miller, D. S., & Elman, L. S. (2008). Psychology trainees with competence problems: From individual to ecological conceptualizations. *Training and Education in Professional Psychology, 2*, 183–192.

Freitas, G. J. (2002). The impact of psychotherapy supervision on client outcome: A critical examination of 2 decades of research. *Psychotherapy: Theory, Research, Practice, Training, 39*(4), 354–367.

Friedlander, M. L., Keller, K. E., Peca-Baker, T., & Olk, M. E. (1986). Effects of role conflict on counselor trainees' self-statements, anxiety level, and performance. *Journal of Counseling Psychology, 33*(1), 73–77.

Fouad, N. A., Grus, C. L., Hatcher, R. L., Kaslow, N. J., Hutchings, P. S., Madson, M. B., ... Crossman, R. E. (2009). Competency benchmarks: A model for understanding and measuring competence in professional psychology across training levels. *Training and Education in Professional Psychology, 3*, S5–S26.

Frank, J. D. (1961). *Persuasion and healing: A comparative study of psychotherapy.* Baltimore, MD: Johns Hopkins Press.

Fuertes, J. N. (2012). Multicultural counseling. In J. Hansen & E. Altmaeir (Eds.), *Handbook of counseling psychology* (pp. 570–588). New York: Oxford University Press.

Fuertes, J. N., Alfonso, V. C., & Schultz, J. J. (2005). Counseling South American immigrants. *Journal of Immigrant and Refugee Services, 3*, 155–169.

Fuertes, J. N., Alfonso, V. C., & Schultz, J. J. (2007). Counseling culturally and linguistically diverse children and youth: A self-regulatory approach. In G. B. Esquivel, E. C. Lopez, & S. G. Nahari (Eds.), *The handbook of multicultural school psychology* (pp. 409–427). New York: Erlbaum.

Fuertes, J. N., Bartolomeo, M., & Nichols, C. M. (2001). Future research directions in the study of counselor multicultural competencies. *Journal of Multicultural Counseling and Development, 29*, 3–12.

Fuertes, J. N., Boylan, L. S., & Fontanella, J. (2008). Behavioral indices in medical care outcome: The working alliance, adherence and related factors. *Journal of General Internal Medicine, 24*, 80–85.

Fuertes, J. N., & Gretchen, D. (2001). Emerging theories of multicultural counseling. In J. G. Ponterotto, J. M. Casas, L. A. Suzuki, & C. M. Alexander (Eds.), *Handbook of multicultural counseling* (pp. 509–541), Newbury Park, CA: Sage.

Fuertes, J. N., & Brobst, K. (2002). Clients' ratings of counselor multicultural competency. *Cultural Diversity and Ethnic Minority Psychology, 8*, 214–223.

Fuertes, J. N., Mislowack, A., & Mintz, S. (2005). Multicultural competencies in clinics and hospital settings. In M. Constantine & D. W. Sue (Eds.), *Multicultural counseling competencies: Theory, research, and applications* (pp. 145–159). New York: Wiley.

Fuertes, J. N., & Ponterotto, J. G. (2003). Culturally appropriate intervention strategies. In G. Roysircar, P. Arredondo, J. N. Fuertes, R. Toporek, & J. G. Ponterotto, (Eds.), *2003 Multicultural counseling competencies: AMCD* (pp. 51–58). Alexandria, VA: American Counseling Association.

Fuertes, J. N., Stracuzzi, T. I., Bennett, J., Scheinholtz, J., Mislowack, A., Hersh, M., & Cheng, D. (2006). Therapist multicultural competency: A study of therapy dyads. *Psychotherapy: Theory, Research, Practice, Training, 43*, 480–490.

Fuqua, D. R., & Newman, J. L. (2002). Academic perspectives on the principles for training in consulting psychology. *Consulting Psychology Journal: Practice and Research, 54*(4), 223–232.

Gallessich, J. (1985). Toward a meta-theory of consultation. *The Counseling Psychologist, 13* (3), 336–354.

Geisinger, K. F. (1998). Psychometric issues in test interpretation. In J. Sandoval, C. L. Frisby, K. F. Geisinger, J. D. Scheuneman, & J. R. Grenier (Eds.), *Test interpretation and diversity: Achieving equity in assessment* (pp. 17–30). Washington, DC: American Psychological Assocation.

Gelso, C. J. (1979). Research in counseling: Methodological and professional issues. *The Counseling Psychologist, 8*, 7–35.

Gelso, C. J. (2006). On the making of a scientist–practitioner: A theory of research training in professional psychology. *Training and Education in Professional Psychology, S*(1), 3–16.

Gelso, C. J. (2011a). Emerging and continuing trends in psychotherapy: Views from an editor's eye. *Psychotherapy: Theory, Research, Practice and Training, 48*, 182–187.

Gelso, C. J. (2011b). *The real relationship in psychotherapy: The hidden foundation of change*. Washington, DC: American Psychological Association.

Gelso, C. J., & Fassinger, R. E. (1990). Counseling psychology: Theory and research on interventions. In M. R. Rosenzweig & L. W. Porter (Eds.), *Annual review of psychology* (pp. 355–386). Palo Alto, CA: Annual Reviews.

Gelso, C. J., & Fassigner, R. E. (1992). Personality, development, and counseling psychology: Depth, ambivalence, and actualization. *Journal of Counseling Psychology, 39*, 275–298.

Gelso, C. J., & Fretz, B. R. (1992). *Counseling psychology*. Fort Worth, TX: Holt, Rinehart, & Winston.

Gelso, C. J., & Fretz, B. (2001). *Counseling psychology* (2nd ed.). Belmont, CA: Wadsworth Group/Thomas.

Gelso, C. J., & Hayes, J. (1998). *The psychotherapy relationship: Theory, research, and practice*. New York: Wiley.

Gelso, C. J., & Hayes. J. (2007). *Countertransference and the therapist's inner experience: Perils and possibilities*. Mahwah, NJ: Erlbaum.

Gerstein, L. H., Heppner, P. P., Aegisdottir, S., Leung, S. A., & Norsworthy, K. L. (2010). *International handbook of cross-cultural counseling: Cultural assumptions and practices worldwide*. Thousand Oaks, CA: Sage.

Gerstein, L. H., & Shullman, S. L. (1992). Counseling psychology and the workplace: The emergence of organizational counseling psychology. In S. D. Brown, & R. W. Lent (Eds.), *Handbook of counseling psychology* (2nd ed., pp. 581–625). New York: Wiley.

Gibson, C. H. (1991). A concept analysis of empowerment. *Journal of Advanced Nursing, 16*(3), 354–361.

Gibson, G., & Chard, K. M. (1994). Quantifying the effects of community mental health consultation interventions. *Consulting Psychology Journal: Practice and Research, 46*(4), 13–25.

Gibson, G., & Froehle, T. C. (1991). Empirical influences in organizational consultation. *Consulting Psychology Bulletin, 43*, 13–22.

Giorgi, A. (1985) Sketch of a psychological phenomenological method. In A. Giorgi (Ed.), *Phenomenology and psychological research* (pp. 8–22). Pittsburgh, PA: Duquesne University Press,

Glass, G. V., McGaw, B., & Smith, M. L. (1981). *Meta-analysis in social research*. Beverly Hills, CA: Sage.

Gold, R. J. (2009). Letter to mandated reporters. Office of Children, Youth, and Families. Commonwealth of Pennsylvania, Office of Public Welfare, Philadelphia, PA

Goldman, L. (1971). *Using tests in counseling*. Englewood Cliffs, NJ: Prentice Hall.

Gonsalvez, C. J. (2008). Toward the science-informed practice of clinical supervision: The Australian context. *Australian Psychologist, 43*(2), 79–87.

Goodheart, C. D., & Carter, J. A. (2008). The proper focus of evidence-based practice in Psychology: Integration of possibility and probability. In W. B. Walsh (Ed.), *Biennial review of counseling psychology* (pp. 47–69). New York: Routledge.

Goodyear, R. K., Bradley, F. O., & Bartlett, W. E. (1983). An introduction to theories of counselor supervision. *The Counseling Psychologist, 11*(1), 19–20.

Goodyear, R. K., & Benton, S. L. (1986). The roles of science and research in the counselor's work. In A. J. Palmo & W. J. Weikel (Eds.), *Foundations of mental health counseling* (pp. 287–306). Springfield, IL: Charles C Thomas.

Goodyear, R. K., Murdock, N., Lichtenberg, J. W., McPherson, R., Koetting, K., & Petren, S. (2008). Stability and change in counseling psychologists' identities, roles, functions, and career satisfaction across 15 years. *The Counseling Psychologist, 36*, 220–249.

Griner, D., & Smith, T. B. (2006). Culturally adapted mental health interventions: A meta-analytic review. *Psychotherapy: Theory, Research, Practice, Training, 43*, 531–548.

Groth-Marnat, G. (2009). *Handbook of psychological assessment* (5th ed.). Hoboken, NJ: Wiley.

Grove, W. M., & Lloyd, M. (2006). Meehl's contribution to clinical versus statistical prediction. *Journal of Abnormal Psychology, 115*, 192–194.

Gushue, G. V., & Constantine, M. G. (2007). Color-blind racial attitudes and white racial identity attitudes in psychology trainees. *Professional Psychology: Research and Practice, 38*, 321–328.

Hahn, M. E. (1955). Counseling psychology. *American Psychologist, 10*, 279–282.

Hart, G., Borders, L. D., Nance, D., & Paradise, L. (1995). Ethical guidelines for counseling supervisors. *Counselor Education and Supervision*, 34, 270–276.

Haverkamp, B. E. (1993). Confirmatory bias in hypothesis testing for client-identified and counselor self-generated hypotheses. *Journal of Counseling Psychology, 40*, 303–315.

Hawkins, E. J., Lambert, M. J., Vemeersch, D., Slade, K., & Tuttle, K. (2004). The effects of providing patient progress information to therapists and patients. *Psychotherapy Research, 31*, 308–327.

Hays, D. G. (2008). Assessing multicultural competence in counselor trainees: A review of instrumentation and future directions. *Journal of Counseling and Development, 86*, 95–101.

Hellkamp, D. T., Zins, J. E., Ferguson, K., & Hodge, M. (1998). Training practices in consultation: A national survey of clinical, counseling, industrial/organizational, and school psychology faculty. *Consulting Psychology Journal: Practice and Research, 50*(4), 228–236.

Heppner, P. P., Casas, J. M., Carter, J., & Stone, G. L. (2000). The maturation of counseling psychology: Multifaceted perspectives. In S. D. Brown & R. W. Lent (Eds.), *Handbook of counseling psychology* (3rd ed., pp. 3–49). New York: Wiley.

Heppner, P. P., Kivlighan, D. M., Jr., & Wampold, B. E. (1999). *Research design in counseling.* Pacific Grove, CA: Brooks/Cole.

Heppner, P. P., Kivlighan, D. M., & Wampold, B. E. (2008). *Research in counseling* (3rd ed.). New York: Brooks/Cole.

Hess, T. H. (Eds.). (2008). *Psychotherapy supervision: Theory, research, and practice* (2nd ed.). Hoboken, NJ: Wiley.

Hill, C. E. (2004). *Helping skills: Facilitating exploration, insight, and action* (2nd ed.). Washington, DC: American Psychological Association.

Hill, C. E. (2001). *Helping skills: The empirical foundation*. Washington, DC: American Psychological Association.

Hill, C. E. (Ed.). (2011). *Consensual qualitative research: A practical resource for investigating social science phenomena*. Washington, DC: American Psychological Association.

Hill, C. E., Helms, J. E., Speigel, S. B., & Tichenor, V. (1988). Development of a system for categorizing client reactions to therapists' interventions. *Journal of Counseling Psychology, 35*, 27–36.

Hill, C. E., & Williams, E. N. (2000). The process of individual therapy. In S. Brown and R. Lent (Eds.), *Handbook of counseling psychology* (3rd ed., pp. 670–710). Hoboken, NJ: John Wiley & Sons.

Holland, J. L. (1973). *Making vocational choices: A theory of careers*. Englewood Cliffs, NJ: Prentice-Hall.

Holland, J. L. (1985). *Making vocational choices: A theory of vocational personalities and work environments* (2nd ed.). Englewood, Cliffs, NJ: Prentice-Hall.

Holland, J. L., Magoon, T. M., & Spokane, A. R. (1981). Counseling psychology: Career interventions and related research and theory. *Annual Review of Psychology, 32*, 279–305.

Holloway, E. L. (1982). Interactional structure of supervision. *Journal of Counseling Psychology*, 3, 309–317.

Holloway, E. L. (1984). Outcome evaluation in supervision. *The Counseling Psychologist, 12*, 167–175.

Holloway, E. L. (1992). Supervision: A way of teaching and learning. In S. D. Brown & R. W. Lent (Eds.), *The handbook of counseling psychology* (2nd ed., pp. 177–216) New York: Wiley.

Holloway, E. L., Freund, R. D., Gardner, S. L., Nelson, M. L., & Walker, B. R. (1989). The relation of power and involvement to theoretical orientation in supervision: An analysis of discourse. *Journal of Counseling Psychology, 36*, 88–102.

Holloway, E. L., & Gonzalez-Doupe, P. (1999, August 23). *Empirically supported intervention programs: Implications for supervision as a training modality*. Paper presented at the American Psychological Association Annual Conference, Boston, MA.

Holloway, E. L., & Neufeldt, S. A. (1995). Supervision: Its contributions to treatment efficacy. *Journal of Consulting and Clinical Psychology, 63*(2), 207–213.

Holloway, E. L., & Poulin, K. (1995). Discourse in supervision. In J. Siegfried (Ed.), *Therapeutic and everyday discourse as behavior change: Towards a micro-analysis in psychotherapy process research* (pp. 245–276). Norwood, NJ: ABLEX.

Holloway, E. L., & Wolleat, P. L. (1981). Style differences of beginning supervisors: An interactional analysis. *Journal of Counseling Psychology, 28*, 373–376.

Holloway, E. L., & Wolleat, P. L. (1994). Supervision: The pragmatics of empowerment. *Journal of Educational and Psychological Consultation, 5(1)*, 23–43.

Howard, K. A. S., Ferrari, L., Nota, L., Solberg, V. S. L., & Soresi, S. (2009). The relation of cultural context and social relationships to career development in middle school. *Journal of Vocational Behavior, 75*, 100–108.

Illback, R., Maher, C., & Kopplin, D. (1992). Consultation and education competency. In R. L. Peterson, J. D. McHolland, R. J. Bent, E. Davis-Russell, G. E. Edwall, & K. Polite (Eds.), *The core curriculum in professional psychology* (pp. 115–120). Washington, DC: American Psychological Association and National Council of Schools of Professional Psychology.

Imel, Z. E., & Wampold, B. E. (2008). The importance of treatment and the science of common factors in psychotherapy. In S. D. Brown & R. W. Lent (Eds.), *Handbook of Counseling Psychology* (4th ed., pp.249–267). Hoboken, NJ: Wiley.

Inman, A. G., & Ladany, N. (2008). Research: The state of the field. In T. H. Hess (Ed.), *Psychotherapy supervision: Theory, research, and practice* (2nd ed., pp. 500–517). Hoboken, NJ: Wiley.

Ivey, A. E. (1979). Counseling psychology the most broadly-based applied psychology specialty. *The Counseling Psychologist, 8*, 3–6.

Jacobsen, C. K. (1985). Resistance to affirmative action: Self interest or racism? *Journal of Conflict Resolution, 29*, 306–329.

Jane, J. S., Pagan, J. L., Turkheimer, E., Fiedler, E. R., & Oltmanns, T. F. (2006). The interrater reliability of the Structured Interview for DSM-IV Personality. *Comprehensive Psychiatry, 47*, 368–375.

Johnson, S. C., & Arbona, C. (2006). The relation of ethnic identity, racial identity, and race-related stress among African-American students. *Journal of College Student Development, 47*, 495–507.

Juntunen, C. L. (2006). The psychology of working: The clinical context. *Professional Psychology: Research and Practice, 37*, 342–350.

Kagan, N. I., & Kagan, H. (1990). IPR: A validated model for the 1990s and beyond. *The Counseling Psychologist, 18*(3), 436–440.

Kanfer, F. H., & Saslow, G. (1969). Behavioral diagnosis. In C. M. Franks (Ed.), *Behavior therapy: Appraisal and status* (pp. 417–444). New York: McGraw-Hill.

Kaslow, N. J. (2009). Culture of competence. *Psychotherapy Bulletin, 44*, 2–5.

Kaslow, N., Borden, K. A., Collins, F. L., Forrest, L., Illfelder-Kaye, J., Nelson, P. D., … Wilmuth, M. E. (2004). Competencies conference: Future directions in education and training in professional psychology. *Journal of Clinical Psychology, 60*, 699–712.

Kaslow, M. J., Grus, C. L., Campbell, L. F., Fouad, N. A., Hatcher, R. L., & Rodolfa, E. R. (2009). Competency assessment toolkit for professional psychology. *Training and Education in Professional Psychology, 3*(4 Suppl.), S27–S45.

Kaslow, N. J., Rubin, N. J., Bebeau, M. J., Leigh, I. W., Lichtenberg, J. W., Nelson, P. D., … Smith, I. L. (2007). Guiding principles and recommendations for the assessment of competence. *Professional Psychology: Research and Practice, 38*, 441–451.

Kavanagh, D., Spence, S. H., Stron, J., Wilson, J., Sturk, H., & Crow, N. (2003). Supervision practices in allied mental health: Relationships of supervision characteristics to perceived impact and job satisfaction. *Mental Health Services Research*, 5, 187–195.

Kennard, B. D., Stewart, S. M., & Gluck, M. R. (1987). The supervision relationship: Variables contributing to positive versus negative experiences. *Professional Psychology: Research and Practice, 18*(2), 172–175.

Kenkle, M. B., & Peterson, R. L. (2010). *Competency-based education for professional psychology*. Washington, DC: American Psychological Association.

Kidd, S. A., & Kral, M. J. (2005). Practicing participatory action research. *Journal of Counseling Psychology, 52*, 187–195.

King, P. A., & Howard-Hamilton, M. (2003). An assessment of multicultural competence. *NASPA Journal, 40*, 119–133.

Kitchener, K. S., & Anderson, S. K. (2000). Ethical issues in counseling psychology: Old themes—new problems. In S. D. Brown & R. W. Lent (Eds.), *Handbook of counseling psychology* (3rd ed., pp. 50–82). New York: Wiley.

Knapp, S., & Tepper, A. M. (1995). Revised child protective services law: What are the implications for Psychologists? *The Pennsylvania Psychologist Quarterly, Feb*, 20–22.

Knapp, S., Tepper, A. M., & VandeCreek, L. (1993). Questions and answers about privileged communications. *The Pennsylvania Psychologist Quarterly: Special Section: Ethics, May*, 22–23.

Knapp, S., & VandeCreek, L. (1982). Tarasoff: Five years later. *Professional Psychology, 13*(4), 511–516.

Knapp, S., & VandeCreek, L (1987). *Privileged communications in the mental health professions*. New York: Van Nostrand Reinhold.

Krishnamurthy, R., Vandecreek, L., Kaslow, N. J., Tazeu, Y. N., Milville, M. L., Kerns, R., & Benton, S. A. (2004). Achieving competency in psychological assessment: Directions for education and training. *Journal of Clinical Psychology, 60*, 725–739.

Kurpius, D. J. (1985). Consultation interventions: Successes, failures, and proposals. *The Counseling Psychologist, 13*(3), 368–389.

Kurpius, R. S. E., Fuqua, D. R., Gibson, G., Kurpius, D. J., & Froehle, T. C. (1995). An occupational analysis of Consulting Psychology. *Consulting Psychology Journal: Practice and Research, 47*(2), 75–88.

Kusy, M. E., & Holloway, E. L. (2009). *Toxic workplace! Managing toxic personalities and their systems of power*. San Francisco, CA: Jossey-Bass.

Kvaal, S., Choca, J., & Groth-Marnat, G. (2003). The integrated psychological report. In L. E. Beutler & G. Groth-Marnat (Eds.), *Integrative assessment of adult personality* (2nd ed., pp. 398–433). New York: Guilford Press.

Ladany, N., Constantine, M. G., Miller, K., Erickson, C. D., & Muse-Burke, J. L. (2000). Supervisor countertransference: A qualitative investigation into its identification and description. *Journal of Counseling Psychology, 47*, 102–115.

Ladany, N., Ellis, M. V., & Friedlander, M. L. (1999). The supervisory working alliance, trainee self-efficacy, and satisfaction. *Journal of Counseling and Development, 77*(4), 447–455.

Ladany, N., & Friedlander, M. L. (1995). The relationship between the supervisory working alliance and trainees' experience of role conflict and role ambiguity. *Counselor Education and Supervision, 34*, 356–368.

Ladany, N., Inman, A. G., Constantine, M. G., & Hofheinz, E. (1997). Supervisee multicultural case conceptualization ability and self-reported multicultural competence as functions of supervisee racial identity and supervisor focus. *Journal of Counseling Psychology, 44*, 284–293.

Ladany, N., & Lehrman-Waterman, D. E. (1999). The content and frequency of supervisor self-disclosures and their relationship to supervisor style and the supervisory working alliance. *Counselor Education and Supervision, 38*, 143–160.

Ladany, N., & Walker, J. (2003). Supervisor self-disclosure: Balancing the uncontrollable narcissist with the indomitable altruist. *Journal of Counseling Psychology, 59*, 611–621.

Lambert, M. J. (2004). *Bergin and Garfield's handbook of psychotherapy and behavior change*. New York: Wiley.

Lambert, M. J., Harmon, C., Slade, K., Whipple, J. L., & Hawkins, E. J. (2005). Providing feedback to psychotherapists on their patients' progress: Clinical results and practice suggestions. *Journal of Clinical Psychology, 61*(2), 165–174.

Lambert, M. J., & Ogles, B. M. (1997). The effectiveness of psychotherapy supervision. In C. E. Watkins, Jr. (Ed.), *Handbook of psychotherapy supervision* (pp. 421–446). Hoboken, NJ: Wiley.

Lambert, M. J., & Ogles, B. M. (2004). The efficacy and effectiveness of psychotherapy. In M. J. Lambert (Ed.), *Bergin and Garfield's handbook of psychotherapy and behavior change* (pp. 139–193). New York: Wiley.

Lambert, M. J., & Vermeersch, D. A. (2008). Measuring and improving outcome in routine practice. In R. Lent & S. Brown (Eds.), *Handbook of counseling psychology* (4th ed. pp. 243–248). Washington, DC: APA Press.

Lambert, M. J., Whipple, J. L., Harmon, C., Shimokawa, K., Slade, K., & Christofferson, C. (2004). *Clinical support tools manual.* Provo, UT: Department of Psychology, Brigham Young University.

Lambert, M. J., Whipple, J. L., Vermeersch, D., Smart, D. W., Hawkins, E. J., & Nielsen, S. L. (2002). Enhancing psychotherapy outcomes via providing feedback on client progress: A replication. *Clinical Psychology and Psychotherapy, 9*, 91–103.

Lave, J., & Wenger, E. (1991). *Situated learning: Legitimate peripheral participation.* Cambridge, England: Cambridge University Press.

Le, T. N., & Stockdale, G. (2008). Acculturative dissonance, ethnic identity, and youth violence. *Cultural Diversity and Ethnic Minority Psychology, 14*, 1–9.

Lee, R. M., Noh, C-Y., Yoo, H. C., & Doh, H. S. (2007). The psychology of diaspora experienced: Intergroup contact, perceived discrimination, and ethnic identity of Koreans in China. *Cultural Diversity and Ethnic Minority Psychology, 13*, 115–124.

Leonard, M. M. (1977). The counseling psychologist as an organizational consultant. *The Counseling Psychologist*, doi: 10.1177/001100007700700230

Leong, F. T. L., & Leach, M. M. (Eds.). (2008). *Counseling psychology.* Burlington, VT: Ashgate Publishing.

Lewak, R., & Hogan, L. (2003). Applying assessment information. In L.E. Beutler & g. Groth-Marnat (Eds.), *Integrative assessment of adult psychopathology (2nd ed).* New York: Guilford Press.

Lewin, K. (1951). *Field theory in social science: Selected theoretical papers.* New York: Harper Collins.

Lichtenberg, J. W., Goodyear, R. K., & Genther, D. Y. (2008). The changing landscape of professional practice in counseling psychology. In S. D. Brown & R.W. Lent (Eds.), *Handbook of counseling psychology* (4th ed., pp. 21–37). Hoboken, NJ: Wiley.

Lichtenberg, J. W., Portnoy, S. M., Bebeau, M. J., Leigh, I. W., Nelson, P. D., Rubin, N. J., … Kaslow, N. J. (2007). Challenges to the assessment of competence and competencies. *Professional Psychology: Research and Practice, 38*, 474–478.

Liu, W. M. (2002). Exploring the lives of Asian American men: Racial identity, male role norms, gender role conflict, and prejudicial attitudes. *Psychology of Men and Masculinity, 3,* 107–118.

Loganbill, C., Hardy, E., & Delworth, U. (1982). Supervision: A conceptual model. *The Counseling Psychologist, 10*(1), 3–42.

Lopez, I. (2008). "But you don't look Puerto Rican": The moderating effect of ethnic identity on the relation between skin color and self-esteem among Puerto Rican women. *Cultural Diversity and Ethnic Minority Psychology, 14,* 102–108.

Lopez, S. J. (2009). *The encyclopedia of positive psychology.* New York: Wiley.

Lopez, S. J., & Edwards, L.M., (2008). The interface of counseling psychology and positive psychology: Assessing and promoting strengths. In S.D. Brown & R.W. Lent (Eds), *Handbook of counseling psychology* (4th ed., pp. 86–99). Hoboken, NJ: Wiley.

Lopez, S. J., Hodges, T., & Harter, J. (2005). *Technical report: Development and validation of the Clifton Strengths Finder.* Princeton, NJ: Gallup Organization.

Lopez, S. J., & Magyar-Moe, J. L. (2006). Positive psychology that matters. *The Counseling Psychologist, 34,* 323–330.

Lowman, R. L., Alderfer, C., Atella, M., Garman, A., Hellkamp, D., Kilburg, R., & O'Roark, A. (2002). Principles for education and training at the doctoral and postdoctoral level in consulting psychology/organizational. *Consulting Psychology Journal: Practice and Research, 54*(4), 213–222.

Mahalik, J. R., Pierre, M. R., & Wan, S. S. C. (2006). Examining racial identity and masculinity as correlates of self-esteem and psychological distress in black men. *Journal of Multicultural Counseling and Development, 34,* 94–104.

Mallinckrodt, B., & Gelso, C. J. (2002). Impact of research training environment and Holland personality type: A 15-year follow-up of research productivity. *Journal of Counseling Psychology, 49,* 60–70.

Mangione, L., & Nadkarni, L. (2010). The relationship competency: Broadening and deepening. In M. B. Kenkel & R. L. Peterson (Eds.), *Competency-based education for professional psychology* (pp. 69–86). Washington, DC: American Psychological Association.

MacDonald, G. (1996). Inferences in therapy: Processes and hazards. *Professional Psychology: Research and Practice, 27,* 600–603.

Meade, C. J., Hamilton, M. K., & Yuen, R. K. W. (1982). Consultation research: The time has come, the walrus said. *The Counseling Psychologist, 10,* 39–51.

Meara, N. M., Schmidt, L., Carrington, C., Davis, K., Dixon, D., Fretz, B., … Suinn, R. (1988). Training and accreditation in counseling psychology. *The Counseling Psychologist, 16,* 366–384.

Meehl, P. E. (1996). *Clinical versus statistical prediction: A theoretical analysis and a review of the evidence.* Lanham, MD: Rowan & Littlefield/Jason Aronson. (Original work published1954).

Melton, G. B., Ptrila, J., Poythress, N. G., & Slobogin, C. (2007). *Psychological evaluations for the courts: A handbook for mental health practitioners and lawyers* (3rd ed.). New York: Guilford Press.

Meier, S. T. (2003). *Bridging case conceptualization, assessment, and intervention.* Thousand Oaks, CA: Sage.

Messick, S. (1980). Test validity and the ethics of assessment. *American Psychologist, 35*, 1012–1027.

Middleton, R. A., Stadler, H. A., Simpson, C., Guo, Y. J., Brown, M. J., Crow, G., et al. (2005). Mental health practitioners: The relationship between white racial identity attitudes and self-reported multicultural counseling competencies. *Journal of Counseling and Development, 83*, 444–456.

Millon, T. (1983). *Modern psychopathology. A biosocial approach to maladaptive learning and functioning.* Philadelphia: Saunders.

Milne, D. L., Pilkington, J., Gracie, J., & James, I. (2003). Transferring skills from supervision to therapy: A qualitative and quantitative N = 1 analysis. *Behavioural and Cognitive Psychotherapy, 31*, 193–202.

Miville, M. L., Constantine, M. G., Baysden, M. F., & So-Lloyd, G. (2005). Chameleon changes: An exploration of racial identity themes of multiracial people. *Journal of Counseling Psychology, 52*, 507–516.

Morgan, R. D., & Cohen, L. M. (2008). Clinical and counseling psychology: Can differences be gleaned from printed recruiting materials? *Training and Education in Professional Psychology, 2*, 156–164.

Morrill, W. H., Oetting, E. R., & Hurst, J. C. (1974). Dimensions of counselor functioning. *Personnel and Guidance Journal, 52*(6), 354–359.

Morrow, S. L. (2005). Quality and trustworthiness in qualitative research in counseling psychology. *Journal of Counseling Psychology, 52*(2), 250–260.

Munley, P. H., Pate, W. E., II, & Duncan, L. E. (2008). Demographic, educational, employment, and professional characteristics of counseling psychologists. *Counseling Psychologist, 36*(2), 250–280.

Murdock, N. L. (2009). *Theories of counseling and psychotherapy: A case approach* (2nd ed.). Upper Saddle River, NJ: Pearson/Merril.

Murdock, N. L., Alcorn, J., Heesacker, M., & Stoltenberg, C. (1998). Model training program in counseling psychology. *The Counseling Psychologist, 23*, 658–672.

Murray, M. (2003). Narrative psychology and narrative analysis. In P. M. Camic, J. E. Rhodes, & L. Yardley (Eds.), *Qualitative research in psychology: Expanding perspectives in methodology and design* (pp. 95–112). Washington, DC: American Psychological Association Books.

National Center of Educational Statistics. (2000). *The condition of education.* Washington, DC: US Department of Education, Office of Educational Research and Improvement.

National Center for Cultural Competence. (n.d.) *Conceptual frameworks/models, guiding values and principles.* Retrieved January 2011, from the Georgetown University, Center for Child and Human Development, National Center for Cultural Competence Web site: http://www11.georgetown.edu/research/gucchd/nccc/foundations/frameworks.html

Neff, W. S. (1985). *Work and human behavior* (3rd. ed.). New York: Aldine.

Neufeldt, S. A. (2004). Critical factors in supervision: The patient, the therapist, and the supervisor. *Core processes in brief psychodynamic psychotherapy: Advancing effective practice* (pp. 325–341). Mahwah, NJ: Erlbaum.

Neufeldt, S. A., Karno, M. P., & Nelson, M. L. (1996). A qualitative study of experts' conceptualization of supervisee reflectivity. *Journal of Counseling Psychology, 43*, 3–9.

Neuman, G. A., Edwards, J. E., & Raju, N. S. (1989). Organizational development interventions: A meta-analysis of their effects on satisfaction and other attitudes. *Personnel Psychology, 42*(3), 461–489.

Neville, H., Spanierman, L., & Doan, B-T. (2006). Exploring the association between color-blind racial ideology and multicultural counseling competencies. *Cultural Diversity and Ethnic Minority Psychology, 12*, 275–290.

Newman, J. L. (1993). Ethical issues in consultation. *Journal of Counseling and Development, 72*(2), 148–156.

Newman, J. L., & Robinson, S. E. (1991). In the best interests of the consultee: Ethical issues in consultation. *Consulting Psychology Bulletin, 43*, 23–29.

Nezu, C. M., Finch, A. J., & Simon, N. P. (2009). *Becoming board certified by the American Board of Professional Psychology*. New York: Oxford University Press.

Norcross, J. C. (2002). *Psychotherapy relationships that work*. New York: Oxford University Press.

Norcross, J. C., Hedges, M., & Castle, P. H. (2002). Psychologists conducting psychotherapy in 2001: A study of the Division 29 membership. *Psychotherapy: Theory, Research, Practice, Training, 39*(97), 102.

Nutt, R. L. (1977). *A study of consultation services provided by counseling psychologists* (Counseling Psychology, University of Maryland). Dissertation Abstracts International, *37*(5816B)

Oliver, L. W., & Spokane, A. R. (1983). Research integration: Approaches, problems, and recommendations for research reporting. *Journal of Counseling Psychology, 30*, 252–257.

Oliver, L. W., & Spokane, A. R. (1988). Career counseling outcome: What contributes to client gain? *Journal of Counseling Psychology, 35*, 447–462.

O'Neill, P. (1989). Responsible for whom? Responsible for what? *American Journal of Community Psychology*, doi: 10.1007/BF00931040.

O'NET online. (2010). National Center for O'NET Development. Employment and Training Administration, U. S. Department of Labor. http://www.hollandcodes.com/onet.html

O'Roark, A. M. (2007). The best of consulting psychology 1900–2000: Insider perspectives. *Consulting Psychology Journal: Practice and Research, 59*, 189–202.

Orlinsky, D. E., Botermans, J. F., & Ronnestad, M. H. (2001). Towards an empirically grounded model of psychotherapy training: Four thousand therapists rate influences on their development. *Australian Psychologist, 36*(2), 139–148.

Orlinsky, D. E., Ronnestad, M. H., & Willutski, U. (2004). Fifty years of psychotherapy process-outcome research: Continuity and change. In M. J. Lambert (Ed.), *Bergin and Garfield's handbook of psychotherapy and behavior change* (5th ed., pp. 307–389). New York: Wiley.

Osipow, S. H. (1982). Research in career counseling: An analysis of issues and problems. *The Counseling Psychologist, 10*, 27–34.

Osipow, S. H. (1999). Assessing career indecision. *Journal of Vocational Behavior, 55*, 147–154.

Ottavi, T. M., Pope-Davis, D. B., & Dings, J. G. (1994). Relationship between white racial identity attitudes and self-reported multicultural counseling competencies. *Journal of Counseling Psychology, 41*, 149–154.

Packard, T. (2009). Core values that distinguish counseling psychology: Personal and professional perspectives. *The Counseling Psychologist, 37,* 610–624.

Padilla, A. M. & Medina, A. (1996). Cross-cultural sensitivity in assessment: Using tests in culturally appropriate ways. In L. Suzuki, P. J. Meller, & J. G. Ponterotto (Eds.), *Handbook of multicultural assessment* (pp. 3–28). San Francisco, CA: Jossey Bass.

Parsons, F. (1909). *Choosing a vocation.* Boston, MA: Houghton Mifflin.

Paskiewicz, W., Rabe, D., Adams, W., Gathercoal, K., Meyer, A., & Mellvried, J. (2006, January). *2005 NCSPP self study with complementary data.* National Council of Schools and Programs of Professional Psychology, Lake Las Vegas, NV.

Paterson, C., & Seligman, M. E. P. (2004). *Character strengths and virtues: A handbook and classification.* New York: Oxford University Press.

Patton, M. Q. (2002). *Qualitative research and evaluation methods* (3rd ed). Thousand Oaks, CA: Sage Publications.

Patton, M. J., & Kivlighan, D. M., Jr. (1997). Relevance of the supervisory alliance to the counseling alliance and to treatment adherence in counselor training. *Journal of Counseling Psychology, 44*(1), 108–115.

Paul, K. I., & Moser, K. (2009). Unemployment impairs mental health: Meta-analyses. *Journal of Vocational Behavior, 74,* 264–282.

Pearson, C., & Porath, C. (2009). *The cost of bad behavior: How incivility is damaging your business and what to do about it.* Hightstown, NJ: McGraw-Hill.

Pelling, N., Barletta, J., & Armstrong, P. (2009). *The practice of clinical supervision.* Sydney, Australia: Australian Academic Press.

Pepinsky, H. B. (1963). On the utility of bias in treatment (an open letter to the retiring editor). *Journal of Counseling Psychology, 10,* 402–405.

Pepinksy, H. B., & Karst, T. O. (1964). Convergence: A phenomenon in counseling and in psychotherapy. *American Psychologist, 19,* 333–338.

Pepinsky, H. B., & Pepinsky, P. N. (1954). *Counseling theory and practice.* New York: Ronald Press.

Peterson, R. L., Peterson, D. R., Abrams, J. C., & Stricker, G. (1997). The National Council of Schools and Programs of Professional Psychology education model. *Professional Psychology: Research and Practice, 28*(4), 373–386.

Peterson, C., & Seligman, M. E. P. (2004). *Character strengths andvirtues: A handbook and classification.* Washington, DC: American Psychological Association.

Phinney, J. S., & Ong, A. D. (2007). Conceptualization and measurement of ethnic identity: Current status and future directions. *Journal of Counseling Psychology, 54,* 271–281.

Pierce, R. M., & Schauble, P. G. (1971). Toward the development of facilitative counselors: The effects of practicum instruction and individual supervision. *Counselor Education and Supervision, 11*(2), 83–89.

Ponterotto, J. G., Fuertes, J. N., & Chen, E. C. (2000). Models of multicultural counseling. In S. D. Brown & R. W. Lent (Eds.), *Handbook of counseling psychology* (3rd ed., pp. 639–669). New York: Wiley.

Pope, K. S., Tabachnick, B. G., & Keith-Spiegel, P. (1987). Ethics of practice: The beliefs and behaviors of psychologists as therapists. *American Psychologist, 42,* 993–1006.

Pope, K. S., & Vasquez, M. T. (1991). *Ethics in psychotherapy and counseling.* San Francisco, CA: Jossey Bass.

Pope-Davis, D. B., Reynolds, A. L., Dings, J. G., & Ottavi, T. M. (1994). Multicultural competencies of doctoral interns at university counseling centers: An exploratory investigation. *Professional Psychology: Research and Practice, 25,* 466–470.

Prochaska, J. O., & Norcross, J. C. (2009). *Systems of psychotherapy: A transtheoretical approach* (7th ed.). Belmont, CA: Brooks Cole.

Pugh, L. A., & Bry, B. H. (2007). The protective effects of ethnic identity for alcohol and marijuana use among black young adults. *Cultural Diversity and Ethnic Minority Psychology, 13,* 187–193.

Raimy, V. (Ed.). (1950). *Training in clinical psychology.* New York: Prentice-Hall.

Random House dictionary of the English language: The unabridged edition (1967). New York: Random House, Inc., p. 1444.

Richardson, M. S., & Patton, M. J. (1992). Guest editors' reflections on a centennial series in process. *Journal of Counseling Psychology, 39,* 443–446.

Robinson, S. E., & Gross, D. R. (1985). Ethics of consultation: The Canterville ghost. *The Counseling Psychologist, 13*(3), 444–465.

Rodolfa, E., Bent, R., Eisman, E., Nelson, P., Rehm, L., & Ritchie, P. (2005). A cube model for competency development: Implications for psychology educators and regulators. *Professional Psychology: Research and Practice, 36,* 347–354.

Roe, A. (1984). Personality development and career choice. In D. Brown & L. Brooks (Eds.), *Career choice and development* (pp.31–53). San Francisco, CA: Jossey-Bass.

Ross, L., & Nisbett, R. E. (1991). *The person and the situation: Perspectives of social psychology.* New York: McGraw-Hill.

Rounds, J. B., & Tinsley, H. E. A. (1984). Diagnosis and treatment of vocational problems. In S. D. Brown & R. W. Lent (Eds.), *Handbook of counseling psychology* (pp. 137–177). New York: Wiley.

Royalty, G. M., Gelso, C. J., Mallinckrodt, B., & Garrett, K. (1986). The environment and the student in counseling psychology: Does the research training environment influence graduate students' attitudes toward research? *The Counseling Psychologist, 14,* 9–30.

Rubin, N. J., Bebeau, M., Leigh, I. W., Lichtenberg, J. W., Nelson, P. D., Portnoy, S., ... Kaslow, N. J. (2007). The competency movement within psychology: An historical perspective. *Professional Psychology: Research and Practice, 38,* 452–462.

Sandoval, J., Frisby, C. L., Geisinger, K. F., Scheuneman, J. D., & Grenier, J. R. (1998). *Test interpretation and diversity: Achieving equity in assessment.* Washington, DC: American Psychological Association.

Schacht, A. J., Howe, H. E., & Berman, J. J. (1989). Supervisor facilitative conditions and effectiveness as perceived by thinking- and feeling-type supervisees. *Psychotherapy: Theory, Research, Practice, Training, 26*(4), 475–483.

Scheel, M. J., Berman, M., Friedlander, M. L., Conoley, C. W., Duan, C., & Whiston, S. C. (2011). Whatever happened to counseling in counseling psychology? *The Counseling Psychologist, 39*(5), 673–692.

Schein, E. H. (1989). Process consultation as a general model of helping. *Consulting Psychology Bulletin, 41,* 3–15.

Schulte, A. C., & Daly, E. J. (2009). Operationalizing and evaluating professional competencies in psychology: Out with the old, in with the new? *Training and Education in Professional Psychology, 3,* S54–S58.

Schultheiss, D. E. (2006). The interface of work and family life. *Professional Psychology: Research and Practice, 37,* 334–341.

Schwartz, S. J., Zamboanga, B. L., & Jarvis, L. H. (2007). Ethnic identity and acculturation in Hispanic early adolescents: Mediated relationships to academic grades, prosocial behaviors, and externalizing symptoms. *Cultural Diversity and Ethnic Minority Psychology, 13,* 364–373.

Scott, K. J., Ingram, K. M., Vitanza, S. A., & Smith, N. G. (2000). Training in supervision: A survey of current practices. *The Counseling Psychologist, 28,* 403–422.

Sears, R., Rudisill, J., & Mason-Sears, C. (2006). *Consultation skills for mental health professionals.* Hoboken, NJ: Wiley.

Seligman, M. E. P., & Csikszentmihalyi, M. (2000). Positive psychology: An introduction. *American Psychologist, 55,* 5–14.

Seligman, M. E. P., Rashid, T., & Parks, A.C. (2006). Positive psychotherapy. *American Psychologist, 61,* 774–788.

Sellers, R. M., & Shelton, J. N. (2003). The role of racial identity in perceived racial discrimination. *Journal of Personality and Social Psychology, 84,* 1079–1092.

Shapiro, E. S. (2011). *Scaling the mountain: Implementation science in delivering evidence-based interventions in schools.* Invited address to the Annual Meeting of the American Psychological Association, Washington, DC.

Shullman, S. L. (2002). Reflections of a consulting counseling psychologist: Implications of the principles for education and training at the doctoral and postdoctoral level in consulting psychology for the practice of counseling psychology. *Consulting Psychology Journal: Practice and Research, 54*(4), 242–251.

Silvestri, T. J., & Richardson, T. Q. (2001). White racial identity statutes and NEO personality constructs: An exploratory analysis. *Journal of Counseling and Development, 79,* 68–76.

Sireci, S. G., & Geisinger, K. F. (1998). Equity issues in employment testing. In J. Sandoval, C. L. Frisby, K. F. Geisinger, J. D. Scheuneman, & J. R. Grenier (Eds.). *Test interpretation and diversity: Achieving equity in assessment* (pp. 105–140). Washington, DC: American Psychological Association.

Sisodia, R., Wolfe, D. B., & Sheth, J. (2007). *Firms of endearment: How world-class companies profit from passion and purpose.* Upper Saddle River, NJ: Wharton School Publishing.

Skovholt, T. M., & Jennings, L. (2004). *Master therapists: Exploring expertise in therapy and counseling.* Boston, MA: Pearson.

Socarides, C. W., & Kramer, S. (1997). *Work and its inhibitions: Psychoanalytic essays.* Madison, WI: International University Press.

Sodowsky, G. R., Kuo-Jackson, P. Y., Richardson, M. F., & Corey, A. T. (1998). Correlates of self-reported multicultural competencies: Counselor multicultural social desirability, race, social inadequacy, locus of control racial ideology, and multicultural training. *Journal of Counseling Psychology, 45,* 256–264.

Soh, S., & Leong, F. T. (2001). Cross-cultural validation of Holland's theory in Singapore: Beyond structural validity of RIASEC. *Journal of Career Assessment, 9,* 115–133.

Spanierman, L. B., Poteat, V. P., Wang, Y. F., & Oh, E. (2008). Psychosocial costs of racism to white counselors: Predicting various dimensions of multicultural counseling competence. *Journal of Counseling Psychology, 55,* 75–88.

Spokane, A. R. (1985). A review of research on congruence in Holland's theory of career choice. (Monograph) *Journal of Vocational Behavior, 26*, 306–343.

Spokane, A. R. (1991). *Career intervention*. Englewood Cliffs, NJ: Prentice Hall.

Spokane, A. R., Inman, A., Weatherford, R. D., Kaduvettoor, A., & Straw, R. (2011). Ecologically-based, culturally concordant responding following disasters: The Counseling Psychologists role. *The Counseling Psychologist, 39*, 1128–1159.

Sprinthall, N. A. (1990). Counseling psychology from Greyston to Atlanta: On the road to Armageddon? *The Counseling Psychologist, 18*, 455–463.

Stanton, M. (2010). The consultation and education competency. In M. B. Kenkel & R. L. Peterson (Eds.), *Competency-based education for professional psychology* (pp. 143–159). Washington, DC: American Psychological Association.

Stein, D. M., & Lambert, M. J. (1995). Graduate training in psychotherapy: Are therapy outcomes enhanced? *Journal of Consulting and Clinical Psychology, 63*, 182–196.

Stein, J., & Urdang, L. (Eds.). (1967). *The Random House dictionary of the English language*. (Unabridged edition). New York: Random House.

Stephens, N. M., Hamedani, M. G., Markus, H. R., Bergsieker, H. B., & Eloul, L. (2009). Why did they "choose" to stay: Perspectives of Hurricane Katrina observers and survivors. *Psychological Science*, 20 , 878–886.

Steven, D. T., Goodyear, R. K., & Robertson, P. (1998). Supervisor development: An exploratory study in changes in stance and emphasis. *The Clinical Supervisor, 16*(2), 73–88.

Stoltenberg, C. D., Pace, T. M., Kashubeck-West, S., Biever, J. L., Patterson, T., & Welch, I. D. (2000). Training models in counseling psychology: Scientist-practitioner versus practitioner-scholar. *The Counseling Psychologist, 28*, 622–640.

Strauss, A., & Corbin, J. (1998). *Basics of qualitative research: Grounded theory procedures and techniques* (2nd ed.). Thousand Oaks, CA: Sage.

Strong, S. R. (1968). Counseling: An interpersonal influence process. *Journal of Counseling Psychology, 15*, 215–224.

Strong, S. R., Welsh, J. A., Corcoran, J. L., & Hoyt, W. T. (1992). Social psychology and counseling psychology: The history, products, and promise of an interface. *Journal of Counseling Psychology, 39*, 139–157.

Sue, D. W., Arredondo, P., & McDavis, R. J. (1992). Multicultural competencies and standards: A call to the profession. *Journal of Multicultural Counseling and Development, 20*, 64–88.

Sue, D. W., Bernier, J. E., Durran, A., Feinberg, L., Pedersen, P., Smith, E. J., & Vasquez-Nuttall, E. (1982). Position paper: Cross- cultural counseling competencies. *The Counseling Psychologist, 10*, 45–52.

Sue, D. W., Carter, R. T., Casas, J. M., Fouad, N. A., Ivey, A. E., Jensen, M., … Vazquez-Nuttal, E. (1998). *Multicultural counseling competencies: Individual and organizational development*. Thousand Oaks, CA: Sage.

Sue, D. W., & Sue, D. (2007). *Counseling the culturally diverse* (5th ed.). NewYork: Wiley.

Sullivan, B. (2009). Supervision as gatekeeping: Managing professional competency problems in student supervisees. In P. Armstrong (Ed.), *The practice of clinical supervision* (pp. 236–251). Bowen Hills, Australia: Australian Academic Press.

Summerall, S. W., Lopez, S. J., & Oehlert, M. E. (2000). *Competency-based education and training in psychology*. Springfield, IL: Charles C. Thomas.

Super, D. E. (1953). A theory of vocational development. *American Psychologist, 8*, 185–190.

Super, D. E. (1957). Career patterns as a basis for vocational counseling. *Journal of Counseling Psychology, 1*, 12–20.

Swanson, J. L. (1995). Process and outcome research in career counseling. In W. B. Walsh & S. H. Osipow (Eds.), *Handbook of vocational psychology* (2nd ed., pp. 217–259). Hillsdale, NJ: Erlbaum.

Tarasoff v. Regents of the University of California, 17 Cal. 3d 425, 551 P.2d 334, 131 Cal. Rptr. 14 (Cal. 1976).

Tinsley, H. E. A., & Chu, S. (1999). Research on test and interest inventory interpretation outcomes. In M. L. Savickas & A. R. Spokane (Eds.). Vocational interests: Meaning, measurement and counseling use (pp. 257–276). Palo Alto, CA: Davies-Black Publishing.

Teitelbaum, S. H. (1990). Supertransference: The role of the supervisor's blind spots. *Psychoanalytic Psychology*, 7 (2), 243–258.

Tinsley, H. E. A., & Heesacker, M. (1984). Vocational behavior and career development, 1983: A review. *Journal of Vocational Behavior, 25*, 139–190.

Thorndike, R. M. (2005). *Measurement and evaluation in psychology and education* (7th ed.). Upper Saddle River, NJ: Pearson.

Toomer, J. E. (1982). Counseling psychologists in business and industry. *The Counseling Psychologist, 10*(3), 9–18.

Trierweiler, S. J., Stricker, G., & Peterson, R. L. (2010). The research and evaluation competency: The local clinical scientist- Review, current status, future directions. In M. B. Kenkel & R. L. Peterson (Eds.), *Competency-based education for professional psychology* (pp. 125–142). Washington, DC: American Psychological Association.

Tyler, L. (1961). Research explorations in the realm of choice. *Journal of Counseling psychology, 8*, 195–200.

Tyler, L. E. (1953). *The work of the counselor.* New York: Appleton-Century-Crofts.

Umana-Taylor, A. J., & Shin, N. (2007). An examination of ethnic identity and self-esteem with diverse populations: Exploring variation by ethnicity and geography. *Cultural Diversity and Ethnic Minority Psychology, 13*, 178–186.

US Department of Homeland Security. (2011). U.S. Legal Permanent Residents: 2009. Retrieved January 2011, from http://www.dhs.gov/xlibrary/assets/statistics/publications/lpr_fr_2009.pdf

Utsey, S. O., Chae, M. H., Brown, C. F., & Kelly, D. (2002). Effect of ethnic group membership on ethnic identity, race-related stress, and quality of life. *Cultural Diversity and Ethnic Minority Psychology, 8*, 366–377.

Vallance, K. (2005). Exploring counsellor perceptions of the impact of counselling supervision on clients. *Counselling and Psychotherapy Research, 5*(2), 107–110.

VandeCreek, L., & Knapp, S. (1993). *Tarasoff and beyond: Legal and clinical considerations in the treatment of life-endangering patients* (rev. ed.). Sarasota, FL: Professional Resource Press.

Vereen, L. G., Hill, N. R., & McNeal, D. T. (2008). Perceptions of multicultural counseling competency: Integration of the curricular and the practical. *Journal of Mental Health Counseling, 30*, 226–236.

Walker, R. L., Wingate, L. R., Obasi, E. M., & Joiner, T. E. (2008). An empirical investigation of acculturative stress and ethnic identity as moderators for depression and suicidal ideation in college students. *Cultural Diversity and Ethnic Minority Psychology, 14*, 75–82.

Walsh, B. W. (Ed.). (2003). *Counseling psychology and optimal human functioning.* Mahwah, NJ: Erlbaum.

Wampold, B. E., & Holloway, E. L. (1997). Methodology, design, and evaluation in psychotherapy supervision research. In J. C. E. Watkins (Ed.), *Methodology, design, and evaluation in psychotherapy supervision research* (pp. 11–27). New York: Wiley.

Wampold, B. E., Lichtenberg, J. W., & Waehler, C. A. (2002). Principles of empirically supported interventions in counseling psychology. *The Counseling Psychologist, 30*, 197–217.

Wampold, B. E., Lichtenberg, J. W., & Waehler, C. A. (2005). A broader perspective: Counseling Psychology's emphasis on evidence. *Journal of Contemporary Psychotherapy, 35*, 27–38.

Wampold, B. E., Mondin, G. W., Moody, M., Stich, F., Benson, K., & Ahn, H. (1997). A meta-analysis of outcome studies comparing bona fide psychotherapies: Empirically, "all must have prizes." *Psychological Bulletin, 122*, 203–215.

Watkins, C. E., Lopez, F. G., Campbell, V. L., & Himmell, C. D. (1986). Contemporary counseling psychology: Results of a national survey. *Journal of Counseling Psychology, 33*(3), 301–309.

Welfel, E. R. (1998). *Ethics in counseling and psychotherapy.* Pacific Grove, CA: Brooks Cole.

Wheeler, S., & Richards, K. (2007). The impact of clinical supervision on counsellors and therapists, their practice and their clients. A systematic review of the literature. *Counselling and Psychotherapy Research, 7*(1), 54–65.

Whipple, J. L., Lambert, M. J., Vemeesch, D., Smart, D. W., Nielsen, S. L., & Hawkins, E. J. (2003). Improving the effects of psychotherapy: The use of early identification of treatment failure and problem solving strategies in routine practice. *Journal of Counseling Psychology, 50*, 59–68.

Whiston, S. C., Brecheisen, B. K., & Stephens, J. (2003). Does treatment modality affect career counseling effectiveness? *Journal of Vocational Behavior, 62*, 390–410.

Whiston, S. C., & Rahardja, D. (2008). Vocational counseling process and outcome. In S. D. Brown & R. W. Lent (Eds.), *Handbook of counseling psychology* (4th ed., pp. 444–461). New York: Wiley.

Whiston, S. C., Fouad, N. A., Juntunen, C., Schultheiss, D., Rottinghaus, P., Rempel, V., & DeBell, (n.d.). *Guidelines for integration of vocational psychology into professional psychology practice* (unpublished data).

Whitely, J. M. (1984). Counseling psychology: A historical perspective. *The Counseling Psychologist, 12*(1), 3–109.

Woody, R. H., Hansen, J. C., & Rossberg, R. H. (1989). *Counseling psychology: Strategies and services.* Monterey, CA: Brooks/Cole

Worthen, V. E., & Lambert, M. J. (2007). Outcome oriented supervision: Advantages of adding systematic client tracking to supportive consultations. *Counselling and Psychotherapy Research, 7*(1), 48–53.

Worthington, R. L., Soth-McNett, A. M., & Moreno, M. V. (2007). Multicultural counseling competencies research: A 20-year content analysis. *Journal of Counseling Psychology, 54*, 351–361.

Yin, R. K. (2009). *Case study research: Design and methods.* (4th ed.). Thousand Oaks, CA: Sage Publications.

Yip, T., Gee, G. C., & Takeuchi, D. T. (2008). Racial discrimination and psychological distress: The impact of ethnic identity and age among immigrant and United States-born Asian adults. *Developmental Psychology, 44*, 787–800.

Yoo, H. C., & Lee, R. M. (2005). Ethnic identity and approach-type coping as moderators of the racial discrimination/well-being relation in Asian Americans. *Journal of Counseling Psychology, 52*, 497–506.

Yoo, H. C., & Lee, R. M. (2008). Does ethnic identity buffer or exacerbate the effects of frequent racial discrimination on situational well-being of Asian-Americans? *Journal of Counseling Psychology, 55*, 63–74.

Key Terms

Action research—a particularly useful approach to investigating the effectiveness of programmatic interventions in organizational settings.

Actuarial—"statistical methods" that involve data-based estimates of the probability of the occurrence of a behavior or outcome.

American Board of Counseling Psychology (ABCoP)—the certifying board for counseling psychologists in the United States and Canada.

APA's The Ethical Principles of Psychologists and Code of Conduct—the ethical code is an agreed-upon imprimatur for the professional behavior of psychologists.

Assessment—the overall process of psychological appraisal using multiple samples and sources of input, including, potentially, clinical judgments across domains of human behavior.

Assessment of dangerousness—a complex task of balancing the needs of the patient with the need of society for safety.

Association of State and Provincial Psychology Boards (ASPPB)—the association of state psychology licensing boards responsible for the licensure of psychologists throughout the United States and Canada.

Beneficence and nonmaleficence—these principles instruct psychologists to "do no harm" and to safeguard the rights of others by acting on the behalf of the best interests of clients and others.

Biological Bases of Behavior—a core academic area of training in applied psychology and a prominent section of the EPPP that assesses knowledge of biological and neural bases of behavior, psychopharmacology, and methodologies supporting this body of knowledge.

Career maturity—the extent to which the individual is ready to make career choices appropriate to age or developmental stage.

Case conceptualization—the process of aggregating information from assessment and testing to formulate a clinical picture of the client.

Client-centered approach—an approach to treatment based on Carl Rodger's humanistic approach emphasizing empathy in the therapeutic relationship between the client and therapist.

Client outcome—the outcome of the therapy assumed to be mediated through the therapist's interventions, the client's efforts, supervision, and other exogenous factors.

Clinical judgment—the inference or the generation of hypotheses about the client based on behavior and information observed during interviews.

Clinical psychology—an applied specialty in psychology that places more emphasis on the study and treatment of psychopathology and on tailoring treatments to target specific symptoms.

Clinical utility—the effects of a psychological test, either on the client or the counseling process.

Cognitive-Affective Bases of Behavior—a core academic area of training in applied psychology and prominent section of the EPPP that assesses knowledge of cognition and its neural bases, as well as theories and empirical bases of learning, memory, affect, emotion, and factors that influence cognitive performance.

Cognitive and behavioral treatments—a form of psychotherapy that emphasizes the importance of scrutinizing thought processes and behavior in order to diminish dysfunction and/or promote psychological functioning.

Confidentiality—refers to the circumstances under which communications between a psychologist and his or her client(s) are protected from disclosure.

Confirmatory bias—occurs when the psychologist is the source of conceptual material and then seeks to confirm hypotheses generated from the psychologist's perspective.

Consensual Qualitative Research (CQR)—a descriptive inductive methodology created by counseling psychologist Clara E. Hill and her colleagues.

Construct validity—the degree to which the measure can be demonstrated to be measuring the purported construct.

Constructivist-interpretivist—approaches to inquiry that have the intention of understanding the relative nature of reality and the world of human experience.

Consulting counseling psychologists—professional psychologists who engage in consultation and training activities in a variety of settings such as community mental health centers, medical centers, educational institutions, and business and industry.

Consulting psychology—the practice of psychology that focuses on consultation to, with, or for individuals and organizations at the individual, group, and or organizational/system-wide levels.

Content validity—the degree to which test items fully represent the content of the construct being assessed.

Core academic areas—the core areas of psychology that have informed and grounded the practice of counseling psychology.

Counseling psychology—an applied specialty in psychology that is guided by the goal of harnessing the individual's talents and abilities to promote psychological growth, personal and vocational development, adjustment, and fulfillment.

Criterion validity (concurrent and predictive)—measures the degree to which a scale or test is associated with a specific measure, behavior, or outcome, either presently (concurrent) or in the future (predictive).

Critical-ideological paradigms—this paradigm of thinking and inquiry has goals of challenging historical, traditional, and/or dominant social structures and norms.

Direct measures—measures that have readily identifiable content and that tap motivation, current status, and skills. They reflect concurrent and predictive validity more accurately than indirect measures.

Duty to warn—the psychologist's duty to protect an identifiable victim from a dangerous patient/client.

Empirically supported treatments (ESTs)—clearly specified psychological treatments shown to be efficacious in controlled research with delineated populations.

Ethnography—the study and systematic recording of human cultures; also a descriptive work produced from such research.

Evidence-based psychological practice (EBPP)—psychological practice that is informed by research and clinical evidence.

Examination for Professional Practice in Psychology (EPPP)—the examination created by the ASPPB and taken by eligible graduates in psychology in order to obtain licensure as psychologists in the United States and Canada.

External validity—the extent to which results can be generalized from the study samples to the populations of interest.

Face validity—the degree to which items on a test are recognized as reflecting the construct being assessed.

Fidelity and responsibility—these ethical principles guide psychologists to behave in a professional manner, including working faithfully on behalf of clients and taking proper responsibility for the welfare of clients.

Foundational competencies—knowledge bases essential to competent practice in applied psychology.

Functional competencies—the actual service delivery abilities that are informed by foundational competencies and other relevant functional competencies.

Grounded theory method—a specific qualitative approach to inquiry concerned with the generation, elaboration, and validation of social science theory.

Growth and Lifespan Development—a core academic area of training in applied psychology and a prominent section of the EPPP that assesses knowledge of age-appropriate development across the life span and the protective and risk factors that influence developmental outcome for individuals.

Health Insurance Portability and Accountability Act (HIPAA)—privacy regulations that are designed to protect and limit access to patient records and information.

Helping skills—the basic skills in psychological interviewing and intervention, including paraphrasing, reflecting feeling, immediacy, open-ended questions, and empathy.

Humanistic—the psychological approach that is influenced by an optimistic view of human nature and understanding the individual factors that contribute to a person's functioning.

Humanistic/existential psychotherapies—a form of psychotherapy that promotes self-awareness and personal growth and aims to help individuals realize their potential.

I-G-O (individual-, group-, organization-level interventions)—general practice specialty of professional psychology with a focus on scientifically based solutions to human problems in work and other organizational settings.

In situ learning—provides a context for the supervisee to reflect on his or her personal practice with a more experienced member of the profession.

Incremental validity—the degree to which a test explains additional variation beyond either clinical judgment and inference or probabilistic determinations from other tests or assessment procedures.

Indirect measures—measures that contain items whose content is not readily connectable to a particular scale or construct and often tap underlying dispositions, structures, and complexes.

Individual and cultural diversity (ICD)—a professional core area in training that emphasizes the value of human diversity and the study of individual and cultural factors.

Individual differences psychology—the measurement of psychological differences that make up individuals, including personality, intelligence and other qualities and talents.

Informed consent—the importance of clients or participants being aware of the nature, potential risks, and benefits of any procedures or interventions to which they might be exposed.

Integrity—this principle guides psychologists to act in a truthful manner, honoring commitments and interacting honestly with others.

Internal consistency—the degree to which items in a test measure a concept in similar ways.

Internal validity—refers to how well a study is constructed and addresses questions of rigor; relatedly, the extent to which a study accounts for threats to internal validity such as maturation, history, and testing effects.

Justice—this principle guides psychologists to promote fairness and provide services to all persons without bias.

Mental health movement—a movement in psychology that influenced the development of centers where mental illness could be treated and where the emotional and psychological well-being of a person could be promoted through psychological intervention.

Meta-analysis—a statistical review of the literature that involves the aggregation of study data across a large body of studies usually involving large numbers of participants.

Model of competency-based education—highly specific foundational and functional competencies for professional training in psychology.

Model Training Program (MTP)—psychological theory, knowledge, and research that have been affirmed as central to training in counseling psychology.

Multicultural competence—refers to the competent delivery of psychological services across cultural groups and that includes knowledge, attitudes, and skills that promote the well-being of immigrants, minorities, and historically oppressed and marginalized populations.

Multicultural counseling—aspects of counseling designed to meet the needs of and provide services to immigrants, minorities, and historically oppressed and marginalized populations.

Multiple-role relationships—a broad term that encompasses instances in which a psychologist acts in more than one capacity or professional role with an individual; multiple-role relationships can be problematic and in certain situations constitute unethical conduct.

Narratology—the study of structure and meaning in personal accounts, stories, and narratives.

Nomological net—consists of rules or hypotheses that specify the relationship of observable properties of hypothetical constructs to each other.

Norming—the process of determining average scores for specified segments of a population.

Parallel or equivalent test forms—test forms that contain different items but both measure a concept reliably.

Participatory action research—a systematic inquiry with the collaboration of those affected by the issue being studied and for purposes of education and taking action or effecting change.

Phenomenology—the study of conscious experience from the first-person point of view.

Populations—the entire group to which research is aiming to generalize.

Positive psychology—the study of human thriving that examines human strengths and how one can become happier and more fulfilled.

Positivist—the approach to research and inquiry guided by adherence to the scientific method and confined to what can be observed and measured.

Postpositivist—an expansion of the parameters for scientific inquiry beyond positivistic experimental and quasi-experimental designs.

Privileged communication—a right accorded to clients/patients to protect information/material associated with treatment from disclosure in legal proceedings.

Psychoanalysis—the school of thought developed and promoted by Sigmund Freud and which emphasizes the influence of the unconscious mind on behavior.

Psychoeducational—a form of psychological practice that focuses on ideals such as lifelong learning and adjustment, and interventions that target other aspects of life functioning such as personal and vocational development.

Psychological test—written, visual, or verbal evaluations administered to assess the cognitive and emotional functioning of children and adults.

Psychometric movement—a movement in psychology that focuses on, among other things, scale development, assessment, and the advancement and use of statistical procedures.

Psychometrics—the field of study concerned with the theory and technique of psychological measurement, including the measurement of knowledge, abilities, and attitudes.

Qualitative designs—approaches to investigation that do not follow the traditional scientific or postpositivist methods but nonetheless represent viable methods of serious, sophisticated, and challenging inquiry.

Racial/ethnic identity—factors associated with identity, development, well-being, and cognitive processes, including assumptions based on socialization, race, racism, and ethnicity.

Relevance—the extent to which results from a study are relevant to questions or needs evident in the field of practice and the extent to which results can be used to address such questions and needs.

Reliability—the degree to which a particular test or scale will consistently measure the concept in question.

Respect for the rights and dignity of clients/patients—this principle guides psychologists to respect and uphold individual rights and cultural differences.

Rigor—deriving and studying complex and elegant research questions by using sound procedures and measures with strong psychometric properties, and by using adequate statistical analyses.

Scientist-practitioner model—a model that emphasizes training in the absorption and generation of knowledge via scientific methods, and the development of applied psychology skills in assessment and intervention.

Settings—the context, environment, or surroundings in which development, interactions, research, assessments, or interventions take place.

Social and Multicultural Bases of Behavior—a core academic area of training in applied psychology and a prominent section of the EPPP that assesses knowledge of interpersonal processes, dynamics, theories of personality, and issues in diversity.

Society of Counseling Psychology—a professional organization comprised of counseling psychologists, students, and other professionals who advance psychological practice, training, research, and education as part of Division 17 of the American Psychological Association.

Solution-oriented—a generally time- and cost-effective form of psychological intervening and communicating with clients directed toward developing and achieving the client's vision of solutions.

Standardization—established procedures for administering a test to a representative sample and constructing population norms using standard scores.

Strength-based psychotherapy—inspired by traditions in counseling psychology and the positive psychology movement, this form of psychotherapy seeks to measure and galvanize treatment focusing on human strengths.

Supertransference—supervisors' biases or distortions based on unresolved past or current conflicts or difficulties in the supervisory relationship.

Supervision—a method of teaching practice that links the foundational knowledge and skills of the field to professional activities and guides the individual supervisee through the learning progression from neophyte practitioner to entry-level professional.

Systems theory—a theoretical framework involving multiple interrelated elements, where the properties of the whole are different from the properties of the parts; systems are viewed as governed by processes of negative feedback (which promotes stability) and positive feedback (which promotes instability).

Test-retest reliability—the stability of the scores of a test when taken over discrete time periods.

Testing—the use of psychological instruments structured around one or more psychological constructs, and having a demonstrated set of psychometric qualities documented in technical and professional manuals.

Training—encompasses graduate-level education, practice, and supervision in psychology and measured in terms of credits, scores, and practice hours that are required for licensure and independent practice.

Trait-factor theories—the idea of matching the abilities of the person with the characteristics of the environment; deriving real-life implications for the selection, training, and placement of an individual into a profession.

Utility—a relatively recent form of validity that indicates the extent to which an instrument is useful or designed for practical use.

Validity—the degree to which a scale actually measures the construct that it purports to measure.

Vocational guidance movement—a movement in counseling psychology that seeks to help people find suitable work that would be conducive to their satisfaction and in which they would be optimally productive.

Index

About the Authors

Jairo N. Fuertes, PhD, ABPP, is licensed as a psychologist and as mental health counselor in New York State and is board certified by the American Board of Counseling Psychology. He is also listed in the National Register of Health Service Providers in Psychology. He is currently associate professor at the Gordon F. Derner Institute of Advanced Psychological Studies at Adelphi University, and he is a psychologist at the Baruch College (The City University of New York) counseling center. He is a fellow of the American Psychological Association and the American Academy of Counseling Psychology and currently is president-elect of the American Academy of Counseling Psychology.

Arnold R. Spokane, PhD, ABPP, is a licensed psychologist in Pennsylvania and is board certified by the American Board of Counseling Psychology. He is currently a professor in the counseling psychology program at Lehigh University and maintains a private practice. He is a fellow of the American Psychological Association and of the American Academy of Counseling Psychology.

Elizabeth Holloway, PhD, ABPP, is a professor of psychology in the Doctoral Program in Leadership and Change at Antioch University and is board certified by the American Board of Counseling Psychology. She has held faculty appointments at the Universities of California, Santa Barbara, Utah, Oregon, and Wisconsin-Madison, and she is a fellow of the American Academy of Counseling Psychology. She consults with leaders worldwide on clinical supervision, mentoring, and incivility in the workplace.

About the Series Editors

Arthur M. Nezu, PhD, ABPP, is professor of psychology, medicine, and public health at Drexel University and special professor of forensic mental health and psychiatry at the University at Nottingham in the United Kingdom. He is a fellow of multiple professional associations, including the American Psychological Association, and is board certified by the American Board of Professional Psychology in cognitive and behavioral psychology, clinical psychology, and clinical health psychology. Dr. Nezu is widely published, is incoming editor of the *Journal of Consulting and Clinical Psychology*, and has maintained a practice for three decades.

Christine Maguth Nezu, PhD, ABPP, is professor of psychology and medicine at Drexel University and special professor of forensic mental health and psychiatry at the University at Nottingham in the United Kingdom. With over 25 years of experience in clinical private practice, consultation/liaison, research, and teaching, Dr. Maguth Nezu is board certified by the American Board of Professional Psychology (ABPP) in cognitive and behavioral psychology and clinical psychology. She is also a past president of ABPP. Her research has been supported by federal, private, and state-funded agencies, and she has served as a grant reviewer for the National Institutes of Health.

CPSIA information can be obtained at www.ICGtesting.com
Printed in the USA
LVOW01s0953040913

350836LV00005B/90/P

9 780195 386448